NAVIGATING SOVEREIGNTY

Navigating Sovereignty
World Politics Lost in China

By
Chih-yu Shih

First published 2003 by
PALGRAVE MACMILLAN™
175 Fifth Avenue, New York, N.Y. 10010 and
Houndmills, Basingstoke, Hampshire, England RG21 6XS
Companies and representatives throughout the world

PALGRAVE MACMILLAN is the global academic imprint of the Palgrave Macmillan division of St. Martin's Press, LLC and of Palgrave Macmillan Ltd. Macmillan® is a registered trademark in the United States, United Kingdom and other countries. Palgrave is a registered trademark in the European Union and other countries.

ISBN 1–4039–6375–4 hardback

Library of Congress Cataloging-in-Publication Data
Shi, Zhiyu, 1958–
    Navigating sovereignty : world politics lost in China / by
Chih-yu Shin.
        p. cm.
    Includes bibliographical references and index.
    ISBN 1–4039–6375–4
    1. China—Politics and government—20th century. 2. China—Foreign relations—20th century. 3. Nationalism—China. I. Title: World politics lost in China. II. Title.
DS775.7.S53 2003
320.951—dc21   2003049866

A catalogue record for this book is available from the British Library.

Design by Newgen Imaging Systems (P) Ltd., Chennai, India.

First edition: December, 2003
10 9 8 7 6 5 4 3 2 1

Printed in the United States of America.

To my mother

CONTENTS

LIST OF TABLES

ACKNOWLEDGMENT

I express gratitude to my institution—the National Taiwan University—for providing me the most liberal research and teaching environment in the country, which has sadly suffered from ethnic finger pointing and labeling. Also through nomination by the institution, I was able to receive the National Chair Professorship from the government that has and will continue to support my research between 2001 and 2004. Finally, I want to thank participants of the Political Science and Cultural Studies Series for their contribution to my critical thinking and my student Kuo Houchih, Randy Liao and Andrea Chen for their excellent editing service.

Chapter 5 is a revised version of "Defining Japan: The Nationalist Assumption in China's Japan Policy," first appearing in pages 539–563 of *International Journal* L, 3 (Summer 1995), a publication of the Canadian Institute of International Affairs.

Chapter 6 is an extended and revised version of "Consuming Part-time Nationalism: China as an Immigrant in Global Society," first appearing in *New Political Science* 25, 3 (2003).

PREFACE

Few will question the fact that the year 2003 had been a difficult year for China—adapting to "foreign" regulations prescribed by the WTO, experiencing the US invasion of Iraq, contending the spread of the deadly Severe Acute Respiratory Syndrome, fighting its surging poverty and the worsening economic recession, and, of course, managing the transition of power to a new generation of leadership. All these challenges are taking place in front of a watchful world, Moscow and Washington above all, concerned about whether or not China can overcome the obstacles and rise into a new hegemon that poses a threat to the rest of the world. Observing from a longer-term perspective, China watchers have always witnessed and experienced eyebrow-frowning and unfolding events or developments that made them feel uncertain of China's rise to power. Even though the Chinese have learned to live with uncertainty, from time to time, they still have to respond to the world about the meaning of Chinese statehood. However, their effort to respond has yet to produce a clearer image of the "state" that can satisfy either the external watchers or the domestic elite stratum.

This book embarks from the dyad puzzle over the inability to articulate the Chinese ambivalence toward the world as well as the world's ambivalence toward China—rendering attempts to speak to or for the entity called "China" unsuccessful. As a result, everything involving China rarely means what people say they are, no matter how sincere the speakers may have intended it to be. The ineffable China therefore made developments in China look promising at times for the concerned watchers; however, at other times, China appears hopelessly stubborn and backward. Consequently, the desire to interpret Chinese affairs in a consistent manner leads to frustration. Learned China experts tend to believe that this is because China is a moving target—constantly undergoing changes in positioning—and the China watchers are the shooters who miss fires at times. By contrast, this book tells how and why the distinction between the target and the shooters is imagined.

I understand that my interpretive method is not popular in social science, and is even less so in the field of Chinese foreign policy. In response to the growing concern for identity politics emerging everywhere in the world, China watchers need to reconsider the relationships between the researcher and the researched, the theoretical analysis of China and the practice of those acting in the name of China, and the production of knowledge and the reproduction of identity. This book relies heavily on insights from cultural studies. It aims to reinterpret China's place in the world through how the "world" is used in China. This way, I hope to recognize and stress China watchers' participation, albeit unintentionally or unwillingly, in the making of China and the China threat, and, in return, the Chinese contribution to the making of the world. Accordingly, the difficult years that the Chinese have lived are our difficult years, too.

Introduction

Taking Cultural Studies Seriously

China's entry into the World Trade Organization (WTO) seems to have created uncertainties in its identities. The literature on China's role in world politics typically falls into two categories—those who see China as a potential threat in formation and those who anticipate China becoming a "normal" state, one that would observe international norms and behave in accordance with the West's expectations. The question of what China represents is a major subject of debate among Chinese intellectuals, domestic as well as overseas. These discussions echo the familiar disagreement between neorealism and neoliberalism in international relations to the extent that an ontologically unproblematized Chinese state is believed to be torn between political power and economic welfare. In fact, globalization does not change the image of China as being primarily an outsider sitting behind its closed sovereign borders still capable of keeping out waves of globalization. To understand how Chinese authorities have responded to world politics is therefore critical for anyone interested in furthering their understanding of Chinese identities as well as the future of globalization.

In this book I will examine the meanings belonging to the Chinese state from a postcolonial perspective. Instead of looking at China from the outside, using those theoretical frameworks popular in the IR (international relations) scholarship, I will attempt to look at the world from its inside. However, the "inside" is not a territorial home, but the psychological space created when Western modernity and Confucian tradition meet. The outcome of this meeting is undecidable because both modernity and tradition are constantly reinterpreted as policy behavior takes place in different situations. Accordingly, the meanings of the Chinese state are likewise undecidable to those who, for their own reasons, need to fix the meanings of China to a certain set of identities.

I argue that the uncertainty over China's identities does not begin with China's entry into globalization. Globalization is embedded in a style of discourse that is familiar to both the Chinese authorities and intellectuals, since it reminds them of the introduction of modernity as a hegemonic discourse, which has completely dominated China's public space since the late nineteenth century. In short, they think globalization comes from the same "West" they faced a century ago. In response, they resort to various identity strategies, sometimes idly, at other times reluctantly, and at still other times, aimlessly, militantly, or creatively. The study of postcolonial hybridity and the Chinese state's adaptation to Western modernity has not been applied to Chinese foreign policy in the IR literature. Without such analytical exercises, China watchers will mistakenly view the inability of the Chinese authorities to settle on one fixed identity as a threat to them. Once postcolonial adaptation is dubbed as a threat, the prophecy of a "China threat" may very well fulfill itself.

I intend to open up the Chinese state by bringing perspectives of cultural studies, most of which are now familiar to the IR literature, including: postmodernism, Orientalism, nationalism, rational choice, postcolonialism, globalization, and Confucianism. I plan to begin with postmodernism that denies the ontology of the state. I then move on to Orientalism, which alludes to the hybrid characteristics of the state. Then, I introduce nationalism that, as a therapy to hybridity, ironically undermines the territoriality of the state. Next, in my discussions of rational choice, postcolonialism, and globalization, I explore the relations of nationalism to them respectively. In the rational choice section, I view nationalism as a preference that constrains the pursuit of other goals informing the "rational" state. In my discussion of postcolonialism, I treat nationalism, as elsewhere, as a response to postcolonial experiences. After that, I examine the mutual constitution of nationalism and globalization in the new age. Finally, I move on to Confucianism, which I argue recollects an unchanged but different meaning of the state alien to world politics.

The literature that focuses on the identities of the Chinese state in world politics is meager. Most of the existing publications discuss it in relation to state nationalism or patriotism.[1] On the other hand, there are a handful of others who correlate the theme to the question of identity crisis and provide analyses either from a modernist perspective[2] or from other interpretive perspectives.[3] My previous works use mainly psychological and interpretive approaches,[4] except one that includes a feminist critique.[5] These writings fail to look from one important and critical angle or, more specifically, they do not examine the problems of "Chinese state" identity from the "state" side, but only from the "Chinese" side. This book, in contrast, critically assesses both the ontology and the teleology of the state.

The following organization shows the flow of argument in the book. Each chapter uses a particular perspective to answer a question, which serves as a bridge between previous and subsequent questions:

1. Can China be a normal territorial state? The answer lies in postmodern undecidability exemplified by Japanese intellectuals' varied interpretations of Japan's own identity.
2. How do Chinese leaders respond in the name of territorial state? The answer lies in the Orientalist construction of a national identity that downgrades cultural China.
3. Can Chinese leaders preserve the nonterritorial identity of China? They attempt to do so through the nationalist attempt to defend the "people's heart" as the essence of being Chinese.
4. How do Chinese leaders make sense of their nationalist pursuit? We search for the answer in the rational choice that reconciles emotion and national interest.
5. Why can the national interest never be dominant? The answer lies in the postcolonial sensitivity concerning Japan's historical colonization of Taiwan.
6. How does postcolonial sensitivity square with opening to the outside world? We look to a globalization process that tolerates occasional nationalism as a tonic.
7. How is occasional nationalism demonstrated? It is done so through the Confucian pretension that an independent Taiwan continues to belong to a China mandated by a heavenly order.

I begin my discussion with a chapter on how Japan has viewed China since the late nineteenth century and why China as a sovereign state has been in a form of "alterity" right from the beginning. This chapter attempts to demonstrate that the nature of the Chinese state is undecidable. The meaning of China as a sovereign state depends upon the national identities that particular Japanese narrators have for Japan. I also touch upon different Chinese identity perspectives that are posited in the United States and China. As a result of their discourses, China has no fixed meanings that can be shared among parties involved in making policy toward, or in the name of, China.

Then I argue that Chinese foreign policy reflects a mood, which I call "reflexive Orientalism," referring to an ambivalence toward the Western notion of modern state. On the one hand, Chinese authorities accept the standards that Western countries typically use to evaluate the performance of the state. On the other hand, they deny that China should achieve a higher standard based on the Western prescription, which labels China as backward. They acknowledge China's backwardness but not China's lower status. I use Zhou Enlai as an example to explain how Chinese foreign policy has seemingly adopted the norms of the state but with a completely different teleology.

In chapter 3, I analyze the way in which Chinese authorities understand national defense. Chinese practices, which I call dependent nationalism, relies on a Western definition of sovereignty to evaluate China's overall performance. Dependent nationalism, which is accordingly a form of reflexive Orientalism, considers the defense of the "people's heart" from Western influence much more important than that of the defense of the territory of sovereign China. Occasional obsession with and alternate disregard to territorial defense testify to the symbolic use of defense as an identity statement. Dependent nationalism thus begins with the defense of territorial integrity but ironically ends up transcending territorial concerns.

Chapter 4 uses a mathematic model to demonstrate that Chinese nationalism is not national interest–oriented, which realist or liberal IR scholarships assume. The model explains that the cycle of Chinese nationalism in foreign policy is predicated by its postcolonial hybrid identities. The model brings back the temporal dimension by adding the elements of forgetting and forgiving to the rational choice model. By first treating nationalism as a national interest in realist terms, the introduction of the two elements of forgetting and forgiving provide a cure for the amnesia in realist epistemology. Moreover, I want to show how the rational choice model can be useful in defeating the rational choice analysis. This works because postcolonial hybridity disallows the application of one internally consistent preference system across time periods.

Chapter 5 goes back to the case of Japan to show that even when Japan is not directly involved, it is still the most significant reference point of Chinese nationalism and foreign policy. This is because the Japanese colonial occupation of Taiwan for 51 years seriously affected the self-respect of those identifying with Chinese nationalism. The chapter illustrates how the Chinese authorities painstakingly tried to render Japan as the "Other" through its Taiwan policy especially during 1994. The postcolonial emotion of shame leads to China's anti-Japan proclivity to the point where the Chinese state practically lives on anti-Japanism. The Chinese authorities' intuitive, albeit indirect, reference to and targeting of Japan in this chapter serve as an interesting comparison to chapter 1 where Japan struggles with little success in determining China's identities.

Chapter 6 explores the changing nature of Chinese nationalism under globalization. I argue that Chinese nationalism is at best a "part-time" nationalism and economically a potentially profitable discourse. China's entry into the WTO is like an immigrant struggling in a foreign land. Like any immigrant, China is trapped in self-estrangement and is badly in need of mediation. However, nationalism, which enables the imagination of an essential Chinese identity, is also a psychological mechanism that may enable the immigrating state to mitigate its sense of loss when it globalizes. However, nationalism as remedy may also backfire when the Western observers mistakenly view it as anti-foreignism and attempt to re-encircle China, and in turn, compel the Chinese authorities to respond aggressively. Yet, globalization allows the masses to practice nationalism in ways that cannot be determined in advance; thus, diminishing the potential for a backlash at the same time.

The final chapter examines negotiation between China and Taiwan to show that, even at the tactical level, sovereignty means very different things to Confucian leaders. In short, negotiation is sometimes anti-negotiation, aimed at redefining identities of the negotiation parties rather than confirming them. Confucianism is allergic to negotiation that exposes disharmony between two parties supposedly involved in a selfless relationship. Negotiation that aims at reconciliation proceeds in politics of identity. Anti-negotiation as an identity strategy deprives the notion of national interest of any relevance in determining the meaning of the state.

Finally, I discuss how successful the ontology of state is in closing off the evolution of an East Asian ontology that promises its own pride as well as shame. I am mindful of the tendency to become closed off in the construction of the new ontology and look for discursive mechanisms that generate moral responsibility toward ever-evolving alterities.

1

The Postmodern Clue: Defining China as an Alterity

Sovereignty's Alterities

China being a sovereign state means something quite different (potentially to anyone) from, say, the United States being a sovereign state. The difference in meaning is however indescribable if we adhere to realist or liberal traditions of political science. The state as a sovereign agency was an unchallenged ontological component in the IR literature before the 1990s. Even the allegedly reformist constructivism, in response to poststructuralist challenges, "depressingly" maintains that the state is an integral part of the ontology of IR studies,[1] although it granted that human cognition is involved in the construction of this ontology. The notoriously simplified form of the state shared among realists, liberals, and constructivists, with the assumption of the state being self-consistent at any given point of time, cannot help but rely on epistemological devices to absorb other forms of existence that are neither statist nor self-consistent. Applying Emmanuel Lavina's wisdom, I call these forms "alterities of international relations," referring to forms of existence that are beyond the theorization based upon the notion of "international relations."

These alterities include the postcolonial state, mother, multinational firm, diaspora, tree, transnational NGO, slave worker, prostitute, water, mini-state, queer, family, O-zone, class, refugee, child, jihad fighter, or ethnic nation. Statist analyses absorb these forms of existence in an all-encompassing conceptual framework that terminates their relevance. Michael Shapiro elaborates on Lavinas's respect of alterity by stressing, "alterity means absolute alterity," which cannot be subsumed into the same or a totalizing conceptual system that informs the meaning of self and Other.[2] Accordingly, a postcolonial state is, for example, irreducibly a postcolonial state whose ontological aims are not to be specified by statism where the relation with the other state arises within a totality or establishes a totality. In denying ontological meanings to these forms of alterity, sovereignty becomes the exclusive source of meanings in itself. Searching for and recognizing alterity are thus actions of opening, that render the confrontation in the name of absolute sovereignty meaningless. Alterity, in this sense, is also the source of remedy.

To many who study it, China unfortunately represents an anomaly in the uniformed sovereign world, not an ever-changing form of fluidity with its own historical path and contemporary contingencies. Several distinguished Western scholars have argued along this line. Lucian Pye contests that China as a state is a product of pretension;[3] Similarly Samuel Huntington finds Confucianism to be a source of clash of civilizations, prompting its disciples into conflict in the name of the sovereign state.[4] In the same vein, Edward Friedman complains about Chinese nationalism impeding China's democratic prospects.[5] From a slightly different angle, the late Gordon White,[6] along with Merle Goldman,[7] viewed the emergence of civil society and democratic prospects in China with elation as if it had been the same civil society familiar to them. However, the more cautious Andrew Nathan and Larry Diamond hold an opposing position to White and Goldman, but still, both are hoping for liberal democracy in China.[8] Others such as the strategic debate between the nicknamed blue team, which favors containment of China, and the red team, which favors engagement, also reflect the monotonous image of the Chinese state mimicking the U.S. model.

Surprisingly, the U.S. inability to define the true nature of the Chinese state and its concomitant China policy today is similar to the puzzlement that Japanese intellectuals as well as political leaders suffered over a hundred years ago when Japan became a "state." This parallel alludes to the possibility that this Japanese incomprehension, which is rarely voiced, actually testified to the long existence of a different kind of state, namely China, which has existed for at least a hundred years. Similarly in the U.S. China policy at the turn of the twentieth century, the nature of China was incomprehensible. This reflects the discursive inability of realists (etc.) to reduce an alterity coexisting ontologically with the state system to just another state. This is not much different from the situation where advocates of civil rights struggled over the political humanity of slaves and women in the past and present.[9] In this book, I intend to analyze the sovereign domain in China that was created by, yet differentiated from, realist sovereignty. In the creation, I argue that those acting in the name of Chinese sovereignty have responded, improvised, and struggled outside the familiar state ontology. As a result, today we have the opportunity of opening up the realist hegemony for a horizon that welcomes alterity.

In this chapter, I first begin by reviewing the bewilderment of the Japanese regarding China as a neighboring community, which reflected the confusion about the meanings of Japan itself on becoming a modern state. Next, I note particularly the discursive strategy of the literature up to the 1930s that perceived China as an alterity, even though some others seemed to hold the counter-position. Third, I follow Chinese responses that began in the 1950s, which painstakingly suppressed feudal China and imperialism as new China's own alterities, and revealed an internal split and, psychotherapeutically, an illusion of modernity.

In general, this book concerns China's international relations. However, I do not intend to define international in general or East Asia in particular as the book problematizes both the notion of East Asia as well as international. In this book I rely on discourses, not detached theory, nor "historical facts." I use China, a country of East Asia, and demonstrate that as a state it has a unique nature that conceptually disallows the country from being treated as just another typical state in international relations. Once China is portrayed successfully as not just another East Asian state, the concept of East Asia as a geographical unity, a system, or a civilization is simultaneously contested. Since the composition of an East Asian state is never clear, one must wonder for whose purpose such a concept (of East Asia or international) ultimately serves if not for cold war hegemons or the global forces.

FAILED DESIRES: THE JAPANESE NARRATIVES

Political and academic leaders in Japan were the first to consider the meaning of China as a state or, more precisely, whether or not China was and should be a state. Debates on how to treat China were intrinsically connected with how Japanese intellectuals as well as political activists interpreted the relationship between Japan and the world, especially with the countries of Europe and North America. It was essentially a problem based on Japan's identity, which carried a heavy Chinese legacy. The prospect for the future of China, which had been the political, economic, and social model that Japan imitated for generations but also having the potential to become a "normal" Western-style state, implies how advanced Japan could eventually become. Therefore, if China cannot be taught to behave like a normal state and if it was indeed excluded from the world of sovereign states, then Japanese narrators would have to truncate Japan's China connection in order to clear their self-doubt about Japan's status of normalcy. On the other hand, if this connection is thought of as being much too deep to be disregarded, then China must be taught standard state behavior to save Japan from the embarrassment of possibly being a pseudo-state.

Koichi Nomura summarizes the ambivalence present in the Japanese intellectual circles,[10] during the years between the two Sino-Japanese wars of 1894 and 1937, toward China's potential to become a normal state. There was in addition a wide range of views. For example, there was the realist view that China must be made into an open land.[11] According to this view, Japan and England should cooperate to guarantee that China would benefit the world equally. Advocates of this view considered England to be the highest civilization and Japan, together with England, had the duty of providing the best possible arrangement for China to benefit the rest of the world. China was guilty of inducing world conflict in the sense that its inability to catch up to world civilization led to a gap that naturally induced the higher civilized one to invade the lower civilized one. The realists believed that the guarantee by England and Japan was the only way to save China from perishing completely.

Seemingly contrary to the realist view was the idealist narrative that Japan had a duty toward China.[12] From a Christian perspective, the advocates of this view were critical of England's hypocrisy. In contrast with England's suppressive action in South Africa and the division of China by forces from America, Russia, and France, the idealist narrators argued, Japan was the only true Christian state in the world. The whole purpose of the Japan–England alliance should be to turn China into a great civilized state. Japan's military adventure in China was legitimate to the extent that war could awaken China, so war with China was still consistent with the law of human evolution and conducive to the interests of the world. Japan's religious character and China's prospects for upgrading were mutually ensured here. Ironically, while the idealists hoped for a rising Chinese state, they promoted a harsh China policy.

There was also the fascist view of China.[13] The narrators of this view strove to maintain the distinction between the West and the East. The fascists believed that both Japan and China belonged to the latter, and denied the superiority of the West. They would like to see a Chinese state that is able to stand on its own feet. For that reason, some awakening method would be necessary, but definitely not one that would make China prey on or dependent on external financing. For the same reason, therefore, the fascists supported Chinese nationalism even if it meant resistance against Japan. Further, some of them entertained the idea of a Sino-Russo war as a starting point of China's rise to a respected state, an advocacy analogous to the Russo-Japanese war that paved the road for Japan's rise as a world power.

That China was not and could not be an ordinary state was equally apparent in the statist view of China as in realist thought.[14] In the statist narrative, however, Japan was to execute a takeover instead of providing an open-door guarantee. For the statists, China was, at most, a retarded state. They felt that Chinese society was composed of self-centered, local, parochial groups whose low development was unusual by any standard. It was impractical to expect Chinese people to develop a view of state that would allow China to be perceived as normal. The best option was for China to be Japan's protectorate. The statists argued that opening up China to the rest of the world could not save it. Opening up China was not very different from dividing it up, for it would require actions that threaten China's sovereignty.

Between the statists, the fascists, and the idealists are the neo-traditionalists who speak highly of Chinese civilization.[15] They maintained that China's problem was not about culture but about politics. Even if the Chinese state could not sustain the pressure and collapsed, there was no doubt, in this view, that Chinese culture should and would still enlighten the world. The neo-traditionalists agreed that it was wishful thinking to expect Chinese people to work toward making their state thrive. Japan's role accordingly was to educate Chinese people through economic infiltration. Japan's occupation and development of Manchu in the 1930s was an archetypal example in this regard. The neo-traditionalists emphasized the indigenous perspective where local autonomy was believed to be the foundation of Chinese society. This culture of autonomy was practical in that local patriarchal leadership was always willing to strike a deal with any rulers, native as well as foreign, as long as local prosperity and safety could be maintained. On this foundation, the neo-traditionalists promoted the idea of federalism. For the neo-traditionalists, one major setback was Chinese anti-Japanism, which targeted Japan's intrusions in Manchu.

The democrats too were stricken by this anti-Japanism.[16] According to the democrats, Japan must avoid militarist and statist ambitions. They welcomed the May Fourth Movement not because it was anti-imperialist as portrayed by the fascists but because it was a truly spontaneous campaign led by real Chinese nationals. In turn, they were critical of Japan becoming an imperialist state. Interestingly, democrats continued to struggle with short-term expediency; for the sake of countering other imperialist states, they perceived the imperialist policy of 21 Demands as being acceptable. Alongside the democrats were the humanists who admired the humanity embedded in the Chinese cultural tradition.[17] The expectation that China would eventually become a great country was present in their analysis. In general, they were against war. At the same time, the humanists seemed deeply puzzled by the process of events and changing images. In their narrative, any presentation of China appeared to be reluctant, nebulous, and inconsistent.

The socialist perspective regarded the Revolution of 1911 as one of capitalist revolution that would initiate modern state building in China.[18] However, they felt that the real revolution was yet to come. The socialist narrators expected that as long as Chinese nationalists continued to resist imperialism, the real revolution would eventually arise to oppose capitalism. In the socialist interpretation, the Revolution of 1911 was a power struggle launched against the bourgeoisie in advanced capitalist countries by indigenous Chinese bourgeoisie. The socialists read into this struggle positive implications for the proletarian revolution. Like democrats and humanists, those socialists who were critical of Japan found China to be full of opportunities. On the other hand, none of Japan's internal critics were ready to reevaluate Japan's official policy toward China believing that these policy positions would not obstruct the opportunities identified in their narratives. China as a sovereign state was never the premise of their analysis.

More extreme than the socialists were the revolutionaries who denounced the former as sheer "translation" socialists who lacked an indigenous root.[19] Filled with a socialist, humanist spirit nonetheless, the revolutionaries perceived China as the most important base for a world revolution. In comparison, a revolution in Japan would have been of little significance to a world revolution. There was supposedly no meaningful distinction between the Chinese and the Japanese in terms of a world socialist revolution. China was not China in any real sense. The identity problem arose, nonetheless, since the revolutionaries who considered themselves internal to the Chinese revolution were Japanese. They were critical of the barbarity of contemporary civilization. In the same vein, Japan's China policy, depicted as shameless, dirty, and arrogant, treated China as a lower kind of state and incurred the criticism of revolutionaries. Similar to the aforementioned narratives, the revolutionaries' image of China was determined by their decision on what Japan should represent.

The latest views included communist as well as populist perspectives. The former emphasizes the revolutionary explosiveness of China's nationalist movement. Accordingly, the nationalist movements in China represented semi-colonial forces challenging world capitalist development. This analysis did not block the recognition of the inconsistency that existed in the nationalist united front in which the proletarian revolution should eventually rise. However, they were disappointed at the seemingly irrevocable confrontation between China and Japan.[20] In contrast, the populists strove to reveal the Taoist elements in Chinese society that had been widely overlooked. Based upon the Taoist tradition, autonomous local organizations were ready to resist the state effectively. It was here that the populists found the establishment of the puppet Manchuguo (Manchukuo) regime acceptable for it appeared to comply with the populist ideal of a decentralized Chinese polity.[21]

Japanese intellectual discourses on China did not completely determine the path the Chinese state took later on. Clearly, China was not simply an open land for the world, nor was it the base of the world revolution. The Sino-Japanese Asiatic front never materialized. In fact, Chinese intellectuals as well as revolutionaries were extremely wary of China becoming fragmented. Many were once hopeful of Pan-Asianism but became the most aggressive anti-Japan speakers after the outbreak of World War II. In any case, there was no doubt that the quest for the meaning of Chinese state building proceeded in the context of Japan's own destiny and the derived role expectation of China. China was almost in a position of responding to the various specifications provided by the Japanese activists thinking of the future of China. This was not to say that there was no position from within China.[22] Indeed it was precisely the variety of perspectives within China that reinterpreted contending Japanese narrators' expectations and failed the latter's inconsistent desires.

Both "Orient," and later on "East," and "Pan-Asianism" were ambiguous concepts from the beginning. The relationship between culture and state was also puzzling on the eve of the twentieth century. Similarly, the question of whether or not China and Japan were two separate states, each endowed with its own destiny and duty, constantly bothered most intellectuals of the time, a question that did not seem to have parallels in international relations among the

European states. The desire for a China that satisfied certain Japanese narratives however always presupposed an unproblematized Japanese state. One must wonder to what extent this sense of an unproblematized Japanese state was arrived at ironically through the indetermination of the nature of the Chinese state. This indetermination forced Japan to take a decisive position. To ponder over the China puzzle thus created desires that were not meant to be satisfied. It was the action of desiring that meant much more than meeting the desires. Multiple desires interestingly set forth a condition where the meaning of Chinese state building was undecidable. The undecidability exposes the responsibility that the narrator of each statement of positioning must bear. For this undecidability implicated that it was the choice of the narrators, not the necessity built in external structures, that resulted in the China puzzle.

The notion of East Asia as a combination of East and Pan-Asianism is inevitably a disputed concept in itself. After the Korean War of the early 1950s, East Asia seemed to be itself an unproblematized geographical specification. East Asia, divided by an abstract containment line, led to Japan's ambiguity concerning the meaning of the Chinese state. On the other hand, with Russia being an ally, leaders in China were able to develop perspectives that did not directly respond to the China puzzle in Japan. Japan lacked a correspondent target in China to collude on discourses that could breed a sense of certainty. On the contrary, Japan had gradually become an object of interpretation for Chinese narrators of the time. I demonstrate this in chapter 5. East Asia replaced prewar China to condition the Japanese narrators in their thinking of Japan's identity. However, as the old China puzzle remains unresolved, East Asia, which theoretically included China, would continue to receive multiple meanings as desires became increasingly fluid and uncertain when d'etente started in the later 1960s.

Engaged Estrangement: The American Narrative

When China was under the reign of the Manchu court, many Americans arrived in China with the belief that the Chinese would eventually accept American values. This belief was particularly reflected in the legacy of American missionary activities, which had begun its journey across the Pacific long before the Republican period.[23] Indeed people under the celestial reign had been the most important target of American overseas missionary projects. Missionaries arrived with philanthropic purposes, wanting to rescue subjects of the all-under-heaven. Even until the 1960s, textbooks printed by missionary schools in the United States still portrayed the Chinese as people living in darkness and in the shadow of death.[24] Consciously or not, the missionaries had implicitly held the view that they were coming from a more advanced civilization during their preaching. Their selfless, altruistic charity to the Chinese living in poverty reproduced and reinforced their self-image of being the vanguard of history and provided them with a sense of mission.

Many United States–China experts during the Cold War were actually children of the early missionaries in China. With their childhood spent in China, there was no denying that many of them retained a strong passion toward China. As they belonged to different political parties and held divergent ideological perspectives, their policy positions varied widely. Nonetheless, in their voluntary defense of the happenings in China or in their criticism of Chinese authorities, they shared one common perspective—that something needed to be done regarding China's underdevelopment. Some understood China's defensiveness and unwillingness to accept international assistance, but others blamed the Chinese for their self-closure. Either way, every United States–China watcher wanted to help China through or bypassing the Communist regime. This discourse of helping and the accompanying act of watching consolidated the progressive self-image of the United States in China.

The initial contact between the Americans and the celestial subjects was only commercial in nature. The U.S. representative successfully forced a treaty with the Manchu court immediately after the Opium War in the early 1840s, when the court was the most vulnerable. The United States did not demand a more favorable position to be put in writing, but it did ask the Manchu court to "shoulder the responsibility of protecting the lives and properties of the American people in China," "honor the neutrality of the American merchants during a confrontation between China and a third party," and "rescue the American ships in times of need along the China coast."[25] Thus, China was still considered as a sovereign country with jurisdictional capacity.

Since officially the U.S. government possessed little territorial ambition or few strategic concerns in Manchurian China, its involvement in court politics was not as aggressive as that of the Great Britain, France, or Russia. However, after Japan defeated China in 1895, the United States realized that Chinese territory faced the danger of becoming divided by the imperialist powers. To the imperial powers China was little more than a piece of land to the extent that each of these countries desired something from it: to support their expeditions elsewhere and maintain the unstable balance of power in Europe.[26] As a result, Secretary of State John Hay proposed an open-door policy with the hope of keeping China intact. However, in the exchange of letters between the United States and the other Western powers, Chinese territory was referred to as all territory "in" China rather than "of" China,[27] alluding to China's status as a territorial object rather than as a sovereign actor. This signals a shift in perception.

Although the U.S. open-door policy kept Manchu China from being divided, many Chinese scholars nowadays do not appreciate the U.S. assistance because most believe that John Hay did what was best for the United States, not for China. The fact, however, cannot be so clear-cut. The United States aided China, which was caught between the celestial order and the sovereign order, at a critical moment and this not only guaranteed Chinese people's amicable attitude toward the United States but also paved the way for the philanthropic role of the United States in China. Subsequently, it was easier for the American people to develop a discourse on their mission to help China. Whatever the true intention was behind Hay's open-door policy no longer mattered. Indeed during the 1899 Boxers' Rebellion, the United States distinguished itself by wanting to deal with some capable local authorities in China instead of making unilateral arrangements from within the Allied forces. Though implying China's incapacity to take care of itself, the U.S. position in 1900 was to keep intact Chinese territorial sovereignty and administrative jurisdiction:

> ...We regard the condition in Peking as one of virtual anarchy, whereby power and responsibility are practically devolved upon the local provincial authorities....We regard them as representing the people, with whom we seek to remain in peace and friendship....
> [T]o act concurrently with the other powers, the policy of the government of the United States is to seek a solution which may bring about permanent safety and peace to China, preserve Chinese territorial and administrative entity, protect all rights guaranteed to friendly powers by treaty and international law, and safeguard for the world the principle of equal and impartial trade...[28]

Compared with the aforementioned first treaty between the United States and the Manchu court, the United States could not delegate the responsibility of protecting American people in China to the Manchu authorities. Instead, this was the concurrent responsibility of all countries having vested interests in China. The United States nonetheless wanted to see a government capable of defending its sovereignty in accordance with international law. Again, whether or not this was a selfish act on the part of America was irrelevant. The sense of trust that the Chinese people already had in the United States determined their growing expectations of U.S. protection.[29] When World War I broke out, for example, after China declared neutrality, it immediately asked the United States to urge the warring parties, on behalf of China, to respect China's neutrality. This sense of trust grew even stronger after the establishment of the Republican regime in 1911.

The Republic of China received its first greeting from the U.S. Congress. The U.S. government decided to follow domestic public opinion and recognized the Republic of China 17 months later. U.S. recognition was aimed at preventing other countries from taking advantage of the ambiguous political situation in China. In addition, the U.S. was not extensively involved in warlord infighting later on as did most other countries and was the first country to express willingness to return tariff rights to Chinese authorities. After the Mukdan incident, Secretary of State Henry Stimson announced his policy of not acknowledging Japanese military action that threatened the independence of Chinese sovereignty or territorial and administrative integrity.[30] According to Stimson, the world should trust in the prospect of a bright future for the Chinese people. Their success would come in time if the world treated them with justice, patience, and mutual respect and empathized with their backwardness and difficulty.[31]

Certainly, Sino-American relations were not separable from affective factors such as care, self-confidence, sympathy, and goodwill. For the American people subscribing to Christian values and sovereign order, the prospect that China would eventually become just another liberal democratic society with a rational, scientific, political system, and reproduce their own identity was attractive. Despite the fact that there were American people who despised and feared the presence of the Chinese people, they, together with others who cared for and constantly worried about China, cognitively fixed China in an awkward historical position, a position only someone from a superior standpoint looking for the new Frontier could identify. An equally profound influence was capitalism in the United States, which also determined China's backward position. Under capitalism, owners of capital had the power of hiring laborers, and larger owners made hiring decisions internationally. Areas that could only provide healthy laborers could not determine their own fate in the international capitalistic system. Workers from their communities left subsistence sectors to look for monetary opportunities in labor sectors, henceforth securing a subsidiary niche for themselves in the capitalist system. Although workers periodically mailed home part of their feeble salary, this did not alleviate the increasing income gap between the subsistence sector and the capitalist center. The traditional sectors thus further depended on exporting healthy laborers. The capitalist employment relationship, income gap, and family background formed a permanent unequal relationship between owners of capital and laborers.

The United States acquired treaty rights so that it could employ Chinese laborers to work in the United States, as a reward for the U.S. assistance in resolving the British–French Allied invasion in 1860. The presence of Chinese workers and prostitutes in the United States produced unintended but inevitable social consequences. First, they lived in the same neighborhood and were not assimilated into the mainstream. The melting pot of nations found it difficult to incorporate the Chinese. Second, exported laborers typically included social rascals and criminals, begetting negative images. In addition, most Chinese immigrants worked extremely hard and were believed to cause local unemployment problems. Gradually, an atmosphere hostile to Chinese workers emerged in society and the popular term used against them, "Yellow Peril," clearly portrayed the mood. Consequently, latecomers including students, tourists, as well as workers were humiliated at the port of entry. Some were dispatched, others committed suicide, still others died of disease due to bad medical conditions at the detention site.[32]

The Chinese government was incapable of extending its protection or registering a protest against the deliberate media slurs against the Chinese.[33] Canton, where most immigrants came from, once launched a boycott against American goods, but there was a lukewarm response from other areas in China. Picking up on a major issue as an example, Liang Qichao, a famous late Qing writer, was critical of all sides:

In the spring of the year of Gengzi, the Honolulu authorities burned millions of people's properties for the sake of curbing an epidemic. The majority of such properties belonged to Chinese merchants. Immediately afterwards the Honolulu authorities promised to repay. Three years have passed without any signs of actualization.... Overseas Chinese all over Honolulu sticking out their necks, awaited the much needed repayments which were blocked by one House member at the

final moment, who crossed out relevant items from the budget....
Millions of our Chinese investments were gone.

The so-called first-rate civilization, or the so-called fatherland of the
liberal political system acted entirely like a charlatan and a robber....
It was not that our government did not intervene, but that it did not
know the issue at all; it was not that it did not know the issue, but that
it did not know there were Chinese at the place; it was not that it did
not know there were Chinese, but that it did not know there existed
such a place in the world.[34]

The Manchu court was truly mediocre; more importantly, it lacked
the motivation to act like a sovereign state. Discrimination against
overseas Chinese occurred all over the world; the court as well as
the subsequent Republican state was too busy managing internal
affairs to pay any attention to their subject's plight. Equally noteworthy was the fact that Chinese media reported little about the fact that
even the "most friendly" Americans were taking advantage of China's
backwardness. Compared with the Japanese-directed intervention in
Chinese affairs, such as 21 Demands and the Shandong Issue—which
revealed Japanese territorial ambition in China, the American
anti-Chinese sentiment seemed insignificant. Especially since at
approximately the same time, the U.S. government voluntarily turned
China's indemnities for the U.S. losses in the Boxers' Rebellion into
an educational fund to support China's development. This friendly
gesture from top American leaders had a much higher visibility and
was consistent with the dependent image of the Chinese government.

Ironically, the anti-Chinese sentiment in American society might
have actually reinforced the backward image of China and provided
an additional rationale for the government to help China. Under the
influence of Anson Burlingame, who was the first Chinese ambassador to Europe, Mark Twain, for example, linked the poor Chinese
workers in the United States to a poor China. According to a Chinese
translation, Twain was quoted as having regretted that nobody loved
Chinese people, nobody was friendly to them to the extent that even
an easy move to relieve them from suffering would not be considered
by anyone. Twain accused everyone, every community, and every
state that disliked, abused, and oppressed these alien workers.[35]
Twain then asked if the German authorities were likely to tell their
soldiers to tramp the United States, kill American people, leave no
land in peace but just kill, kill, and kill in order to open a road for the
offended religion of theirs and reach the core of the United States.
Twain wondered if Germans would do the same thing to Britain or
France: or was this only something people would do to China?[36]

SPLIT IDENTITY: THE CHINESE NARRATIVE

Since the late nineteenth century, Chinese intellectuals had been struggling to define the meaning of being Chinese. This puzzle originated exclusively from their encounter with the West, whose forces intruded into all aspects of Chinese culture—the military, religious, political, and financial spheres. The lack of conceptual capacity in the Chinese culture to interpret this encounter had continuously caused emotional confusion in the political and intellectual community, with some determined to learn from the West, perhaps through Japan, others wanting to strengthen the existing indigenous culture, and still others wanting to try some blend of the Orient with the Occident. These different approaches in confronting the West resulted in psychological as well as political confrontations among the Chinese themselves.

Basically, political leaders and intellectuals could be classified into two affective complexes: "progressionism," which has the confidence that eventually an ordinary Chinese could fully utilize all Western institutions, knowledge, and technology; and "conditionism," which holds the belief that somehow Western practices had to be introduced in line with the appreciation and the preservation of Chinese indigenous conditions and revised accordingly. Except for the very radical, who either conceived of anything Chinese as completely worthless or considered anything Western as totally nonsense, both progressionists and conditionists wanted to see China as strong as and equal to the West.

In fact, progressionists and conditionists were not two distinctively separate groups as many Sinologists conventionally believed.[37] They shared a common affective orientation toward the West. Even if progressionists did not necessarily like the West, they felt relatively more comfortable with the Western lifestyle. Sometimes one was both progressionist and conditionist, depending on the occasion. A progressionist became a conditionist when imperialism arose but returned to progressionism upon seeing the much regretted cycle of conservatism in China resurface.

The political infighting between the two different approaches in China continued throughout the twentieth century. This infighting occurred inside the mind of every Chinese intellectual, including both conditionists and progressionists. Political expediency could lead one individual to accuse another of excessive progressionism (i.e. total Westernization, and subsequently incur the countercharge of being xenophobic). It seems that what both sides did was to control the much feared total Westernization or extreme xenophobia inside each of them. Thus, the easiest way out was to select as a target the feared tendency within and act in the opposite way to demonstrate one's own rationality. As a result, a progressionist could periodically appear and behave conservatively and a conditionist could at times sound enlighteningly progressionistic.

The projected contradiction within was always emotionally stimulating because it was related to one's deep identity as a Chinese national. Consequently, one could be an emotionally progressionist at one time but a conditionist at another. Although in awe of the West, few Chinese would want to be labeled "Western," nor would a xenophobe like to be called anti-Western. Neither Western nor anti-Western, this was the predicament of Chinese nationalism: wanting an identity and also fearing it. Indeed, there was the fear of being pinned down as a progressionist or a conditionist although it was improbable to be both at the same time. An ordinary policy dispute could, under psychocultural circumstances, turn into a fierce identity struggle between any two of those once opportunist groups of politicians, warlords, and bureaucrats. Pure politically expedient manipulations easily turned into serious emotional struggles.

Constantly searching for an "Other" to prove, through contradiction, what one was or was not, composed a typical modern Chinese political drama. This Other could be either internal, such as feudalist, counterrevolutionary, compradors, or defectors, or external, such as anti-Chinese, imperialist, or Japanese militarist. This way of fighting the unwanted self in the disguise of fighting one another involved a psychotic element in that people were incapable of seeing themselves entirely, historically, and open-mindedly. The fear of being identified as, for example, a feudalist conditionist or a comprador progressionist left no psychological home to which one could return, hence there was a need to have a clear, permanent, and omniscient enemy to help one evade the ultimate identity question through opposing this inimical Other. I call this dependent nationalism. It is discussed further in chapter 3.

The infighting among as well as inside each Chinese (and obviously Japanese intellectuals, too, though of a different nature) reflected a deeper clash of civilizations. However, the West was not a direct participant and therefore enjoyed the privilege of being able to determine when and how its various agents wanted to join the battle. At first glance, there was no similar identity struggle in the minds of these Western intruders. Yet, the struggle inside the intruders in a deeper sense actually motivated the intervention of the West (and later Japan) under the camouflage of universal progressionism. For many China watchers in the West, China had always represented an outdated "Other" to be developed or rescued. Western sympathizers of Chinese conditions, who were generally cynical of their own society, were either critical of the Beijing government for its lack of vision, or protective of it because their own governments disallowed China a fair chance. Either way, they usually wanted to help. In fact, a lot of these predominantly male China watchers married Chinese women, reflecting as well as reinforcing their love for Chinese people.

From the Chinese perspective, this pitiful love was hard to digest. Chinese intellectuals were wary of how China was being treated conceptually as well as practically in the West. Whenever China was conceptually feminized, it was assisted wholeheartedly by the West, but few Chinese intellectuals could cope with the ambivalence thus aroused. Moreover, when this kind of benign colonialism met resistance from China, Eurocentrism in the West shifted toward its racist end for a period of time, which easily provoked further xenophobic sentiment from China. For the Chinese people, therefore, the inability to cope with feminizing love also indicated their own internal split between progressionism and conditionism. An imperialist move from the West served as a perfect Other for the Chinese to resolve their temporal need to evade a substantive identity.

It was in this historical context that Chinese revolutionaries struggled with the meaning of China being a sovereign state. In the process of state building, it was difficult to cope with the predicament that the ordinary Chinese hardly appreciated being autonomous citizens of their state, which was a rational design to protect them from the Dark Ages and to promote their influence in the non-Christian world.[38] What the Chinese state protected, by contrast, however was its distinctive cultural identity. A loose kind of Orientalism prevailed in the external view of China. Orientalists are those who, consciously or not, lock those under study in a space called "Orient," as an exotic object to be discovered, collected, and deprived. Conditionists resented this loss of Chineseness while progressionists adapted to it. What is interesting is that there emerged an unnoticed consensus among Orientalist and counter-Orientalist writers that China, as a sovereign state, was first a piece of territory like every other state but different in nature in its political culture and economic backwardness.

To fairly interpret Chinese foreign policy thus requires a rereading of the meaning of state by incorporating the function of emotion in state building. In short, the state was for the Chinese a tool to counter Western influence. Since China as a state was believed to be inferior by all standards intrinsic to a Christian state, such as religious conviction, civic participation, property rights, or defense capacity, state building inevitably reproduced a sense of inferiority among the Chinese. Once Chinese statesmen were completely engrossed in this dilemma and lost their access to discursive mechanisms beyond the rationality of state, the only solution left was to strive to beat the Western state by having a Western-styled state in China. Unfortunately, this Western-styled state in China could not help but define Chineseness, which it supposedly protected, by economic backwardness and cultural collectivism. That is to say, the Chinese counter-state deprived Chineseness of its superior cultural identity. Its sole meaning lay in its countering function. As a result, the counter-state and the sense of inferiority form one dominant discourse. This self-alienation was the origin of "reflexive Orientalism" arising out of the fusion of conditionism and progressionism. This is the subject of chapter 2.

A Moral Critique

Competing narratives in Japan did not stop the statist perspective from finally persevering over all other competing ideologies and consequently leading to a war against China. It may look like the discursive analysis provides no explanation to the realist world. Nonetheless, the drive to eliminate the alterity form of existence is clearly present in the statist narrative, as in the other narratives. However, it should not be statism per se that explains the violence because even totalizing idealists could be equally violent. As Levina worried that subsuming alterity into a totality inevitably leads to violence, it is not difficult to see that almost all killings in history were done in the name of some totalizing philosophy. One major goal of the international relation theorization, which produces this realism, idealism, as well as constructivism, is to trace the process of nation building and the formation of the international system. If one does not consider international and East Asian systems to be open-ended and to be continuously developed, would not any analysis of how far the nation building or formation of the international system is from the end be an act of violence? On the contrary, recognizing the international system as an open-end system would allow states to be a constantly fluid form, then any state is in itself a legitimate formation that cannot be denied. Without the fear of being denied, the drive for a violent solution to cope with alterities would diminish.

The explanation of violence thus lies not merely in the contents of any specific narrative such as realism or the socioeconomic background that gives strength to its ultimate rise, but also lies deeper in the discursive incapacity of modern statists (including both realists and liberals, and even constructivists) to accept alterities as absolute alterity. When alterity is not discursively absolute, the drive to eliminate it is imperative because the sheer presence of an irreducible alterity would mean self-denial. In this chapter, I tried to show the readers how the attempt to establish a totalizing framework is fruitless and has caused violence and self-doubt. In this way of thinking, realism is not an explanation of a scheme, but is a scheme to be explained. The moral failure of realism is not just about its negligence toward humanity, but also about its totalizing discursive style. The formation of international and East Asian systems on an open-ended, fluid, and alterity-recognizing horizon is a necessary though not sufficient condition for China and its watchers to avoid violence.

2

THE ORIENTALIST CLUE: EQUALIZING THE COUNTER-STATE

INTRODUCTION

Ambiguities concerning China's identity in world politics were largely resolved with the beginning of the Cold War. Few students of China are interested in analyzing the purpose of Chinese foreign policy precisely because the goal seems too clear to be questioned. Chinese academics and politicians, as well as those who study Chinese foreign policy typically hold that key factors of national interest defined in terms of territorial security, national reunification, and modernization are undoubtly what China aims to accomplish in the post–Cold War era. In fact, leading analysts tend to interpret all other purposes, such as nationalism, into a national interest calculus.[1] In response, Chinese diplomacy witnesses repeated rhetoric of sovereign integrity, peace and development, and strategic partnership, reflecting the wisdom of classic realism. The question, which I want to tackle in this chapter, is whether or not the rhetoric effectively conveys the meaning of foreign policy to those who enlist in the rhetoric. In other words, to what extent the rhetoric of national interest suppresses the expression of motivation underneath each foreign policy move taken.

My questioning of the notion of national interest in general, and foreign policy in particular, stems from the seemingly ineffable rise of nationalistic sensitivity in China toward the United States in the last decade of the twentieth century. Despite the show of self-restraint by the Chinese, Beijing leaders and the intellectual strata have on private occasions consistently expressed great anxiety concerning a perceived U.S. conspiracy to separate Taiwan from China and to subvert Chinese sovereignty pertaining especially to the human rights issue.[2]

In other words, many of those who have opined about China's U.S. policy do not like what they see even though they by far abide by classic realism.[3] This suggests that the foreign policy circle in China does not necessarily enjoy its own pledges. This emotional dimension, while missing in the mainstream scholarship on the subject, is nonetheless relevant, for frustration may have accumulated to such an extent that the range of policy options in the years to come would be reduced severely. Interested readers can find a mathematic model on this in chapter 4.

Contemporary scholarship on Chinese foreign policy usually concentrates on national interest and capability questions.[4] However, foreign policy made in the name of the Chinese state has an origin and repercussions outside of the state establishment. Historically, foreign policy was not foreign to the Chinese territory of "under-heaven." "Foreign" or "alien" used to mean "barbarian," "peripheral," or "frontier." It is not clear how well Chinese statesmen today have exempted themselves from the "under-heaven" legacy. Nonetheless, popular hindsight in China is that since the end of the Opium War in 1842 China has suffered imperialist intrusion, thus China must now have a strong state to protect its people from suffering yet another humiliation. Being unaware of the implication (or this being exactly intended), Chinese intellectuals had used the term "national family" (*guojia*) to signify the notion of territorial, sovereign state. The use of "family" insinuates that states are cultural gatherings and their ranks depend on their cultural proximity to Confucianism. In contrast, however, territoriality in the context of the contemporary state simply makes irrelevant the notion of a superior culture. This means that Confucian standards could not determine the criteria of what a good country should be like.

To continue the discussion on Chinese sovereign identity in chapter 1, I discuss the Western Orientalism view of the Chinese state, responses from China in the form of reflexive Orientalism, and the impacts of reflexive Orientalism on the purpose of state as reflected in Chinese foreign policy. Next, I attend particularly to the way Chinese statesmen present China's foreign policy concerns. In this regard, I will use Zhou Enlai as my primary example. Finally, I attempt to provide an alternative interpretation of Beijing's foreign policy in the beginning of the new Millennium.

ORIENTALIST VIEWS OF THE CHINESE STATE

Edward Said's critical study of Orientalism, embodied in scholarship and literature on the so-called "Orient,"[5] challenges all area studies to the extent that it discloses the subject under study as being the making of students of the areas. According to this broad view of Orientalism, all area studies, including China studies, cannot claim political innocence or value-neutrality. The positions of the narrator who determines what is to be observed with which referent points are argued to provide meanings to the subject studied. Therefore, China scholarship is an intrinsic element in defining what is China, not a field of knowledge exterior to it. In an extreme sense, even Said himself cannot be excused of the making of Orientalism for the simple fact that he enlists the term "Orientalism." While he means to be critical, he reproduces (or creates) "the Orient" as a cognitively expedient and powerfully constraining category.

Since historically China was not understood as a territorial state, students of China who treat it as a piece of sovereign territory and claim knowledge of China cannot be exempted from Orientalism. All of us use "China" in our daily language even though some of us are consciously aware of the problem of the term.[6] Nowadays, the spatial dimension has dominated the temporal dimension when speaking of China. This is especially true in foreign policy analysis because the term "foreign" presupposes territorial limitation of China. What ostensibly exists inside of territorial China accordingly attracts more attention than how celestial China has become territorial China. This quest for an objective China typically examines China in terms of its distance from the model of liberal state, hence the operation and existence of civil society is critical to all political analysis.[7] The concern for civil society in China culminates once a year in the U.S. human rights report, which painstakingly details cases involving violations in China. Stories of violations such as slaughter of female babies, jailing of dissidents, and suppression of religious freedom, and so on, easily take up front pages. All this portrayal of lacking civility carries with it a referential power that determines the location and the angle from which one approaches China as a territorial state.

Films that are not meant to be critical of China often reproduce an image of China that lacks humanity, suggesting the essential relevance of China's backward image in the audience's acquaintance of the Chinese state. "Taipan," for example, juxtaposes a static, dependent, and feminine China (reified through Chen Chong) against active, independent Western visitors implicitly constructing an image of an inactive China versus a lively West. "Big Troubles in Little China" represents Chinese in the underground—a mysterious world. "The Year of the Dragon" similarly duplicates a lawless, brutal, yet feminine Chinese culture. This negative view of Chinese society and culture distinguishes the Chinese state from Western states and later supports

Taiwanese authorities' polemic with China concerning Taiwan's sovereign independence. For example, in his 1996 inauguration speech, President Lee Teng-hui specifically charged China as being feudal, despotic, poor, and backward.[8] Seeing China as an external (and therefore territorial) state, Taiwan needs and acquires the discursive tool (of civil society) that renders the narrator a location (outside the Chinese state) to set the standard of observation.

This last instance regarding Taiwan's status actually reiterates a suspicion regarding the Chinese state, a suspicion that has existed since the Boxers' Rebellion. The suspicion is that China does not have the defense capacity required of an ordinary state. Contemporary analyses of Beijing's Taiwan policy always question the rationality of using force to reunite with Taiwan,[9] this despite the constant miscalculation of Chinese deterrence in modern history. For example, the Allied forces did not believe that the Kuomintang (KMT) troops were able to fight Japan alone. Today, remarks about China's military forces vis-à-vis the United States, who presumably will defend Taiwan, are generally skeptical. In reality, not only did Republican troops hold on for eight years during the second Sino-Japanese War, but the People's Liberation Army also intervened in Korea in 1950, countered the Indian troops in 1962, and launched a punitive war against Vietnam in 1978, all to the surprise of China watchers.[10] I analyze of China's defense culture further in chapter 3. The suspicion continues nonetheless that China will be considered rational only if it chooses to cooperate.[11]

The case of Taiwan touches upon another dimension of the modern state, namely, the level of development. The use of economics as a criterion of state performance does not initially come from within China and, understandably, leaders in China have struggled with it.[12] In any case, there is no denying that China has been lagging economically allowing the statist analysts to argue reasonably that Chinese leaders place priority on modernization. On the one hand, Taiwan is, according to the popular impression, more modern than China from the marketization point of view. Chinese leaders thus need to compete economically to win legitimacy for reunification. On the other hand, emphasis on modernization unavoidably shifts resources away from military sectors and may render China increasingly vulnerable to Taiwan's quest for independent statehood. With modernization being the criterion, sympathy for independent Taiwan is rising among China specialists and this sympathy comes with the perception of the maturing of civil society in Taiwan.[13]

To summarize, the paradigm of territorial state, which places China in a cultural vacuum, enlists an Orientalist device that contains at least four discursive mechanisms: civic culture, modernization, human rights, and national defense. In contrast, what the Chinese education system used to teach was heavenly order, cyclical pattern, selfless virtue, and moral appeal. Even today, in addition to the value prescribed for territorial China, school children and young cadres continue to read about filial piety, party rule, duties, and patriotism. As a result, the Chinese state appears to be no more than a territorial enclosure of a dependent society, with low development, collectivism, and irrational emotion. All this Orientalist specification influences students of China negatively, who then perceive China as a potential threat to the rational denomination of state, but may have the good-will of wanting to help China evolve into a progressive society.

Chinese leaders and intellectuals, trapped in the notion of state sovereignty, can be very frustrated for not being able to resume historical superiority to which they thought China was entitled. This frustration led to a variety of responses. I use the term "response" because the rhetoric of the Chinese heavenly order is no longer legitimate and one can only choose to accept or refuse the statist paradigm. If one divides the Orientalist dimension of thought based on image and action, one can logically break responses from China into four categories depending on whether one accepts or refuses the images and actions. I label these four categories as progressionism, postcolonialism, indigenization, and reflexive Orientalism (see table 2.1). The latter three types together form conditionism, which I discussed in chapter 1. In the next section, I introduce the first three categories briefly and its implications for Chinese foreign policy. Then I discuss the last category separately because I think it is this category that is still guiding China's foreign policy in the beginning of the new millennium.

Table 2.1 Chinese responses to the Orientalist view of China

Responses Images and action	Progressionism	Postcolonialism	Indigenization	Reflexive Orientalism
Orientalist images	Yes	No	No	Yes
Orientalist prescription	Yes	Yes	No	No

Chinese Hybrid Responses to Orientalism

The irrelevance of Chinese culture cannot be more obvious than that in the advocacy of complete Westernization. The earlier representatives of this progressionist response were May-Fourth intellectuals who introduced to China a variety of Western thoughts among which there were liberalism, socialism, empiricism, humanism, and so on.[14] The common thread of all these thoughts was their determined pledge to jettison anything Chinese. For them, Chinese tradition represented suppression of human nature and indeed many argued that there was no room for reconciliation between China's feudal past and Western modernity.[15] The magic word for the early liberals was "rationality," the breeding of which in the Chinese mind accordingly required the liberation of the soul from the Confucian establishment such as family.[16] Like Orientalists who treat China as a symbol of backwardness, early progressionists also held negative images of China. They prescribed a solution for China embedded in "science" and "democracy." The whole idea of modernization was to rescue a dying culture by creating agency for its individual citizens.

To take a closer look at progressioists' anti-feudal campaign would, however, show a different reading of their motivation. Progressionists acknowledged that China as a state was backward. While they all wanted to help China, this beloved China could not be understood in territorial terms. As argued in chapter 1, liberalism and other Western thoughts were basically an instrument to strengthen China in the face of Western challenges.[17] For example, liberals specifically promoted individuals to fight against certain family conventions. They had no trust of their fellow citizens' spontaneous initiatives and wanted them to consciously and actively perform liberalism. In other words, liberalism was not much more than a weapon to destroy Confucianism. Since the purpose of promoting liberalism and democracy was really about Chinese patriotism, progressionists were able to move back and forth between individual freedom and national freedom and conceived the latter as being the ultimate goal.[18] Few progressionists were ever interested in instituting Christianity in China,[19] so the souls liberated from feudal tradition had to find residence in the Chinese state that was intended to be an instrument to oppose imperialism, which was a synonym of "West" to early progressionists. The predicament lies precisely in the de-constructive emptiness of early Westernization thoughts that took destructive anti-feudalism as the only sensible path to opposing Western imperialism.

The instrumentality of liberalism has declined during and after the interlude of Communist Party rule between 1950 and 1990. Liberals in China have reemerged in the 1990s.[20] Liberals at the turn of the century examine liberalism more from perspectives of Western liberalism than from the need of China to protect itself from imperialism.[21] Some raise the possibility of having a kind of civil society that has distinctive Chinese characteristics.[22] Without specifying forms of Chinese civil society (because this should supposedly evolve spontaneously) liberals in the new century are nonetheless suspicious of the role the Chinese state can play in the process. The worry of imperialist intrusion is not so apparent in contemporary liberals as in early progressionists. Some are openly skeptical of nationalism that once motivated May-Fourth progressionists.[23] The solution is typically to withdraw state from society instead of making it strong. They clearly deny the Party of any significant achievement in its 50-year reign.

In comparison with the weak tradition of liberalism in China, there has been an even smaller number of postcolonials who refuse the Orientalist specification of backward China, but welcome assistance from the West. These public figures actively favor the introduction of Western thoughts and institution into China but criticize the construction of the Orientalist images of their polities. During the Republican period, Madame Chiang Kaishek was probably the best example of this thinking. Her contemporary counterpart is possibly President Lee Teng-hui of Taiwan between 1988 and 2000. These are postcolonial politicians struggling with their own identities. Unlike the progressionists, they resent the specification of their political system as primitive or backward. Recognizing the inevitability of learning from the West, they strive to present to the West how modern their citizens have become. Madame Chiang did this by painting a democratic and capitalist China for U.S. congressmen to appreciate. With her perfect English and attractive Oriental look, she was able to enlist dramatic sympathy from her audience.[24] Domestically she transformed her husband's Confucian renaissance campaign, which was officially entitled New Life Movement, into a Christianization campaign.[25] Later she served as the first Chinese Air Force commander, devoted to the building of a modern military for China.

Similarly, Lee wants to avoid being associated with the low images of China. He does this not by showing how progressive the Chinese state has become but by constructing a separate image for Taiwan.[26] He has been consistent in his presentation of Taiwan as a model of Chinese democracy and never fails to criticize human rights violation in China when giving a public speech. He tries painstakingly to demonstrate that his Taiwan is no longer a part of China by skillfully contriving periodical political confrontations with China. Having successfully invited the United States to wedge the difference between China and Taiwan,[27] Lee ably meets the democratization expectations of U.S. congressmen and secures much sympathy for his confrontational policy. Unlike earlier progressionists whose ultimate motivation continues to register in a deep-seated anti-West sentiment, postcolonial politicians are more concerned with being accepted by the West.

In contrast to pro-Western values of both progressionists and postcolonials, there has been a strong and populist anti-Western force in China. The Chinese state as a counter-state starts with these indigenizers, who believe that a return to China's own tradition is the only valid solution to Western encroachment on China's social order.[28] An earlier quintessential representative were the Boxers, who relied on the spirit of folk heroes to fight imperialism. Anti-Manchurian racism once prevailed among the Han Chinese majority in the early twentieth century.[29] Republican intellectuals in this stream debated progressionists from perspectives that denied the superiority of Western values as well as institutional designs. While not necessarily opposing modernity, indigenizers believe that transformation of Chinese culture is not the same as overthrowing its tradition.[30] Some sort of combination and harmony between the Chinese and the Western is not only possible but desirable. They anticipate a rebirth of Chinese culture.[31] In fact, most politicians, including Mao, have held this view during both the Republican and the Communist periods (with the exception during the Cultural Revolution).[32] Indigenizers do not trust the West. They generally reserve the use of foreign capital in developing China. On the other hand, they hold the conviction that the Chinese people are able to find their own path to modernity.

Contemporary indigenizers are critical of globalization and the policy of openness to the outside world or socialist market reform. While indigenizers disagree among themselves on a variety of issues, all parties share the conviction that the solution to China's problems does not come from the West and that the situation in China cannot be evaluated by Western standards. The behavioral relevance of indigenizers' perspective is significant in that there emerges an Occidentalist tendency.[33] To oppose the West, the Chinese state as a counter-state ironically reproduces China's low images in the eyes of the Western countries and reinforces the confrontational tendency between China and the West, hence a vicious circle is created.

Progressionists, postcolonials, and indigenizers represent three conditionist styles of response to the referential framework imposed

Table 2.2   Hypotheses explaining choices of response

Responses	Westernization	Postcolonialism	Indigenization	Reflexive Orientalism
Background conditions	No access to power (the intellectuals)	No location (the Taiwanese)	No exposure to new knowledge (the nationalists)	With power, location, and knowledge

by the paradigm of territorial sovereignty (see table 2.2). Foreign policy implications within each stream are unique with, for example, progressionists favoring openness and indigenizers preferring selection. While postcolonials seek dependence, the other two share the mission of national revival. Their background is distinctively different in the sense that necessary conditions for a person to belong to one of the three approaches are not the same. Inductively speaking, Progressionists have fewer access to power, most of them have been intellectuals. Postcolonials typically have an identity problem, being hybrid in their cultural composition. They lack a clear location to speak and suffer what Homi Bhabha calls unhomely inbetweenness.[34] Finally, indigenizers are those who have relatively less exposure to Western knowledge. When all three—access to power, Western knowledge, and a position to speak—are present in a person, he or she is likely to be a reflexive Orientalist.

REFLEXIVE ORIENTALISM AS A RESPONSE

Reflexive Orientalism refers to the acceptance of Orientalism by Chinese intellectuals and politicians and the development of new identities with a sense of subjectivity accordingly. As a result, the Orientalized Chinese may assert Orientalist images upon him/herself. Instead of seeing these images negatively, however, reflexive Orientalists establish their own justification for the images that they accept. There is nothing bad about having backward economics, undeveloped civil society, collectivistic human rights, or relatively limited national defense capability. The key here is that reflexive Orientalists are able to jettison the teleology of linear modernity. In substitute, they place China in its historical path without specifying its definite destiny. One is able to explain away the seemingly backward images by stressing national uniqueness, which territorial sovereignty implicitly protects. The counter-state arises when the purpose of the state is no more than a deep-seated emotion to oppose the Orientalist prescription set by Western countries.

For reflexive Orientalists, backwardness acquires new meanings that are not familiar to the sovereignty adherents for now backwardness no longer predicates upon a fixed direction. Since modernity had no fixed form for them, the advanced nature of Western countries in establishing civil liberty lose their advantage in China's search for a remedy. China need not look to the West for models of development. This way, backwardness in China as indicated by the paradigm of sovereignty ironically proves the existence of alternative routes of development. Being an alternative further contributes to the sense of uniqueness in China. Reflexive Orientalism thus deprives sovereignty of its original taste for liberal democracy and market capitalism. What remains for reflexivists is the legitimacy to use force to exclude foreign influences that are judged not conducive to the Chinese alternative still under making.

In this sense, globalization is neither a progressionist's gospel, nor an indigenizer's nightmare, but an opportunity to realize new possibilities.[35] To force modernization modeled upon European experiences would be tantamount to distorting personality and culture. Chinese leaders should accordingly pace modernization and democratization to avoid causing anxiety due to the rupture of the historical path.[36] Furthermore, neither should a reflexivist trust liberal spontaneity, nor authoritarian leadership. Some combination of creativity and intervention is inevitable. To gain room for trial and error sovereign defense is necessary to keep foreign intervention from taking place. On the other hand, the political system in China should adapt to the new configuration of a state–society relationship brought about by economic changes.

The role of the counter-state in foreign policy looms large in reflexive Orientalism. China's sovereign territory must be well guarded before nationals have room for creative adaptation. However, what counts as foreign intrusion is not always clear under globalization. Negotiation between the locals and the Communist Party center as well as between the center and the foreign countries is equally important in determining the perception of the Chinese leaders concerning foreign intervention. The opposite is true, too. When negotiations between China and the foreign countries encounter difficulties, differences between the locals and the center will more easily be interpreted as involving foreign intervention. Foreign policy usually appears to be lacking consistency as the mood varies with situations. A model of this position shifting in chapter 4 expresses the embedded inconsistency of postcolonial as well as reflexivist foreign policy.

To begin with, the Orientalist definition of China's backwardness is omnipotent because reflexivists, with some knowledge of modernization linearity, learn to internalize it. Then the dispute over the proper role of the Chinese state naturally arises between reflexivists and foreign Orientalists. Orientalists would consider the protective shield that the Chinese state presents in front of Western influences as a historically outdated tool of control, believing that the fate of China lies in the transformation of backwardness into Western modernity. Reflexivists can counter that position out of a conviction that Western modernity at best suffocates other indigenous alternatives that may lead to some version of modernity with Chinese characteristics.

In other words, reflexive Orientalism prepares interstate confrontation and interstate confrontation in turn consolidates reflexivists' reliance on the mechanism of the state. On the one hand, reflexivists' historical experiences produce very different feelings about state in China than in the Western countries. These feelings demand that reflexivists must not act in complete accordance to Western expectation. Without developing their own perspectives on the state system or appreciating their state being counter-state, however, reflexivists' most expedient solution to the maintenance of uniqueness is to be confrontational. Reflexivists do not have an alternative conceptual framework to signify Chineseness except state sovereignty. This sovereignty-related sensitivity is exacerbated whenever interactions between China and the West escalate as if assimilation into Western modernity would be taking place. Compared with postcolonialists whose histories are composed of hybrid interpretation, reflexivists are clear about their wish to represent an authentic China and therefore are not psychologically prepared to act dependently without hurting their self-dignity.

On the other hand, modern knowledge of reflexivists alerts them to the backwardness of China. This is why they are more tolerant toward new possibilities than indigenizers who feel antagonistic toward anything Western. Ambivalence of this sort can explain inconsistencies and cycles in reflexivist foreign policy. There is a need to act independently, and there is also a need to act expediently. Sensitivity toward violation of sovereignty varies by mood or by situation. It is quite possible that something conceived of as a violation in one situation is accepted without being questioned in another.[37]

For a reflexivist, a sense of inferiority is inevitable because the sovereignty paradigm judges one's ranking partly by looking at the strength of civil society. Reflexivists acknowledge that civil culture is not ripe in China, protection of individual human rights is flawed, and economic growth depends on the technology, market, and management of the outside world. Nonetheless, reflexivists maintain that civil society may not be the most appropriate form of participation in China. They further argue that collectivism, correctly identified by Western analysts as a feature of Chinese politics, is reality that is not subject to changes over night. In short, Orientalists and reflexivists agree on most observations that come out of Orientalist perspectives. Reflexivists try to overcome the sense of inferiority by stressing equal sovereignty.

Progressionists are outcasts in Chinese politics even though they may be heard often and even loudly in the academic fields, both domestic as well as overseas. Postcolonials are rare in China because not many politicians in China have experienced colonial cultural conquering. It is the battle between indigenizers and reflexivists that shapes the ups and downs in Chinese foreign policy. For reflexivists, the job is primarily defensive while for indigenizers there is a drive for offense, retaliation, or self-assertion. Reflexivists do not often assert specific solutions, at least not necessarily resulting in some sort of indigenous campaign, such as the Great Leap Forward, the Cultural Revolution, or the anti-bourgeois liberalization. The more moderate position often incorporates the reflexivists' initial inferior position. On this moderate position, even China could not possibly remain static and has already witnessed tumultuous changes.

Reflexivists believe that changes are irrevocable and the mission of the Chinese counter-state is to make sure that China does not sink once again to the status of colony. Reflexivists do not hesitate to use the state to mobilize economic production as well as anti-imperialist campaigns. Since the motivation is to substantiate the claim of Chinese characteristics vis-à-vis the West, the nature of being a counter-state remains true even in domestic politics. The substitution of counter-state for liberal-styled passive state in China insinuates reflexivists' lack of confidence in Chinese nationals' own initiative in finding solutions, hence the distrust toward spontaneity that powerless twenty-first-century progressionists/liberals always worship.

In sum, reflexivists accept the Orientalist description, but not the Orientalist prescription. The acceptance is the result of their cognitive incapacity to move beyond the paradigms of modernity and sovereignty. The refusal of prescription carries with it a kind of amorphous, atavistic resentment against historical imperialism and the suspicion that contemporary imperialism lingers on. Their knowledge about modernization alleviates the absurdity indigenizers may display in anti-Western campaigns. Their access to power leads them away from downgrading their own national identity through anti-Chinese campaigns. Finally, their historical memory of imperialist intrusion reduces sympathy toward hybrid postcolonials. As reflexivists, they are armed with a dubious hope for the future that is periodically relegated to oblivion due to the confrontational approach that the sensitive counter-state is made to adopt every once in a while.

ZHOU ENLAI AS A REFLEXIVE ORIENTALIST

Zhou Enlai was probably the most prominent reflexive Orientalist in the People's Republic's diplomatic history.[38] On all the aforementioned conditions that affect one's response to the device of sovereignty, Zhou had the proper background to be grouped into the reflexivist category. For example, he studied in France and was always in touch with foreign affairs before coming to power. In other words, he had access to Western knowledge. Having participated in coalition with the KMT and later the Long March, he played a key role in the Communist Party's coming to power. This gave him an indigenous location of voice when coping with foreign affairs. Finally, he was among the top government leadership since the beginning of the People's Republic.

Zhou's followers in the Foreign Ministry respected and learned a great deal from his style.[39] This made Chinese diplomacy an archetypal host of reflexive Orientalism. Basically, Chinese reflexive Orientalists believe in science and technology, sovereign independence, and national development. At the same time, they accept that China is economically backward, militarily weak, and ideologically and socially collectivistic, but they do not accept that collectivism is the cause of backwardness. In their perspective, Chinese culture is a factor not relevant to the sovereign world. The solution to China's backwardness ironically lies in one specific Orientalist reality, namely, the preservation of collectivism and this requires another Orientalist value, that is, sovereign protection.

Zhou Enlai did not question standards set up in the Orientalist–statist paradigm when evaluating newcomers to the state system. Encouraging Chinese people to have confidence in the future of China, he told them how well China had performed a year after the revolution on all those aspects that an ordinary Orientalist would be most concerned with. He acknowledged that the new government faced problems such as inflation, fiscal balance, resource supplies, transportation, and postwar recovery. Having faced "colossal challenges and difficulties," he pronounced victory, not on cultural or moral, but on economic, political, and military fronts:

> The imperialists repeatedly claimed that the young People's Republic will be struck out by all this seemingly irresolvable problems and will beg them for rescue. The past year proved that the prediction made by the imperialist is bankrupt. The Chinese people have achieved victory on the economic battlefront as they did on the military and political battlefronts.[40]

It is to be noted that he was equally concerned with defense strength and economic growth. Although he proclaimed victory, the motive of his remark was to show that China did not welcome foreign interference—not to deceive the Chinese by exaggerating victory. This motive was clear as he constantly worried about how a backward China could develop. The direction of China's development was nonetheless Western for he more than once cautioned his audience to be mindful of China's backwardness in the field of science, modernization, and defense capacity. For example, he recognized that China was economically no more than a "sub-colony," but advised people that China not rely on "imperialist countries who made us a sub-colony." He was confident that China could find a "profitable market for our own goods."[41] His analysis and general prescription could not have been very different had he asked a Western friend except that he refused assistance from the West to avoid damaging China's independence.

Zhou's remarks on science were particularly interesting for he considered the lack of science a major reason for China's backwardness. He complained that since Western science had come to China, China benefited very little because science was used as an instrument of "exploiting, oppressing and massacring Chinese."[42] He never questioned the importance of science in the Chinese context. For him, the problem was not science or science education, but control and use of science by imperialists. Now that "the situation has changed completely and the revolution for a new democracy has won," Zhou believed that science would eventually contribute to "China's transformation from an agricultural state to an industrial state."[43] Here, his goal of modernization echoed more classic realism than communism. He could not help but wonder "how many scientists we really need?"[44] Later he reiterated the sense of being backward by saying that the transformation "will take a very long time."[45] Unless transformed, he thought that China would not have modern defense, nor a high culture.[46]

Zhou then soothed all the scientists in China by promising: "we will get better and better everyday." Accepting China's backwardness and the ultimate importance of material development, he wanted scientists "who suffer material shortage to celebrate their spiritual liberation."[47] By spiritual liberation, he meant not having to work for imperialists. In other words, while there had to be some remedy to the backwardness in science, a necessary condition is sovereign protection of patriotic collectivism. He explained his optimism by pointing to the invincible power of science when science and collectivism combined in a certain way.

Zhou found that Chinese scientists coming from different backgrounds did not work well with one another, for example there was confrontation between those from Germany and Japan on the one hand and Britain and America on the other. As an advocate of collectivism, he urged scientists to "oppose individualism which is despotic in nature in a class society." Zhou said, "once we achieve real progress and freedom, we can use all the human power to struggle with the natural environment."[48] Zhou welcomed scientism's drive to exploit nature, but this Westernized goal was possible for China only if China adamantly subscribed to collectivism. Here, backwardness and collectivism, both of which were considered essentially Chinese by many China watchers (even today), were conceptually no longer mutually reinforcing. The Orientalist specification of collectivism became the reflexive Orientalists' solution.

Zhou specifically argued that communism in China developed hand in hand with "state nationalism" (*guojiazhuyi*). He thought *guojiazhuyi* was bad because it had the potential to make China an aggressor. What China needed was independence. For him, communism was welcomed because it promoted anti-imperialist independence.[49] This suggests how constraining the device of sovereignty was on Zhou's worldview. He thus reiterated the importance of "having strong defense capability."[50] The fact that he did not use Chinese cultural superiority in his quest for independence was illuminating. Not only was culture not a familiar force in the paradigm of sovereignty, but it was a sign of weakness for him. Zhou worried about the demise of Chinese culture, he warned, "imperialist influences since the past hundred plus years remain strong and deep in China's economics and, above all, in its culture."[51] No one can legitimately deny China as a sovereign state although people may not respect Chinese culture. Understanding this, one would not be surprised to hear why Zhou reemphasized in many speeches the importance of remembering that "diplomacy is about state-to-state relationship."

To put it differently, Zhou opposed globalism but promoted internationalism for the latter presupposed equality between sovereign states. Only as a state was Zhou's China ready to learn from other states or not to show arrogance when dealing with other states. I suspect that Zhou's well-known modesty might well reflect his anxiety of losing Chinese cultural identity. The notion of sovereignty helped him avoid the sense of inferiority stemming from the breakdown of cultural confidence in China. Zhou specifically touched upon this inferiority sensitivity when he explained the essence of patriotism (*aiguozhuyi*):

> Socialist patriotism is not narrow state nationalism, but is patriotism supported by national confidence, which is achieved under the guidance of internationalism. Some of our comrades worship capitalist countries' civilization because we were a semi-colony state in the past. They forget to examine its poison elements, blindly embracing them, and waver on principles. It is wrong to say that all about China is good or all about it is bad. We should critically accept Chinese and foreign cultures. *Dagongbao* used to have a column called "China the First." Where does China have that many "firsts"? It is wrong to have the column. Later, the column was unable to continue indeed. The new China is better than the old China for certain and the motherland is lovely. But, we have to learn from the foreign countries.[52]

His anxiety about Chinese backwardness continues well into the People's Republic's years ahead. He spoke about China's need for modern weapon, machinery, and transportation all the time. Most importantly, however, was his apprehension that the feudal legacy might sneak up behind his back:

> In China, there is feudalism with Chinese characteristics. We may have overthrown feudalism, but feudalist, bureaucratic conventions are still alive in society. China's past ruling classes used to be far away from the masses, lofty on top, peculiar in life style, and pretentious on appearance. We can become that easily, too. From top to bottom, all those with a title of director (*zhang*) easily receive special treatments from others. This is why outdated social customs often encroach upon us if we do not consciously and constantly prevent them, this is so even after socialism has rooted in the Chinese soil.

One can now return to Zhou's preoccupation with the definition of diplomacy as a state-to-state relationship. He reminded his audience that diplomacy had to be based upon people's support, but that this was not a diplomat's job. In his personal note to Zhu De, he advised that reports on diplomacy and on domestic governing be separated. Accordingly, the latter was dropped from the speech.[53] His famous five principles of peaceful coexistence reiterate his position that differences in domestic ideology and political system should not affect the state-to-state relationship. While indeed at that time Zhou could be rationally formulating a policy to break diplomatic isolation,[54] one cannot miss the ease with which he disregarded supposedly superior Chinese culture. In fact, he remarked a few lines later, "we Asian and African countries, including China, are *backward* in economics and *culture*" (italics added).[55] This statement, the most dramatic ever made in public abroad by a Chinese leader, provides a clue to a potentially revisionist account of Zhou's diplomacy in the early 1950s. His gesture was so low that classic realism could not make sufficient sense. He was very likely speaking out of anxiety about China's low culture, determined and camouflaged by the sovereignty discourse.

Nonetheless, Zhou could not possibly hide his cultural background totally. He used inter-personal relations to analogize state-to-state relations and reasoned accordingly. For example, he specifically instructed that, according to the advice of many foreign friends, terms such as "bandit," "imperialist," "fascist," and "devil" be dropped from news releases in order not to provoke bad feelings.[56] Here, "feeling" obviously belongs to an interpersonal rather than interstate phenomenon. On many other occasions, he used "brotherly relations" to describe interactions between China and its allies. In other words, for Zhou, in state-to-state relations, nothing should be personal, but the analogy of personal relations can be used to promote state-to-state relations. The personalization of the diplomatic rhetoric brought comfort to Zhou who was deprived of cultural confidence in the state-to-state relationship.

CONTEMPORARY REFLEXIVIST DIPLOMACY

Various themes have appeared in foreign policy statements made by Chinese leaders since Zhou Enlai came to power, including anti-imperialism, internationalism, revolution, peaceful coexistence, anti-hegemonism, peace and development, and independence and autonomy.[57] Each of these themes has emerged to provide legitimacy to foreign policy in specific historical contexts. While contexts have been constantly evolving so that themes may appear more or less frequently, depending on situations, the basic assumptions concerning the nature of the Chinese state remain stable. This is true despite the fact that disputes over the proper foreign policy position occur between indigenizers and reflexivists.[58] In this book, I am interested in those basic assumptions that have made the disagreement and debate possible and meaningful to those involved.

My argument is that Chinese leaders and intellectuals have adopted these assumptions from Western countries, although specific themes and policies vary widely across time and leadership. These assumptions provide a conceptual base upon which China as a state has been perceived and, in response, Chinese leaders have interpreted and reinterpreted the encountering with the West. Specifically, the conceptual treatment of China as a "backward state" constrains the way Chinese leaders perceive the world. Both "backward" and "state" contradicted Chinese self-images when the encounter with Western influences began. When it was clear that extant Chinese worldviews no longer made sense following the encounter with Western influences, Chinese intellectuals and leaders learned to accept China as being a backward state, jettisoning the image of being culturally superior.

What contemporary Chinese leaders have yet to realize is that "backward" and "state" are not separable concepts. China's backwardness is intrinsically a conceptual derivative of the state paradigm. This is where Said's Orientalism provides guidance. Studies of Orientalism can help point to a politics of forgetting, which erases the meaning of state in its inception. Indeed the notion of state carries rich meanings, however, those from Europe who practice politics in the name of state feel no need to clarify the meaning among themselves. These meanings direct them to look into certain aspects of other societies that they encounter during their venture into the world. In this sense, Orientalization of China means that China is not Christian, nor economically developed, militarily strong, civic, or liberal. The notion of state that is historically a protective shield against the city of gods, anarchy, fascism, communism, anathema such as Islam and Confucianism, and human rights violation defines what is to be interpreted as backward.

When Chinese leaders accepted China as a state, they at the same time denied a long history of cultural superiority that Chinese leaders had for generations aspired to. This lost sense of superiority frustrated Chinese of all strata and classes in their quest for collective rebirth. The device of state provides no outlet for this frustration, nonetheless the Chinese look to statism for a solution and therefore reinforce their inexpressible anxiety.[59] The more Chinese hope for a future, strong Chinese state, the more they remind themselves of its backwardness, discursively as well as practically. Responses mentioned earlier include total Westernization, postcolonial adaptation, indigenization, and reflexive Orientalism. Chapter 3 will study how responses of this sort could turn violent. At the present time, I suspect that most of those working in foreign policy sectors adopt an approach of reflexive Orientalism.

Reflexivists are conspicuous in terms of their acknowledgment of China's backwardness. They are adamant on the sovereignty issue, though. They are able to do this because for them state and backwardness are not mutually definable. Reflexivists share little historical background of the old-fashioned European states and often consider the Orientalist specification of collectivism as a base for prescribing a remedy to China's backwardness. As a result, they take Chinese collectivism seriously, which explains to them why China is not right for individual liberalism in human rights as well as for civil society. The habitual resort to the rhetoric of sovereignty ironically offers a pretext to Chinese leaders for deliberately not making changes toward the Western model of development.[60] However, the enlistment of the same rhetoric weapon deprives Chinese leaders of cultural superiority that may be useful in explaining away, and thus soothing, anxiety. The Chinese state means counter-state in the sense that it is reactive, anti-Western, and occasionally suppressive.

Reflexive Orientalism is present in China's human rights argument, which emerged on China's foreign policy agenda after Jimmy Carter took office in the White House and has become a galvanizing issue since the 1989 Tiananmen massacre. Being unable to move beyond the discussion of civil society, reflexivists cannot help but acknowledge that China is not ready for individual human rights. Their arguments are nonetheless Orientalist. First, it is their own business, said reflexivists, as regards coping with the human rights issue in China because the issue is domestic and not to be determined by foreign forces.[61] They do not understand the long tradition of sovereignty that sets apart state and society and the endogenous distrust toward the state in civil society. As Chinese leaders use sovereignty to ward off Western criticism, they only reinforce the backward image of the Chinese state, and the resulting uneasiness felt in the West prompts further interference.[62]

Second, reflexivists contend that China has human rights, but of a different nature. It is collective human rights concerning national survival facing imperialist intrusion, and concerning national development facing capitalist exploitation.[63] Note that both survival and development arguments presuppose a stereotyped backward country that is militarily weak and economically underdeveloped. In other words, the legitimacy of collective human rights argument comes from a standard of evaluation provided by the paradigm of sovereignty. Third, reflexivists say that because of its backwardness China needs sovereign protection against further imperialist intrusion, the menacing example of which is precisely Western interference with Chinese human rights issues. Coming full circle, reflexivists can adeptly use the Orientalist observation of weak sovereignty, backwardness, and collectivism to justify their transformation of state into counter-state. They have yet to apply Confucianism, Daoism, or Legalism in their argumentation, or even socialism or Marxism.

China's rebuttal turned offensive in recent years as charges of U.S. violation of human rights on a variety of collective databases such as child abuse, domestic violence, abortion, and racism escalated into antagonism.[64] The rebuttal does not represent attempts to overthrow sovereignty because, through refutation, Chinese leaders agree, by implication, that human rights are universal and border-crossing, the unit of observation is individual not collective, and China's backward development deserves exemption from the criteria applied to higher levels of development. Implicit in antagonism and polemics is the message that anger felt in China did not really come from U.S. interference in domestic affairs. It comes from the discursive inability to have a different set of standards that can immune China from Western value–laden dialogue.

This inability leads to Zhou Enlai's style of response, namely, using sovereignty to protect collectivism to resolve backwardness. Foreign policy themes such as peaceful coexistence, peace and development, and independence and autonomy, though serving different purposes in different periods, all point to one common goal: China's desire to use its own method to enter modernity, which is modeled after the West only in material terms. Contemporary Chinese foreign policy continues to follow this path.[65] The desire is predicated upon the availability of a Chinese method with which the search for a meaning of Chineseness can quietly begin. For Deng Xiaoping, this process of searching is called "crossing the river by touching a stepping stone one step after another." For Jiang Zemin, it is "the primary stage of socialism" wherein almost anything non-socialist is legitimate. Obviously, Chineseness is not something tangible. It represents an attitude of searching. This attitude guarantees that China's twenty-first-century foreign policy will proceed with an occasional stance of counter-state. Amidst the value-laden device of sovereignty, the Chinese state is playing an embarrassing role by using the concept of Western sovereignty almost obsessively to refuse Western advise on how to approach modernization, yet acknowledging Western specification of China's backwardness and direction of development, thereby taking the stance of reflexive Orientalism.

3

THE NATIONALIST CLUE:
DEFENDING PEOPLE'S HEART

INTRODUCTION

The National People's Congress of the People's Republic of China passed the National Defense Act during its annual session in March 1997. The objective of this new legislation, however, has been a cause of concern for foreign China watchers, since there is an unambiguous emphasis on what can be called "inward defense." According to the Act, one of the major functions of national defense is to prevent any potential internal split of the nation, a mission that immediately incurs concern from observers in Taiwan, where a separatist movement has been gaining increasing ground in the past decade.[1] Similarly, the call for "inward defense" also raises worry of another harsh crackdown on "subverting internal forces" (according to the Chinese official point of view) much like the Tiananmen incident of June 4, 1989 where the People's Liberation Army forcefully stopped a rare pro-democracy rally.

A more recent example would include the military actions that took place in the Taiwan Straits in 1995 and 1996. Serving as a warning against any potential international interference in the Taiwan Straits and as a means to silence the "internal Taiwanese separatist movement," Beijing launched a series of missile exercises to assert its sovereign claim over Taiwan.[2] Another example of concern for "inward defense" is evident in the reversion of Hong Kong to China on July 1, 1997. Despite the warning from London that the PLA entering Hong Kong would cause local anxiety, the PLA nonetheless went in on the grounds that there could be subversive elements in Hong Kong. With the presence of the PLA, Deng Xiaoping argued that those who may have thought of creating troubles would naturally think twice.[3] Summer of 2002 witnessed a rally of 500 thousands in protest of the proposed legislation of national security act drafted by the Hong Kong autonomous government, making inward defense an increasingly sensitive issue in China. By expanding the definition of national defense, this Act therefore targets those whom national defense, in its conventional definition, is meant to protect.

Inward defense, though a common phenomenon in the history of modern state building, is a concept seldom analyzed in Western defense circles. In fact, the concept of inward defense may well arouse anxiety from political and military observers since it seems to be the antithesis of the conventional meaning of national defense.[4] China's National Defense Act not only provides a legal basis for the military to engage in military actions against its own civilians, it is also a reflection of China's distinct national defense concept; contrary to the territorially oriented national defense concepts in the West, I argue that national defense in postcolonial China responds to an anxiety about disharmony in society. In accordance with traditional conceptions, the Chinese regard territorially oriented defense as an indication of the moral decay of an emperor. Similarly contemporary Beijing authorities cannot entertain the idea of a great Chinese civilization being territorially contained, hence the reiteration of China's modality for Third World countries.[5] Nonetheless, since the failure of the Boxers' Rebellion (1899–1900) whereby the Allied forces of eight countries completely demoralized the Chinese dynastic court, the proclivity to obtain a correct human relationship among all the people under heaven has evolved into an obsessive pursuit for a unified national front to resist external imperialism.

In brief, while national defense presupposes the existence of a permanent threat outside Chinese sovereign borders, inward defense aims to prevent a harmonious social being from splitting. Without such internal cohesion, national defense, which juxtaposes external threat and internal order, would lose its bearings. Inward defense therefore refers to the mechanism that justifies as well as practices the prevention of dissenting voices from arising within sovereign borders. Accordingly, national defense, by targeting external enemies, inevitably presupposes, in an ultimate sense, a united social order within territorial boundaries.

Consequently, contemporary Chinese identity is less defined by one's relationship with the emperor, as a Son of Heaven, than with the Chinese nation in its confrontation with an invading imperialist Other. Although this defensive mentality has led the Chinese military in both the Republic and the People's Republic eras to defend territories that the Chinese considered as their own, the military practices continue to demonstrate that national defense embraces an essentially introspective state of mind.[6] It is not merely a material, objective capacity for sovereign, excluding power; rather, it is a determined search for a path to return to a pure national identity that no longer exists. As a result, the Chinese military could either jettison territory with a feeling of superiority, or display a compulsive attachment to a piece of land regardless of the sacrifices required. All this performance, in the end, enacts a position of moral incorruptibility with a spirit reaching far beyond secular territory, therefore reproducing a difference that distinguishes the Chinese from the imperialist Other. Ironically, Chinese nationalism that supports this difference itself becomes highly dependent on the maintenance of that difference. As a result, national defensive mobilization becomes a discursive force in perpetuating and identifying imperialist threats and, in turn, reproduces nationalism through the presumed presence of imperialism.

A HISTORICIST READING OF NATIONAL DEFENSE

It is not possible or, at least, not easy to provide a full account of Chinese national defense behavior without referring to the recent critical literature on sovereignty. Unfortunately, mainstream research on Chinese external behavior has yet to establish a dialogue with a number of nascent schools of thoughts. Postmodern,[7] feminist,[8] as well as postcolonial[9] writers, have questioned foreign policy studies' assumption of sovereignty, since it is exercised to the disadvantage of those living in the border areas, physically as well as conceptually.[10] Indeed the sovereign order, which assumes a chaotic outside world, cannot persist without each country preparing for a defense against some external enemy.[11] If there is no enemy outside, then there is no need for sovereignty, nor national defense. Especially for an immigrant society such as the United States, an enemy outside is particularly important in that immigrants belonging to a nascent and imagined community can only create a collective national identity by confronting a common external enemy.[12] National defense, which perpetuates the feeling of being threatened, sustains a nation discursively rather than physically.

Postmodern critics hold that diplomacy, which supposedly manages mutually exclusive sovereign relations, is in fact both a product and, indirectly, a reproducer of states' mutual estrangement from one another.[13] The unstated position that people represented by diplomats are one harmonious whole is obviously unattainable, but when disputes among sovereign actors happen, the presumption of harmony, that is solidarity, gains strength. As a result, the forces that contradict the assumption of harmony become elements of anti-diplomacy, for they defy the very foundation of the sovereign binary of order: the orderly inside versus the chaotic outside. Chapter 7 provides a case study in this regard. Similarly, all national defense behavior is precisely an act of mutual estrangement and forces that contradict the harmony assumption are consequently "anti-defense." Anti-defense is much more serious than anti-diplomacy because, unlike the discursive nature of diplomacy, national defense, physically as well as discursively, demands expressive loyalty from those encompassed by it.

Sovereignty-based national defense, which almost all states universally practice today, nonetheless requires more efforts to implement in China than in the Western nation-states. This is because national defense based on territorial security is historically a product of the Western sovereign order. Under the traditional Chinese hierarchical worldview, where the Chinese celestial court was assumed to be the sole ruler of all lands, no secular leaders (or any Great Wall) possessed the legitimacy of permanently separating others; leaders were leaders because they won the hearts of people everywhere, nor could they discriminate others on a territorial basis. All were subjects of the sovereignty of a morally or religiously supreme being. In contrast, and by definition, the goal of modern sovereign defense is to protect the nation from foreign intrusion. An imagined enemy becomes critical in that the national defense establishment must decide upon or justify the amount of resources considered sufficient for the defense build-up. A balance must be struck between the unlikely prospect that a nation can prepare itself to fight all the countries in the rest of the world, and the risk of under-investment in the defense sector.[14] In addition, to have each individual citizen invest in their own defense on the market would be obviously inefficient, for rarely would a nation face simultaneous attacks from all directions. National defense thus conceived is predicated on three assumptions that reinforce one another, yet none are familiar to traditional Chinese thinking: clear national borders to be defended, an imagined enemy or group of enemies, and professionalism of national defense. For example, if no defined borders existed, there could be no enemy located outside national borders; if no professional army exists to guard the borders, resources can cross boundaries at will to a point that may render a state borderless; if there is no imagined enemy, why would one need professional defense?

Indeed no exaggerated image of the enemy could occur in a cultural vacuum. The construction of any imagined enemies relies upon certain psycho-cultural foundations to make them appear real for the citizen-defenders. One component of these foundations deals with the specific political context of the defending nation. For example, the specification of the USSR as the enemy of the United States emerged partially as a product of the U.S. self-image as a capitalist, democratic country, yet the perception of socialism's evil and its fundamental confrontation with capitalism takes place outside the conventional definitions of national defense.[15] Therefore, the defense sectors cannot help but reproduce the image of a Soviet threat actually created by politicians and society's ideologues.

At a deeper level, national defense reflects a profound need of anyone acting in the name of the state to consider its external environment to be hostile.[16] As a matter of fact, the origins of sovereign states can be traced back to a number of religious wars. Sovereignty as a theory grants a prince the right to determine to which religion his state would subscribe. Sovereignty of the people later replaced sovereignty of a prince as capitalism and democracy overthrew the monarchy. Not much change occurred, though, in terms of the external hostility each civilized state faced except that it was no longer the Dark Ages, the city of Gods, or the heresy, but the authoritarian, socialist, feudalist regimes. National defense in the West is supposed to prevent these regimes from engaging in any external intervention.

This second level provided the persistent motivation for states in the modern era to search for enemies outside territorial boundaries.[17] Earlier colonialism reflected this mentality by establishing colonies for religious as well as secular reasons, forgetting that often these reasons were themselves mutually incompatible throughout European history. As a result, secular expansion of capitalism and the missionary movement together promoted colonialism and eventually caused World War I among the contending colonial masters. Germany, demoralized after the war and struggling to breathe in their imagined "living space," cooperated with a Japan determined to throw all White races out of Asia. Both acted in the name of establishing a rightful boundary, that is, a "living space" for Germany and the Great East Asian Co-prosperity Sphere for Japan, to camouflage racist sentiment.

National defense as a mechanism to secure an enemy for the European states survived after World War II. Colonies gained independent statehood one after another, providing increased anxiety toward the possibility that their immaturity would expose them to co-option or coercion by their enemy. The U.S. national defense, for example, must therefore defend the borders of its strategic postcolonial allies.[18] Actions that targeted domestic groups of these allies exemplified a kind of inward defense that occurred outside of the U.S. borders but within the confinement of the allies' borders, which the U.S. national defense claims to protect.[19] Inward defense of one's own ally thus secured the sense of an enemy's threat to oneself. This is especially true for a global sovereign power such as the U.S.

The practice of inward defense of allied states incurs anxiety for the American people. Inward defense allows a government to impose terror on its people and violates democratic principles, which justify the existence of national defense against potential threats posed by external authoritarian regimes. The need to overly stress the threat of the enemy develops, an enemy said to be in collusion with the targets of inward defense in the ally states, be they the fifth column, the communist rebels, or simply dissident intellectuals. With the power of religious and capitalist ideologies, the U.S. government seemed to have worried its own people much less than an allied state's citizens, who were believed to be dependent, traditional, and weak, and hence vulnerable to subversion.

In other words, there is a fundamental difference in how Western states view sovereign borders. Sovereign borders for them are protective shields against external threats of human rights violation, but for the non-Western states, sovereign borders appear to be a way of covering up human rights violation. Indeed all this discursive practice of distrust toward non-Western sovereignties justifies itself, yet also undermines the sovereign order. For a non-Western state such as China, national defense is harder to maintain since their sovereignty is imbedded in a historically essential and fundamentally different concept and multiethnic society, but easier with the identification of external imperialist intervention appearing as a real threat.

Contemporary inward defense emerged from the expansion of Western civilization. Newly independent states became aware of national defense, implanted during their colonial legacy. Their definition of national defense and their enemies naturally was heavily influenced by their former colonial masters. However, these states became states without sharing a common religious or cultural root as their European counterparts. The European sense of common roots was embodied in a shared anxiety toward a certain external interference. As the symbol of a typical European state changed from the prince to the citizens, the perceived external threat concomitantly shifts from being the church to colonial competitors, communists, and more recently authoritarian regimes. Today any state that does not share the same respect for the citizens' subjective position, primarily defined in property and participatory rights, threatens the

Western states.[20] I discussed this point in chapter 2. This emphasis on civic culture does not exist in the newly independent states, including China.[21]

Many newly sovereign states won independence through war with their colonial masters or their neighbors. The colonial master is simultaneously both friend and enemy since colonialism assists in defining the path of future national development, yet, in spirit, denies equal sovereign status to its former colony. The obscurity of national identity in many of these states creates ambiguity along the national borders drawn by the former master. For newly independent states, therefore, the national defense issue is intrinsically a national identity issue, and thus an internal issue from the European perspective. Once national defense becomes an internal identity issue, the military unavoidably enters in all political struggles, damaging its professionalism and credibility in specifying the imagined enemy for the whole country,[22] whose borders were arbitrarily drawn by colonialism.

However, internal defense is not restricted to the newly independent states. Domestically, Western states have derived a kind of internal defense, though in a more indirect manner. Colonialism historically absorbed a great number of immigrants whose descendants have generally acquired citizenship in the master country generations later. Many of these immigrants left home unwillingly and were regarded at best as secondary citizens. The immigration actually continues into the current postcolonial ages. Collectively, they easily become scapegoats of the mainstream particularly when things go wrong.[23] Chinese immigrants, for example, evoked the image of Yellow Peril more than once in modern U.S. history. Once inside others' borders, these religiously, culturally, ideologically, and socially different classes of people naturally maintain a strong attachment to their homelands and thus are considered as potential external threats due to their pledge of nationalism or socialism. They become the targets of inward national defense for the Western capitalist states.[24]

Since their native countries are typically non-Christian, authoritarian, and sometimes socialist states, which are themselves portrayed as, or at least vulnerable to, an enemy, the descendents of people originally from these countries unavoidably subvert the integrity of the colonial master states by simply residing inside them. American Indians, Africans, Chinese, Japanese, and Arabs experienced similar discrimination in different historical periods. Globalization at the end of the twentieth century has led to deeper identity crises within both the immigrant groups and the mainstream societies.[25] The drive to clarify or even purify one's own identity continues to obscure the national boundaries upon which national defense build-up rests. Globalization detracts from the amount of loyalty a national identity can claim and diverts resources a national government can control. This trend exacerbates the concern over the likelihood of foreign intrusion in a nonmilitary form.[26] The notion of national defense concomitantly broadened to include issues such as the war on drugs, trade merchandise dumping, and foreign political contributions. Conceptually unprepared for this change, national defense sectors are perhaps compelled to greatly exaggerate the threat imposed by an imagined enemy.

THE INTROSPECTIVE NATIONAL DEFENSE

First, the ambiguous relationship between nationalism and state sovereignty in modern China helps explain China's mal-adaptation to the sovereign order. Since the Republican Revolution of 1911, there has been a tendency to define Chinese nationalism in terms of patriotism, a middle ground between nationalism and the sovereign order.[27] Yet the Chinese defense of sovereignty has clearly been motivated by anti-foreignism, which is neither liberal nor Christian in nature. In addition, this anti-foreignism presupposes a Chinese national that is in actuality torn among different ethnic groups as well as people with different foreign connections. The construction of a modern Chinese nation is thus discursively dependent on the notion of sovereignty.[28] However, this address of sovereign concerns ignores people's feelings as an irrelevant issue. The emphasis is inevitably on strength and independence, something the Chinese are historically reluctant to express.

Consequently, the meaning of sovereignty in China falls back on one ultimate, familiar task—people's final awakening—and because of this aspiration, family, society, and the emergence of the Chinese sovereign state are morally indivisible, as a postcolonial writer notes:

> [T]he solution to the problem posed by the multileveled structure of family-state-nation-society would come about as a natural result of humanity's "repentance from the origin, amelioration of error and fresh start" and thus "renovate his heart and blood entirely, in order to renew the moral quality."[29]

Accordingly, the anti-Confucian campaign in the name of scientism in the early Republican period was essentially not Westernization as it may have appeared; the whole purpose of the Westernization school was to enable China to defend itself against Western intruders.

Therefore, the movement's contents involved "aspects of morality," "family and state system," and "the future of mankind."[30] But since the reformers demanded that all traditional elements be first modernized, the process of modernization appears to be a call for Westernization. As a result, those involved in nation building were divided into several camps—the progressionists and condionists accused each other of moral crimes of the worst kind. Interestingly, the same fear of an internal enemy persists among Chinese defense reformers in the 1990s even if the so-called progressionists are rare in China. One People's Liberation Army–related publisher in the aftermath of the Tiananmen crackdown reflected this type of worry:

> [The imperialist forces] substitute contacts for containment, interaction for blockade, thought infiltration for open subversion, nurturing of internal forces of change for external military, political intervention. If fire can burn people to death, water can also drown people to death...Struggles seem to have lessened on the surface, but have escalated to a more intense and complex level in reality.[31]

Second, the modern Chinese state did not entirely model itself on other postcolonial states. To begin with, no such dominant colonial power existed in China to the extent that the subsequent building of Chinese sovereignty could not possibly follow the path laid down by one external master. In contrast to the colonial legacy elsewhere, therefore, the specification of just one external enemy was not enough for solidifying a united nation. In addition, the sheer mass of the Chinese territory disallowed colonial powers from dividing and occupying the entire Chinese lands. There remained a strong, indigenous voice in China that never succumbed to the colonial powers.[32] The subsequent independence claimed by the Chinese after the Republican Revolution of 1911 posed a particular threat to the extant sovereign states in that the assimilation of the Republic into the European sovereign state system seemed unlikely to succeed.[33] For the Chinese, the construction of a Chinese identity was not to clarify relationships with just one colonial master, but to expel them all.[34] Nonetheless, each former colonial power could identify certain forces within the Chinese sovereign borders to be their faithful clients. China's total expulsion approach thus encountered enormous difficulty from within.

The concerns over internal disagreement probably explains why the late Premier Zhou Enlai once claimed and the last Foreign Minister of the 20th century Qian Qichen repeated that a good diplomat must first clean his own house before inviting a guest.[35] These are not just thoughts of diplomats of past and present. Under pressure that the Chinese people must show unity in the face of imperialism, apprehension of internal disagreement often escalates into one about subversion, which has been the fundamental national security issue in China up till the twenty-first century. Extreme views articulated by the leftists in the mid-1990s deserve attention in this regard for their widely circulated work—Ten Thousand Words I, II, III, IV—recalls a kind of discourse familiar to perhaps all Chinese politicians and intellectuals since the first Foreign Affair Movement (*yangwu yundong*) in the 1860s. Volumes I and II directly discuss national security issues, they are entitled "Certain Factors Affecting Our National Security" (1995), and "Preliminary Study of External and Internal Environments and Major Threats to Our National Security in the Ten to Twenty Years to Come" (1996) respectively.[36]

The four factors mentioned in Volume I are property structure, class relations, social consciousness, and the condition of the ruling party, none of which is the subject of mainstream national security research, be it sovereignty-related or enemy-driven. Volume II divides national security threats into two groups: those jeopardizing the interests of the Chinese nation and those jeopardizing the social system. Further, It lists four categories of fundamental threats: a new cold war offense, internal peaceful evolution, separatism, and territorial disputes, with peaceful evolution considered "the key." Eight forces leading to these threats are described as:

> (1) Western anti-Chinese, anti-communist forces; (2) local hegemonism and expansionism along the borders; (3) separatist and anti-communist forces in Taiwan and Hong Kong; (4) Overseas and domestic antagonistic forces and nationalist separatists...; (5) Bourgeois liberals in the Party; (6) Corrupt elements in the Party and the regime as well as local patriarchalism and bureaucratic forces; (7) Nascent bourgeoisie who attempt to resist proletarian leadership or change socialism; and (8) Criminals of felony, economic criminals, and ugly social forces.

Third, the Dao discourse in traditional Chinese politics, compared to the tangible territorial sovereignty, is highly abstract and subject to no boundary. Dao is an expression of sincere regard for people's welfare, a spirit of selflessness, and capacity for empathy. Chinese Confucians, Legalists, as well as Daoists all speak of the spirit of Dao when dealing with issues concerning national unity.[37] The universal nature of Dao prescribes that a prince should win people's hearts but warns against the open use of coercion and rewards lest this would tarnish the supreme incorruptibility of a prince. People's hearts remain the sole judgment of a prince's legitimacy. As a corollary, all enemies are internal, for it must be the prince's misconduct that has alienated people's hearts or lost the respect of the outsiders. The solution lies in the rectification of mind, referring to the return of everyone to his/her rightful roles.

In fact, a certain reading of people's hearts may compel national leaders to take drastic moves as the empress dowager explained to Li Hongzhang, the major modernizer of the Qing dynasty, that upon knowing the people's heart in Peking she had no alternative but to declare war on all the treaty countries during the Boxers' Rebellion at the next-to-last turn of the century. In fact, the debate at the Qing court on the eve of war was precisely about how reliable is the "people's heart". The hawks stressed the imperative mandate of the people's heart and demanded actions to be taken, while the doves suspected its utility and consequently did not want to wage the war.[38] A different reading of the people's heart may on the other hand lead national leaders to adopt particular defense strategies as Chiang Kaishek called for the building of a Great Wall of the people's heart during the second Sino-Japanese War in the 1930s upon the retreat of his troops. He said:

> The final victory...relies upon the broadly based and unified heart of the people in the countryside. My people of the countryside clearly understand that it is unavoidable that the enemy will swallow [land]..., [but] the forty million square li of our nation's land can be built into a strong wall of defense, both tangible and intangible.[39]

Since colonialism became an unbearable burden for the Chinese sense of superiority, expulsion of the White race has occupied the agenda of all Chinese national leaders, who disagreed with one another over how soon and through which practical measures the expulsion should be executed. Having been a countermove in the face of imperialist and colonial invasion, this expulsion approach by no means released the people from attending to the issue of people's hearts.[40]

The national defense establishment provides a conceptual tool of transforming this internal enemy into one outside territorial borders. Even there, the Daoist legacy remains strong. For example, the troops are the "people's liberation" army, and the troops sent to Korea in 1950 were the "people's voluntary" army. The justification of sending troops was understood to benefit the Korean people as if they were a part of the Chinese under-heaven. Therefore, the official discourse on China's intervention was not merely the familiar national interest argument but that helping Koreans was considered assisting a "neighbor," and helping a neighbor was "to protect families and the nation" from imperialism.[41] In the Chinese under-heaven conception, there were no sovereign borders to separate one people from another; all were subjects of the rulers' concern. There were no such things as territoriality, sovereignty, or national borders.

While the sovereignty principle assumes the lack of order among sovereignties, Daoist concerns for people were universally applied norms regardless of which land territory was in question. Political campaigns and counter-revolutionary movements were always associated with involvements in war,[42] indicating the intimate relationship between the rectification of public consciousness and national defense. Zhou Enlai's celebration of the victory of land reform during the Korean War signified that the war was and, perhaps, had to be on two fronts simultaneously. The purpose of any mass rally during the Korean War was necessarily against both imperialism and feudal land ownership:

> The Chinese Voluntary Troops...have pursued the [American troops] from the Yalu River back to the 38th Parallel..., the land reform movement...has been the most comprehensive and complete ones in the Chinese revolutionary history...and has included ninety million agricultural population, the national militia has developed [to recruit] twelve million and eight hundred thousand people...[and] a great victory has been achieved in oppressing the domestic anti-revolutionary struggle.[43]

Chinese national identity is not always a product of sovereign territory. In the sense that the display of military strength does not serve to protect national borders, national defense cannot be a tool of state sovereignty. No doubt the Chinese have accepted the Western discourses of national defense and seem to treat national territory as an intrinsic element of national identity; yet between the lines, the logic has been modified to be Chinese. For example, Chinese national leaders proclaim that they would rather lose thousands of troops than give up one inch of their land and that they would sacrifice and bleed to protect territory.[44] This seems to be an intensified version of the rationality of the sovereign state. National territory should never be absolute but fluid in accordance with the nation's capacity as well as the choice of its citizens.

To elaborate further, territory is absolute for the Chinese when dealing with subversion, whether it is real or fabricated. The uncompromising criterion is to show one's wholehearted devotion to Chinese nationalism. This does not imply anything essential about Chinese territoriality being ready to be protected;[45] rather it is some territorially based anti-foreignism that produces and reproduces nationalist narratives for the citizens of the new Republic. Yet there exists many instances whereby the Chinese gave up territory without feeling inferior, or gained legitimacy despite a retreat (discussed later). Both absoluteness and casualness in the Chinese approach to territorial integrity imply the ultimate insufficiency of territory in maintaining Chinese state identity. In other words, the emphasis on people's hearts distracts concerns for defense of any specific territories, and that the discourse of national defense is far more important than the achievement of national defense.

Given that Chinese moral incorruptibility is all-compassing, preoccupation with territorial integrity would look awkward if not self-contradictory. The selfless propensity calls for a disdain for trivial battles over land. However, when the Chinese need to signal their willingness to sacrifice for the cause of nationalism, the national defense of a seemingly worthless land may become absolute; the occasional casualness, on the other hand, implies China's transcendence over the secular issue of state sovereignty. Sacrifice as well as transcendence stress humanity and morality over territorial integrity. These ethics frustrate many Western defense watchers of China. A late observer of Chinese national defense even claimed that virtually no rule existed to explain Chinese defense behavior.[46]

NON-TERRITORIAL DEFENSE THINKING

Historical incidents show that territorial security was not a priority in any emperors' battle to win people's heart. On the contrary, a relatively flexible approach to the acquisition and relinquishing of territory was considered to be in line with a moral outlook. What worried the Chinese leaders the most involves symbolic issues relating to the emperors' place vis-à-vis barbarians. The most important rationale behind Chinese defense was that of moral principles. Failure to appreciate this non-territorial based Chinese defense culture may lead an expert to misinterpret a display of moral superiority as a rational offensive initiative.[47]

As early as the seventeenth century, for example, China's Qing dynasty yielded a large quantity of land to Czarist Russia, and a missionary who cared little about China's territorial integrity carried out the negotiations. Even Emperor Kangxi, considered to be one of the few expansionist leaders in Chinese history, relinquished the land without much thought to Russia. Later in the nineteenth century, Emperor Daoguang yielded to the British the island of Hong Kong and agreed to open five trading ports for the sole purpose of placating the "barbarians" so as to limit their activities to the periphery of China. Upon signing the Treaty of Nanjing to honour these concessions, Daoguang deliberately neglected his earlier call to expel the barbarians. Likewise, for the Chinese, when facing choices between face-saving and the loss of territory or of sovereignty, the latter is often treated as if an unimportant issue. Daoguang demonstrated this when he instructed:

> if the barbarians show regret, [we] can take the opportunity to enlighten [them]...As to trade, we have never rejected it, as to begging for peace, you have never mentioned, if [you] would like to think of this idea [of peace], I will let you accomplish [peace].[48]

The heated issue that led to the 1860 invasion of Beijing by the British–French allied forces was unambiguously the right of the "barbarians" to station diplomats in Beijing, a right Emperor Xianfeng found extremely difficult to accept. Having known perfectly well that he would lose and had actually fled before the defense of Beijing ever started, he would still rather be defeated than simply grant their wish. In fact, however, with weak artillery, small numbers, and the onset of winter, the allied forces would have been in trouble if serious resistance had been mounted. The walls of Beijing were as much as 40 feet high and 60 feet thick while the Chinese forces were still potentially formidable. The capture of 37 allied hostages by the Chinese could have been a portent of things to come. The escape of the emperor, who ordered the fight but refused to win, simply turned the balance of power through the collapse of Chinese morale. Obviously Xianfeng's willingness to fight had little to do with the chance of victory, but with the position that the "barbarians" should not enter the heart of the dynasty on an equal footing.

Equally dramatic was the Sino-French war in 1885 wherein China refused to yield to France its protectorate status over Vietnam. The exchange of fire between the two warring parties in Vietnam, Taiwan, and along China's coast afforded the French forces virtually no advantage at all. China then decided to yield its sovereign position in Vietnam to France in order to preserve their then existing achievement of having not been defeated. The emperor who was worried that the French would revenge their earlier defeats, instructed the officials:

> If...we do not take advantage of the victory and withdraw...
> the whole design will be destroyed...War affairs cannot be totally
> controlled...Now that [we] have won, why should we not plan the
> ending...[You] should make a cease fire and withdraw, without delay
> in order to avoid other changes.[49]

The land of Vietnam clearly held less importance than the supreme
moral status of the dynasty. In other words, to prove that China continued to occupy a superior position, the moral emperor bestowed
upon the French a land toward which he should have had no concern.

The Sino-Japanese war that occurred a decade later witnessed the
most humiliating defeat in Chinese modern history. For the Chinese
could not imagine themselves defeated by the "dwarf" Japanese,
especially since, if the Chinese "treated the Korean people well," they
would assist in "isolating the Japanese troops" and the Chinese troops
"could move anywhere at will."[50] Despite top military advisor
Li Hongzhang's urge to avoid military confrontation, the court
scorned any diplomatic resolution lest this would damage China's
national dignity and even began to suspected Li Hongzhang's intention. It was believed that if the court called back the diplomatic
delegation, "the national face can be saved and the people's will
can be solidified."[51] At the end, nothing worked for China and it was
compelled to yield Taiwan to Japan. The dynastic court, however,
expressed no eagerness in retrieving the land in the aftermath. Instead,
the court focused on other events, conceding to other imperial
powers some treaty rights and treaty ports in order to secure their
support for collusion between the empress dowager and court
officials to install a new emperor. Apparently, even after the dynasty's
repeated defeats in the past four decades, the loss of sovereign
integrity still proved an inadequate criteria in judging the empress's
legitimacy.

The empress and her followers became furious and frustrated on
coming to know that all the imperialist powers supported the incumbent Emperor Guangxu, who supported reform, and eventually
forced her to abort the installation of a new emperor. Projecting its
fury, the court then summoned the Boxers to kill the "barbarians."
When the Boxers entered Beijing, the indulged empress could not
resist calling the hearts of the people symbolized by the Boxers and,
in 1900, declared war on all foreign countries that established treaty
relations with China. But what China did was puzzling at best.

First, it did not develop a war plan or goal,[52] and with 50 times more soldiers and the powerful Krupp cannons, which could have easily decimated the foreign legation walls in one day, only seven symbolic shots were fired. The whole event seemed to be a drama of showing China's displeasure with foreign intrusion. As an onsite observer recalled:

> There had been suspicions that the war against the Legations had not been carried out in a whole-hearted manner. Casualties on the foreign side were high and disturbing but when compared to the number of rounds fired by the Chinese, they were incomprehensibly low. It almost seemed, at times, as if the Imperial soldiers at least were merely putting up a show of attack and seemed content to make things uncomfortable for the foreigners.[53]

Before the Allied forces could catch them, the empress dowager took Guangxu to Xian. Upon leaving, she did not forget to execute those who once cautioned her during the court debate and called them "betrayers." The contrast of the reluctant attacks on the Legations and the resolute execution of one's own loyal officials revealed most vividly where China's enemy resided. This anxiety toward an internal enemy has remained till today and reduced national defense efforts against the external imperialist intrusion to no avail. In the aftermath of the Tiananmen Massacre, a contemporary writer provides a new, long list of internal enemies, all famous writers of the 1980s, and concludes:

> We execute the policy of reform and openness and strengthen the interactions and exchanges with all the countries in the world. This has positively affected the economic growth and all-round development in our country. But, international reactionary forces take advantage of the opportunity to infiltrate political, thought, cultural areas and engage in their conspiracy under the banner of friendly cooperation and through various channels. They want to win the war without fighting.[54]

Before the actual outbreak of the second Sino-Japanese war in 1937, the KMT regime had struggled to avoid armed conflict with Japan, whose troops had first taken over Manchuria and then moved into Northern China. The KMT wanted to eliminate the Communist power contenders before engaging in any premature warfare with Japan. Obviously, Japan's invasion did not fundamentally challenge the legitimacy of the government. In fact, the KMT continued to negotiate for a cease-fire even after the government had officially announced the beginning of the war of resistance. Moreover, the pursuit of cease-fire did not depend upon the return of the territory previously taken by the Japanese troops![55]

The repeated defeats and setbacks of the KMT troops did not invite substantive criticism concerning the government's capacity for leadership. The regime specifically called on the citizens to resist Japan by building a "Great Wall of people's hearts." Further wartime losses seemed ironically to consolidate the regime's legitimacy. The confidence of the government rose after the bombardment of Pearl Harbor since China has now been declared a formal member of the Allies. This confidence did not fade even though Japan continued to dominate on the battlefield for the years after. In fact, the KMT's effort to take the city of Changsha illustrated the symbolic function of territory in China's state-building process. Believing that the whole world scrutinized this front, the KMT felt it imperative to seize the city although it was unable to defend it later. Chiang Kaishek felt that the battle over Changsha was "watched by the whole world" and thus pushed his troops to achieve a victory "at any sacrifice." Upon recovering the city, he celebrated saying: "our supreme moral and spiritual authority has been established now."[56] Becoming a showcase battle decades after the war, the simple performance of taking Changsha, losing, retaking, and again losing it would supposedly demonstrate the courage and the determination of the Chinese troops. The emphasis lies not upon taking the territory, but displaying the unity of "people's hearts" through sacrifice.

Despite the dramatic increase of fighting morale and capacity after 1949, the People's Liberation Army, like many of its predecessors, also disregarded territorial occupation as a central war objective. Several times, the PLA enacted the drama of unilateral withdrawal after gaining ground in the first series of skirmishes.[57] The Western military certainly never encountered the philosophy that all the bloody sacrifice results in telling the opponent that there never had been any territorial ambition. It was difficult to imagine that the military in the West would return the land they capture simply for the sake of sending political signals. Once arriving at a place, it would be extremely difficult to get troops out, even though they were not there to procure territories. For the Chinese, the psychological capability to oscillate between taking and relinquishing land indicates moral supremacy.

The PLA's first display of this approach involved the Korean War. The PLA intervened in the war in the guise of the People's Voluntary Troops to indicate the appearance of peace between the Chinese and American state and the abdication of territorial ambition for the

Chinese. The initial stage of contact effectively pushed the U.S. troops back to the Pacific, yet the Chinese armies did not pursue them. Instead, the PLA unilaterally ceased fire. The Chinese communicated the message that they could win, but would not take advantage and acted purely on defense. One veteran told me a story of PLA self-restraint that he is unable to understand even today. He was involved in a rescue mission offshore during the Korean War, but unfortunately was stuck due to a mechanical problem of the boat. When they were eventually towed away by another rescue craft, the Chinese began to shell the water behind them. I think this indicates a typical Chinese style of confrontation, aimed at showing determination and fearlessness while at the same time executing self-restraint, leaving both sides room to compromise without losing dignity.

The Korean War was fought in the name of defending China's national security. The official discourse was rarely seen in this light, though. Compared with at best scarcely mentioned national security, the "people-"related discourse dominated throughout. In other words, the Korean War could not be understood in the Chinese mind as a war to protect the sovereign order, but as a war between people and the imperialist. As Zhou Enlai declared:

> The Chinese people can never tolerate foreign invasion nor allow the imperialist to invade our neighbor at will without responding. Whoever intends to liquidate and destroy the interests of our one-fourth of the human race and imagine he can arbitrarily resolve any issue in the Orient related to China will break and bleed his head.[58]

Not only did people in China look unified despite suffering from political purges, but also the Chinese and the Korean people claimed to be unified:

> No Asian affairs can be solved without the participation of the Chinese people. It is impossible to solve the Korean problem without the participation of its closest neighbor, China... North Korea's friends are our friends. North Korea's defense is our defense. North Korea's victory is our victory.[59]

It is the American imperialist Other that had helped foster this cross-sovereignty brotherhood and the national security issue for China could no longer be national per se. It is a statement of lofty relations among all Chinese people, Asian people, and people of the world.

In 1958, Mao ordered the shelling of the offshore islands defended by the U.S.-supplied KMT troops. The purported purpose was to cut the supply line to these islands. While this failed to be accomplished, Mao decided to extend the engagement by symbolic shootings every other day. No intention to seize the islands existed, for the simple act of shelling served to symbolically continue the civil war between Beijing and Taipei.[60] Similarly, the Taipei authorities decided to heavily guard the island, which from the American point of view remained unimportant for the defense of Taiwan, to suggest its intention to eventually retake the Mainland. The occupation of the offshore islands was never the real issue. In fact, in a dramatic statement given by Marshall Peng Dehuai, a two-week cease-fire was offered to the Quemoy troops in exchange for their agreement not to depend on the U.S. 7th Fleet for logistical support:

We hope that the authorities on Taiwan respect [Chinese] nationalism. The Quemoy supply problem can be solved by yourself. You should not ask the Americans for protection...Any Chinese with national dignity would never ask a foreigner to represent him to solve his own domestic problem.[61]

Another more intriguing offer was to supply Quemoy from the Chinese side:

You should not be overly dependent [on the Americans] under their roof and let people [i.e. the Americans] take away all your power of leverage. I have ordered the Fujian front not to shell Quemoy's airfield, Lairo Bay's port and shore or [supply] ships on odd days, so that the civilian and military comrades on Quemoy...can consolidate their long run defense...If you [feel] that this is insufficient, as long as you ask [us] we can provide supplies [to you].[62]

While the statement was insufficient to win Taiwanese people's heart, it was a try nonetheless and it was far off the track of national defense thinking from a Western point of view. The dramatic nature of these announcements could not be clearer: the whole point of shelling was a demonstration that Taiwan was a part of China and China was daring enough to resist U.S. intervention even without the Soviet backup.

In 1969, the PLA exchanged fire with the Soviet patrols on Zhenbao Island. The conflict reaffirmed Mao's claim that China was a true world revolutionary, whom both superpowers treated as their enemy. The contact on the islands ceased as the PLA pushed out the Soviet patrols and then unilaterally withdrew. No one could doubt the Chinese claim that they dared to oppose the Soviet social imperialist.

At the CCP's 9th National Congress, Lin Biao reported that China was the true world revolutionary for it was China's honor to fight both superpowers at the same time.[63]

> It is China's honor that the American imperialists and the Soviet revisionists always want to isolate China. We should be well prepared to fight early and vehemently with them. [We should be prepared] to fight a regular war with them and also to fight a great nuclear war with them.

There was apparently no intention to keep the Zhenbao Island after the successful initial seizure. To highlight the Soviet Union as the most formidable enemy of China assumed the utmost importance in this conflict. In fact, Zhou Enlai was ready to make peace with the Soviet Union. The lesson seemed to be that concern about sovereign territory does not explain Chinese national defense behavior, but indeed it provides a clue as to how to resolve conflict once broken out. Thus Zhou Enlai and Soviet premier, Aleksei Kosygin, met eight months later to reach a cease-fire understanding when Zhou stressed the familiar five principles of peaceful coexistence,[64] the first of which was to respect sovereignty. Sovereignty as an expedience provided China breathing room, but rarely motivates specific defense initiatives.

The tactics of unilateral withdrawal appeared also in the Sino-Indian war of 1962 and in the Sino-Vietnamese War of 1979. In the former case, the PLA themselves withdrew 40 kilometers after forcing the Indian troops back 40 kilometers; while in the latter, the PLA withdrew after reaching the city of Liangshan. The PLA demonstrated its ability to defend the territory in 1962 and its determination to punish Vietnam in 1979 while at the same time proving its lack of territorial ambition. This logic presupposes then, that the war must have originated from the other side's territorial intent. In the Indian case especially, the notion of sovereignty as an identity rather than an end cannot be clearer. For the Chinese, the war was imposed upon them, not asked by them. Obviously they felt no anxiety facing the ambiguity in the Sino-Indian border lines, therefore unilateral withdrawal did not hurt Chinese feeling, either. China's willingness to tolerate the lack of clear sovereignty is considered a good place to start building China's image:

> We did not take advantage of military victory, force a solution, or revoke the peaceful consultation approach...Regardless of India's

refusal to negotiate, we ceased fire unilaterally...no one could be made to believe that China wanted to invade India, no Indian people could be made to believe that Chinese people wanted to fight them...To use all possible means of propaganda and to treat various international occasions seriously...allows the people of the world to understand Chinese people...[65]

Similarly, the three missile exercises the PLA launched in 1995 and 1996 in the Taiwan Straits actually suggests no intention to occupy Taiwan as long as the exercises could rebuff any potential foreign intervention. The exercises propounded the political statement that indeed Taiwan belongs to China; occupation would have proved meaningless or even damaging because an armed invasion would only suggest that the Taiwanese people's heart was no longer on the side of the Chinese. Accordingly, it is critical for the PLA to demonstrate that the missile exercises were not aimed at the Taiwanese people. China subsequently repeated its pronouncement that the PLA's job in the Taiwan Straits was to prevent foreign intrusion. In a dramatic statement made in 1995, China's President Jiang Zemin declared that the Chinese would not fight the Chinese, presumably warning separatists on Taiwan to think twice before declaring themselves non-Chinese. In fact, the solution Beijing came up with for the reunification of China and Taiwan is "one country, two systems," presumably to maintain everything in Taiwan as it is after reunification takes place and, perhaps, provide more room for Taipei to participate in international intergovernmental activities. National defense in terms of the right to resort to armed solutions is thus in no way to enhance Beijing's control over the land of Taiwan; rather, it is simply a statement of national unity, which is ironically preserved by granting a separatist type of autonomy for Taiwan. I will discuss this further in Beijing's Taiwan policy in chapter 7.

In brief, national defense in China is psychological defense. The issue of national defense per se did not exist in past Chinese history. Discussions on strategic defense ultimately concerned one's identification with the ancestor, the prince, or the emperor. As a result of their contacts with imperialist invasion, the Chinese only recently began to accept the notion of national defense. Consequently, national defense in modern China embraces nationalism. For Daoguang and Xianfeng, emperors of the Qing dynasty, separating the Chinese from the "barbarian" is their concept of nationalism. For the empress dowager, nationalism referred to the gathering of the people's hearts in Beijing; for the KMT, it alludes to national unity. Finally, for the PLA, nationalism relates to anti-imperialism, the forces that had driven its predecessors to care about national defense in the first place.

In other words, national defense is an emotional rather than a rational project. In the past, Chinese Daoist spirit embraced all of the under-heaven without any boundary. Only when an emperor who personally symbolized the Daoist spirit was humiliated did national defense become a substitute. At this juncture, Chinese character came to be constructed upon China's acquired national territory and not that of an emperor. However, territorial sovereignty has proved to be an insufficient element in defining the Chineseness of China, and yet the way one understands Chineseness defines for oneself the meaning of territorial sovereignty. To establish the lofty and supreme morality of Chinese character relies on the manipulation of territory. Without the emperor, there is nonetheless imperialism, which the Chinese mold into an Other/outsider/invader against whom they no longer worried about their identity.

To show China's higher status vis-à-vis outside imperialism, China can seize lands from imperialist "agents" and then return them as it did in 1962 and 1979. National defense becomes a mechanism to project nationalist emotion,[66] which can be helpful in explaining the timing of Chinese military action. War often occurs when the Chinese feel internally vulnerable and need to demonstrate their moral supremacy. Since the concept of national defense is associated with the experiences of imperialism and colonialism, it is always ready to explode in the face of any reminder of China's past vicissitudes. Any reference to national defense in China would therefore signal a rising nationalism. By the same token, however rational or cool-headed they appear, studies of Chinese national defense would in themselves stimulate nationalism in China if they degrade China to a mere territorial identity.

DEPENDENT NATIONALISM AND THE ENEMY WITHIN

Accordingly, perhaps like all the other examples of postcolonial nationalism, Chinese nationalism is also highly dependent. Nationalism can be called a "dependent nationalism" when nationalistic feeling is not generated per se but dependent on another source. In the Chinese case, national defense is the driving force that reproduces an external imperial threat that solidifies nationalist unity to forge a nationalistic feeling; hence, China is in essence a dependent nationalist state.

Certainly, nationalism follows no scientific mode because its first target is generated inside the minds of the Chinese people. Since these people must prove to themselves that they are intrinsically Chinese, the self-justification process can be accomplished most efficiently through resisting those who deny being Chinese. The psychological dimension of national defense is a vital consideration for defense practitioners. For example, defense against imperialism has conventionally depended on rallying the masses. One famous case would be Xu Guangjin and Ye Mingchen who mobilized villagers to block the British from entering Canton in the 1850s. Other notable instances include the Boxers, the student and worker rioters in the beginning of the Republican period, and campaigners in the subsequent anti-Japan, anti-imperialist, and anti-social imperialist rallies throughout the 1970s. What distinguishes these modern mass rallies from historical anti-foreignism is that they arise primarily out of a position of inferiority, as compared to the former attitudes of arrogance and disdain, which were generally actualized through some punishing sanctions.

Dependent nationalism promotes revolutionary diplomacy as a form of national defense.[67] Revolutionary diplomacy was a term first used in the May Fourth Movement and was later adopted by subsequent leaders until 1978, the year that the term finally disappeared from the media. To engage in revolution, there must be an oppressing Other. The existence of this Other is precisely constructed on the assumption of every military action of the PLA, who usually describes its action as a "self-defensive counter attack."[68] This passive approach suggests that Chinese self-identity comes from an oppressing Other. On paper, though, the Chinese have pursued a sovereignty discourse in explaining the concept of self-defense counterattack:

> [It] can only be territorially-oriented and has passed practical tests of the Sino-Indian, Sino-Soviet border clashes in the 1960s and Xisha Islands and Sino-Vietnamese border clashes of the 1970s. All this fighting occurred when the other side's border patrols invaded the sacred territory of China, killed Chinese border patrols and people, led to bloody incidents, destroyed the peaceful development of border areas, and defied the warning and the protest of the Chinese government and when the Chinese military and people could no long endure. The style of fighting always aimed at maintaining the territorial integrity by expelling the other side's armed forces, regain the taken territory or engaging in limited counter attack.[69]

While in theory self-defense may appear to be territorially based and is in fact conceptualized as the protection of China's sovereignty, yet the mood is invariably nationalistic, which, in turn, is a matter of the individual soldiers' internal rectification in preparation for a final showdown with the imperialist Other. Sovereignty is therefore not to protect individual civil citizens from chaotic external forces, but to protect the Chinese people as a whole by the willing sacrifice of its individual members. The "self" in the "self-defense" discourse is unambiguously the "greater self" of nation instead of the "lesser self" of citizens. As one author of the Modern Defense Series puts it:

> The just war defends our national sovereignty and territorial integrity and defends our national resources and interests of the Chinese nation. Accordingly, our soldiers must be cognizant of their being heirs of Emperor Yan and Emperor Huang, as members of the Chinese nation... To be a People's Liberation Army solider, one's responsibility is to save the Chinese nation.[70]

With this inspirational note, the worry that individual Chinese may fail to pass this nationalist test inevitably takes place each time there is reform to enlist foreign capital, technology, or human resources.

The predicament of dependent nationalism is that there exists a strong element of self-loathing, a form of frustration caused by the realization of unwanted characteristics inside one's identity. This self-hatred stems from the understanding that imperialist cultural institutions were invading and infringing Chinese sovereign establishments long before China had a border to defend. Many others also know that the strengthening of a sovereign Chinese state actually depends on the contributions of merchants, who can bring in capital from imperialist countries: scientists who are educated abroad, the military who purchase weapons from foreigners, and institutionalists who introduce Western systems to China. Therefore, whatever used to grant China its sense of glory in the past now becomes shockingly irrelevant in the domain of the modern sovereign state; instead, all the past splendors are conceived as a soon to be discarded legacy—something to be jettisoned if China wished to be truly modernized.

Self-hatred contains almost inexpressibly subtle ironic overtones.[71] On the one hand, compradors, who facilitate the import of Western civilization to develop the Chinese state, feel superior to their fellow "primitive" citizens. On the other hand, they face their own indispensable inferiority toward their Western masters and a heightened uneasiness about China's dependence on Western power. Thus in some situations these people would like to distance themselves from the less developed China, yet they still hate their helpless attachment to foreign forces and seek self-dignity from indigenous sources.

Taiwanese leaders keenly reflect this ambiguity. With 50 years under Japanese colonial rule and another 50 years under American tutorship, Taiwan is perhaps one of the most modern regions in areas under the Chinese cultural influence. On the one hand, leaders in Taiwan look down upon China as a "feudal, despotic, poor and backward" country;[72] on the other, they possess a sense of self-pity for not being fully recognized by the United States and Japan from whom they have acquired their perspectives on China.[73]

However, the number of compradors inexorably increases. They are at best partial compradors because they also resist foreign influences at times. However, to resist foreign influences also means to resist ones own self, and this makes people frustrated. Similarly, to despise the underdeveloped also implies a rejection of one's own cultural legacy. All Chinese national leaders are trapped in this predicament, for they need to occasionally remind their citizens of China's backwardness thus causing anxiety amongst them over their indigenous identities. They must also mobilize nationalism to ensure that Western value systems do not completely overtake the People's Republic—this is a process that is confusing to those engaged in China's pursuit of equal status under the Western sovereign system. The PLA is affected deeply by this self-hatred. Facing Taiwanese leaders' claim that the recognition and promotion of Taiwan's separate sovereign status in the world is a Chinese achievement, a PLA daily editorial explains this is not true for people in China because Taiwan independence would be a "bitter split of the Chinese people," and hence not an achievement. For the PLA, which "is marching toward modernization," they must stop Taiwan independence for the sake of all the people in the world:

> Experiencing a bitter past, fed up with predicaments, the Chinese nation is about to enter the new century. In the age all countries pursue peace and development and at the moment the Chinese government is ready to resume its sovereign rule over Hong Kong and Macoy, it becomes more urgent to resolve the Taiwan problem and achieve the unification of the mother land. A united, strong, wealthy China can make greater contributions to peace and progress of the world.[74]

The PLA still cannot decide whether it is a modern, Westernizng or a Chinese traditional establishment. The arts and cultural products in the 1990s celebrate PLA's victory in the Civil War much more frequently than it does other wars the PLA had fought successfully. These films portrayed the defeated KMT as feudalistic. The clear message is that the PLA has jettisoned its past legacy and become truly a people's military. The principles of a people's war are concurrently witnessing revision. For example, the PLA no longer advocates the tactics of mingling with the enemy in the face of tactical nuclear weapons, nor do they promote an earlier and greater nuclear war than a later, smaller one. Modernization of national defense, in particular nuclear technology, is called for today.[75] In particular, as Russia is no longer a threat, the PLA is quickly developing the ability to rapidly deploy troops to peripheral areas, including Taiwan. This, ironically, may limit its sovereign ability. As one Western observer notes:

> China's global agenda bears significantly upon its concerns about its territorial integrity, and particularly over Taiwan. China must put considerable effort into maintaining global support for the one-China policy. Maintaining this support constrains its ability to influence international issues and to take sides in international disputes.[76]

Moreover, modernization conveys the concept of cost-efficiency, which, in turn, shifts attention to profit making.[77] The PLA begins to earn money by producing market-oriented goods for both civilian and international military buyers. While modernization demands that the Chinese learn lessons from the capitalist societies, it is nonetheless ironic to see the PLA, which once overthrew the old bureaucratic capitalism of the KMT regime, now lead the way to capitalism. The political attitude of the PLA has changed profoundly.

First, the PLA needs to perform conservatively in the political field in order to distract attention away from their profiteering policy. No one doubts the PLA's loyalty to socialism after the Tiananmen massacre without appearing extremely politically awkward and naïve. This facade allows more room for the PLA to maneuver in the commercial area. Yet with its mission of anti-imperialism, the PLA would inevitably be most sensitive to signs of imperialist influences in China, including the commercialization of the military, for example, to run businesses with military resources for the sole purpose of generating profits. The PLA, more than anyone else, needs to establish that imperialist collusion with its agents in China would eventually prove futile. Therefore, the PLA would have to treat this colluding agent in China seriously. Indeed one author of the aforementioned National Defense Series underscores the dangerous tendency within China itself to loosen up and warns: "the real enemy is amongst us" for the "pursuit of individual interests" has gradually replaced "concerns over national survival and crisis":[78]

> War preparation and war form forge to form a single concept. The only way to avoid losing without fighting is self-strengthening...To self-strengthen is to transcend ourselves and to reform constantly. Only thorough reform can dangerous elements be controlled, so one noteworthy international phenomenon in the tranquillity of "soft war" is that social systems of various kinds as well as states at different levels of development understand themselves more deeply.[79]

The PLA reassures itself regarding its capability of self-control by locating and controlling the colluding agents. Taiwan has become a perfect target as many foreign influences are using Taiwan as a leverage against China, and Taiwanese leaders enjoy boosting the image of Taiwan's success as a Western-style development. Accusing Taiwan of alienation from China serves as a reminder of Japanese colonial legacy in China since Taiwan was Japan's colony for 51 years.[80] A full analysis of Chinese psychological need is discussed in chapter 5. This action both satisfies the anti-imperial anxiety and evokes a sense of shame inside Chinese minds. Inward defense in regard to Taiwan is thus a psychological as well as a national defense, guaranteeing China a chance to cleanse Taiwan, as Japan's postcolonial base, while still including it as part of China's under-heaven. The PLA leaders continue to see the Taiwan issue as a matter of "people's heart." Any move against the conception would be "a serious emotional blow to the Chinese people."[81] Therefore, although sovereignty seems to be a key factor in national defense, it is in fact not—since, in the Chinese discourse, the sovereignty argument is not utilized to defend itself against enemies outside but, rather, to cleanse imperialism from the inside. It is more emotional than rational:

> If...those endeavoring to enlist Western support are determined no matter what [to pursue independent statehood]..., Chinese government and people will not let them be. The entire history of China has demonstrated that whoever split the mother land would eventually become a historical criminal...This is a matter of Chinese sovereignty and territorial integrity, directly in relation to the feeling of 1.2 billion Chinese people.[82]

This feeling of self-loathing is formed during China's encounter with imperialism and colonialism. It is an ineffable emotion both in Chinese as well as in English—due to the poverty of language concerning the hybrid nature of postcolonial thinking. Instead of being a foundation of the Chinese state, territorial sovereignty at best reverts to a tool of identity politics. Fluctuating positions swing from emphasizing territory in one instance to giving it up in another. These instances all make a political statement concerning China's commitment to values at a level much higher than the concept of territorial sovereignty entails. Accordingly, inward defense is not as simple as a regime's oppression of its own people;[83] rather, it is a summons of the people to unite in the name of the state.[84] In essence, however, a deeper reading may indicate that the state is never as important as the nation and territorial sovereignty rarely is more important than the unity of the Chinese people, which usually takes priority when a discourse, such as the following, ends:

> Frequently suffering foreign invasion, the Chinese people cherish state sovereignty and territorial integrity very much, thus the Chinese people, all of whom carry long-lasting patriotic tradition, must fulfill the unification of China. The fundamental condition for a resolution of the Taiwan issue is to do a good job of China's own ventures... Let the Chinese people on the two sides of the Taiwan Strait unite together and work together to fulfill the great engagement of China's unification.[85]

It should be noted that this obsession with national unity informs the meaning of sovereignty, not the other way around. Sovereignty is at best a pretext for China to preclude Western intervention when treating imperialist elements inside Chinese people. It is clear that the PLA leaders regard the Taiwan issue as a Japanese colonial legacy. They cannot understand why the Nationalist Party and the Communist Party could "work together to fight Japan during World War II" while people in Taiwan today can "feel comfortable with a Japanese colonial legacy?" If the Chinese people are to thrive in the world, this post-colonial drive to split China "must be stopped."[86] Worse, "international as well as internal forces will laugh at the Chinese people" if their richest province (i.e. Taiwan) "flies away." These internal forces would include "separatist movements in Xinjiang and Tibet." The Chinese government would have no alternative to a Civil War.[87]

The predicament nonetheless continues in that such psychological defense is meaningful only to the extent an un-Chinese target can be identified, be it feudalism, liberalism, or imperialism. It is always opposition to something that defines national defense in China. The importance of this "anti" defense may grow further in the twenty-first century because the public can no longer identify Chairman Mao or Comrade Deng as the personification of Chineseness. With globalization and China's reform increasing Western influences, the pressure for stronger inward defense is likely to expand. Then, the determination to command seemingly uncontrollable territory and the willingness to relinquish those already under control would likely form a symbiotic relationship deep into twenty-first century China.

CONCLUSION

In light of the military agreement coming out of the Bill Clinton–Jiang Zemin Summit of October 1997 and June 1998, Jiang's two meetings with George Bush in 2002, and a series of mutual visits by high-ranking military officials from China and the United States since 1998, it would seem that China is ready to enter the sovereign world with a style typical and familiar to most Western states. For example, Beijing has agreed to halt its missile sales to Iran, has established a hot line with Washington, and has ceased calling for the withdrawal of all the U.S. troops from Asia. However, I take all these dialogues as Chinese maneuvering to ameliorate the "China threat" image so pervasive in the Western media since the 1990s.[88]

If we look at the current developments between China and the United States from a hundred-year perspective, the result will be quite different from the usual conclusions. In brief, Beijing's effort to meet international standards, which are required for a responsible sovereign state, is perhaps a significant source of pressure on its leaders to keep all the Chinese united. The case in point would be the 15th National Party Congress of October 1997, during which news media were to broadcast how 1.2 billion Chinese have reached an unprecedented unity. Ironically, the report of the Party Congress is that China is facing a serious challenge and pressures ahead, and this is the critical moment for the survival of the Party. The celebration of the Party Congress on past achievement and the calm of Jiang Zemin upon hearing the U.S. human rights criticism of China cannot help but produce an intense, self-contradictory mood.

The National Defense Act passed by the National People's Congress of March 1997 may well cause controversy due to its incompatibility with norms of Western sovereign states. For the Western states, inward defense is to prevent communist forces from utilizing the so-called liberal settings within the states and thus sabotaging the sovereign order. From the same liberal standpoint, however, China's inward defense is to prevent its citizens from succumbing to the allure of Western influences, and thus is disliked by

Western observers. Inward defense in China is therefore considered so undemocratic that it defeats the purpose of having sovereignty, which is to protect liberalism from the threat of outside authoritarianism or communism. Ironically, though, inward defense may distract the Chinese from attempting to achieve superpower status.

However, as argued earlier, inward defense exists in all states albeit indirect in Western states. In all the countries in the world, inward defense possesses a colonial and imperial origin. The difference lies in the fact that in the Western, imperialist country, inward defense does not cause self-hatred because the national defense thinkers in the West come from a stratum that is culturally, ideologically and economically different from the targets of their inward defense. The Chinese defense thinkers and practitioners hold no such fate, for every one of them bears a similar imperial legacy that they acquired from education, work, the market, and the media. Both anti-feudalism and anti-imperialism lead to self-denial due to the hybrid composition of Chinese national identity.

Since the enemy resides within the country, it is impossible to speak strictly of territorially oriented national defense. To win people's hearts, the end of Chinese psychological defense is, first, to deal with and terminate these unwanted hybrid influences on the public consciousness, and, next, to correct those who have been influenced to forge a united national identity. The hybrid influences unfortunately would not disappear; consequently, any purifying projects would require an external as well as an internal target to project this unwanted self and to conquer (in the case of Taiwan) or expel (in the case of spiritual pollution) it. On the other hand, the Western observers of Chinese national defense are equally, if not more, confused and anxious about China's inward defense. China's defensive actions may cross over or stay entirely within sovereign borders, but they are never solely motivated by protection or maintenance of the geographical border. The West either views the Chinese as a threat to their sovereign order (when China moves beyond its borders) or to universal human civilization (when China stays within borders). The differing responses from the West naturally reinforce the strength of dependent nationalism in China. Under this circumstance, those Chinese who benefit from or enlist Western techniques, values, or institutions, including the PLA, must engage in inward defense to prove their purity and identify an external enemy to consolidate their own Chineseness. This self-perpetuating circle, which first originated from Western imperialism in China, is the essence of contemporary Chinese national defense. The resulting nationalist–rationalist cycle in Chinese foreign policy is the focus of chapter 4.

4

The Rational Choice Clue: Curing Epistemological Amnesia

Introduction

Although the impacts of nationalism seem to be on the rise in all parts of the world in the post–Cold War era, it has not become a familiar concept to students of international politics until very recently.[1] For those political scientists dedicated to neorealist analyses, research on nationalism could potentially be unscientific for its tendency to reduce analyses of "international" politics to the "national" level.[2] Or, it could potentially be counterproductive to neoliberal analysts for its inclination to distract attention from the institutionalization of common interests in the process of regime formation.[3] It is thus conventional for realist and liberalist to treat nationalism as a cover of some other genuine values,[4] a policy instrument to mobilize support,[5] or a nostalgia for history writers,[6] but not a topic that has intrinsic academic value in itself.

Nationalism has, very commonly, been associated with conflicts in the last decade of the twentieth century; as a result, political scientists have, along the statist line, begun to see nationalism as a national interest item, juxtaposed with power capacity, economic welfare, human rights, and national security. Via this perception, research on nationalism (and economic nationalism above all) continues to center around the state under neorealism[7] and becomes implicitly an atypical pursuit of autonomous interests under neoliberalism.[8] This treatment of nationalism consequently alienates nationalists from that with which they consider themselves to be emotionally involved.

On the other hand, cultural studies as well as critical literature is not unanimously attractive to nationalism, either, although cultural studies and nationalism in the Third World in general and China, in particular, share an antagonist sentiment toward American neorealism and neoliberalism.[9] For postmodern observers and their allies, Chinese nationalism is at best discursively constructed and can be reinterpreted along with the increasingly contended genealogy of state sovereignty, democracy, and capitalism.[10] This issue will be discussed later in chapter 6. Nonetheless rising nationalism witnessed of late is recognized partially as a response to the unavailability of an oversimplified, all-encompassing collective identity once familiar to Cold War subjects.[11] The obscuring of collective identity is aggravated by highly praised globalization processes and the diaspora of almost all nationalities among us.[12] While feminist writers laud androgyny and postcolonial authors testify to hybridity, fundamentalists of all sorts have anxiously risen to protect their imagined community.[13] Against any claim to authentic identification, many who belong to these post-positivist cultural studies are unable to treat nationalism and identities as nationalists themselves may have experienced these concepts.[14] On this account, they are ironically and, likely, unwillingly related to neorealists, as well as neoliberals.

The fact that stories of Chinese nationalism are prevailing in historical studies[15] reveals the disadvantage of political scientists in dealing with Chinese nationalism. Historians are more interested in the past, while political scientists, the present. For the latter, the past is often presented in numbers and structures, not in memories or pictures. Historians understand the contemporary by tracing its roots in the past; political scientists find the past interesting only to the extent that it confirms what they believe to be universally true today. As a result, contemporary international politics cannot help but treat Chinese nationalism as just another independent preference, a preference free from other preferences, each by itself contributing to China's disposition to a certain degree. Which of these preferences and how much they each determine China's utility may vary over time, depending on the utility function at the time, however, the overall utility function does not change. International politics is thus a business of amnesia, in that memory and its interpretations undergo reconstruction periodically in accordance with the needs of the present.[16] The resulting epistemology in international politics can approach Chinese nationalism if, and only if, Chinese nationalism is exclusively a contemporary phenomenon. This means that if nationalism as a value is not entirely satisfied today, it is not a big deal;

one can always vie for a priority for its realization in following periods, just like economic growth or military security.

What the amnesiac epistemology brings about is a nationalism without a past. Yet Chinese nationalism is no longer nationalism if people do not accumulate past love or hatred, even though its weight can be reduced and its contents reconstructed over time. If people remember and act upon memory as they must indeed, unfulfilled nationalist desires today would inevitably impose higher pressures on subsequent resource allocation as I have hopefully demonstrated in chapter 3. In brief, nationalism is not totally contingent upon international structures, and it never starts all over again at the end of a budget year. In contrast, values associated with economic growth or military security do not vary across time, other things being equal. The scientific power of universality does not usually apply to a utility function or payoff matrix, such as the one involving nationalism, that is not determined exclusively by structural factors and that changes after every game. The way to formally model Chinese nationalism as a value of ever-changing weight in an amnesiac epistemology is the task I undertake in this chapter.

The ensuing two sections develop a model of nationalism in foreign policy and discuss its implications. The first attempts to expand nationalism to allow for a broader application. In the next, I use Sino-U.S. relations as an illustration as to what the model would direct us to expect in understanding the subject matter. Finally, I try a bold reflection on how well the model improves both the neorealist/neoliberal agenda, by attending to nationalism's intrinsic, non-statist logic, and the cultural studies literature, by formally acknowledging the force of hybridity in policy-making.

FORMALIZING NATIONALISM

Let us assume that resources for foreign policy can be divided into two kinds, one for achieving nationalism and the other, national interests in general, excluding nationalism. The division is between functions, not between policies, which can serve both purposes. Let the proportion of resources allocated for national interests in general be p, and for nationalism, $1 - p$. Define $h(p)$ as the current benefit from spending p percent of resources on national interests in general and assume that

$$h(p) = bp; \quad b > 0.$$

Let $g(1 - p)$ be the current benefit from spending $1 - p$ percent on nationalism. We shall assume that the marginal return for more nationalism is decreasing and let

$$g(1 - p) = c \ln(2 - p); \quad c > 0.$$

To take into account the element of memory, let us further assume that for every expenditure on national interests in general, there is a psychological grievance in terms of lost opportunity of nationalism, while the same is not true of national interests in general for each spending on nationalism. Let the grievance be shown against the accruing of benefits in all the subsequent periods, and let the grievance be diminishing over time. For a p proportion of spending on national interests in general in period zero, let the penalty in the tth period be

$$k^t c \ln(1 + p_0); \quad k \in (0, 1),$$

where k is the amnesia coefficient with a smaller value denoting easier loss of memory. Accordingly, the total benefit for period t is

$$F(p_t) = h(p_t) + g(1 - p_t) - \sum k^t c \ln(1 + p_{t-1}).$$

Since $\sum k^t c \ln(1 + p_{t-1})$ is a constant for every tth period, or when $F(p_t)$ is at maximum,

$$\partial F(p_t)/\partial(p_t) = \partial F(p_{t-1})/\partial(p_{t-1}) = \ldots = \partial F(p_0)/\partial(p_0) = 0,$$

we know the optimal solution $(p = p_0)$ is the same across all periods. (Note that I make the computation easier by blocking p from influencing k, so that the result of this exercise can only underestimate the uncertainty in the impacts of nationalism on policy, not overestimate it.) Let δ^t be the forgiveness coefficient, with a smaller value denoting higher forgiveness, so that remedy to the grievance in t periods later will be much less meaningful today when it occurs and its benefit be discounted by δ^t, where $\delta \in (0, 1)$. (Again, I block p from influencing δ.) For an optimal resource allocation, one wishes to

$$\text{maximize } \Phi(p) \equiv \sum \delta^t F_t(p)$$

or to

$$\text{maximize } \Phi(p) = [c/(1 - \delta)] \{(b/c) \, p + \ln(2 - p) - [\delta k/(1 - \delta k)] \ln(1 + p)\}.$$

Since the curvature of $\Phi(p)$ is uncertain, one needs to use simulation to study the problem. Only the values of the two parameters, (c/b) and $(\delta k/1 - \delta k)$, will affect the resolution for the optimal solution and let $r \equiv (\delta k/1 - \delta k)$ and $s \equiv (c/b)$. Since our purpose is to see the effects of the amnesia and forgiveness coefficients, for the purpose of simplicity and illustration, let $s = 1$ and see how p_0 varies with r. The implication of this convenient assumption is not impractical, though. For $h(p) = b$ when $p = 1$ and $g(1 - p) \cong 0.7c$ when $p = 0$, the benefit of pursuing only national interests in general $(p = 1)$ will be greater than that of seeking only nationalism under the circumstance where $s = 1$. In short, the assumption that $s = 1$ means that people suffer less when there is absolutely no nationalism $(p = 1)$ than when there is absolutely no butter, or tanks $(p = 0)$.

A total of four results of the simulation are selected for the sake of illustration. When $r = 0$, that is, where there is either total amnesia or total forgiveness and this would cross out the temporal dimension, the optimal solution for $\Phi(p)$ is at the point $p_0 = 1$; when $r = 0.1$, the optimal solution is close to where $p_0 = 0.95$; when $r = 0.5$, the optimal solution is close to where $p_0 = 0.5$; finally, when $r \geq 0.6$, the optimal solution is where $p_0 = 0$.

Obviously, people do not make resource allocations according to rational calculations of benefit, and they are most likely influenced by resource allocations of the opponent as well as by the dissatisfaction caused by past failures to achieve the optimal solution. For this reason, the modeling of resource allocation must be separated from the modeling of optimal solution. Let p_t be the actual resources allocated for national interests in general in period t, and let p_0, be the universal optimal solution; let q_t be others investment in their national interests in general, and make q_0, the universal optimal solution for other nations. We assume that the actual allocation in the next period is negatively associated with the difference between the actual allocation and the optimal solution in this period (i.e. $p_{t-1} - p_0$), yet it varies positively with other nations' investment in non-nationalism–related interests in this period. Let

$$p_t = \alpha[1 - (p_{t-1} - p_0)](p_{t-1})(q_{t-1}); \quad \alpha \in (0, 1),$$

where α is the sensitivity coefficient reflecting how quickly resource allocation in a certain period responds to the condition in the previous period.[17] In equilibrium,

$$p_t = p_{t-1} = 1 + p_0 - (1/\alpha \; q_{t-1})$$

or

$$p_t = p_{t-1} = 0.$$

The unlikely optimal solution in equilibrium is at the point where

$$p_t = p_{t-1} = p_0 = 0 \text{ (and } \alpha = q_{t-1} = 1)$$

or

$$p_t = p_{t-1} = p_0 = q_{t-1} = 1 \text{ (and } \alpha = 1).$$

As shown earlier, when $p_0 = 1$, one knows that $r = 0$, and thus either amnesia or forgiveness or both is at the maximum. In contrast, whenever $p_0 = 0$, then $r \geq 0.6$. In between $p_0 = 1$ and $p_0 = 0$, or when sensitivity is not at the maximum ($\alpha = 1$), the optimal solution is not available in equilibrium. Furthermore, other nations' solutions must also be $q_{t-1} = 1$, so that the optimal solution in equilibrium can be maintained at the international level. While $r \neq 0$ or $\alpha \neq 1$, as is most often the case, international equilibrium will be off the optimal solution, yet in equilibrium nonetheless. This is achieved by setting $p_t = q_t$ and β as the sensitivity coefficient for other nations, where

$$q_t = q_{t-1} = 1 + q_0 - (1/\beta \; p_{t-1}); \quad \beta \in (0, 1).$$

A state of equilibrium is not always available as the resolution below indicates:

$$p_t = q_t = (\beta - \alpha)/[\alpha\beta(p_0 - q_0)].$$

Obviously, the relative values of the two sensitivity coefficients and of the two optimal solutions in the nation and in the rest of the world determine whether there can be a state of equilibrium between one nation and other nations in the world. One of the necessary conditions is that $(\beta - \alpha)(p_0 - q_0) \geq 0$. In addition, the nation and the rest of the world must both achieve an internal equilibrium at the same time when a global equilibrium can be reached. If $q_t \neq q_{t-1}$, then p_{t+1} and p_t as functions of q_t and q_{t-1}, respectively, cannot reach the equilibrium.

DISCUSSION

Amnesia counts. As one remembers and reflects as well as acts upon one's memory, benefit, which one could have accrued by achieving nationalism but did not in the past, becomes a constraint on one's capacity for national interests in general in the future. Only at the point of total amnesia would one allocate all the resources for national interests in general, disregarding nationalism. Put differently, only when nationalism is just another kind of national interest in general, which creates no grievance in the future policy-making process, would nationalism deserve no special attention. As my illustration of simulation indicates, once leaving the extreme end of total amnesia, the optimal solution necessarily involves resources for nationalism. This involvement increases dramatically to the extent that if one could remember and act upon over 60 percent ($r \geq 0.6$) of the unfulfilled nationalism of the past in the form of grievance, the optimal solution requires complete devotion to nationalism.

In the real world, one can easily imagine that the parameter k would increase during certain renaissance-type campaigns and thus push resources away from national interests in general. The parameter k is constrained by another parameter δ, though; so if one forgives well, what one remembers about the past will not greatly affect what one does today. Low δ is that which is considered rational in neorealism and reflects the spirit of the neoclassic economic proverb, "the sunk cost is sunk."[18] Similarly, the reality is often that some people do not forgive easily. If, for various complicated reasons, a historical event suddenly reactivates grievance in a later period and leads to increases in the magnitude of the forgiveness parameter, one can expect resources to be shifted toward nationalism in that period.

In the controlled simulation, we can expect that the shifting of resources between two kinds of national goals occurs only in accordance with endogenous conditions, primarily the accumulation and the dissolution of past grievance (i.e., $\sum \delta^t \sum k^t g(p_{t-1})$). A possible explanation for the accumulation of grievance lies in the fact that grievance, in terms of nationalism, is largely a matter of affection, in addition to cognitive mapping. An amnesiac epistemology cannot deal with affective values, an expedient pull away from which the value today would unavoidably impose a penalty on policy makers in subsequent periods. If policy makers were entirely rational or forgiving so as to disregard nationalist grievance in benefit calculation, the optimal solution would not vary across time to merit the dictum, "the sunk cost is sunk." Two other factors that must be taken into account are inertia and environment. My formulation thus makes actual resource allocation contingent upon these two factors.

As shown in the last section, the state of equilibrium disallows the optimal solution unless the amnesia or forgiveness coefficient is 0, and the sensitivity coefficient is 1, that is, unless nationalism is irrelevant or unless nationalism totally dominates when $r \geq 0.6$. Even if history began without nationalism at $r = 0$, this equilibrium would be unstable, for once nationalism enters into the picture, p would be pulled away from equilibrium as $p_t \neq p_{t-1}$ and $q_t \neq q_{t-1}$. In reality, resource allocation always reflects policy makers' concerns over resource allocation in the rest of the world, and amnesia and forgiveness are usually imperfect. This complicates even the search for the state of equilibrium, not to mention the impossibility of finding the optimal solution.

Disregarding the goal of reaching the optimal solution, whether or not one can locate the state of equilibrium still depends on the null optimal solution, for policy makers naturally adapt to the distance from the optimal solution in each previous period. The ultimate equilibrium would reflect the difference between the nation and the rest of the world in the proportion allocated for nationalism (and national interests in general as well) $(p_0 - q_0)$. If the equilibrium is available, it would also depend on the difference between the two sensitivity coefficients $(\beta - \alpha)$. As mentioned earlier, the results of these two computations must be either both positive or both negative, and this is reasonable. In common sense, amnesia and sensitivity are opposite characters: A high p_0 connotes a low r (i.e., more amnesia or forgiveness), so the sensitivity coefficient α is plausibly small; the same holds for the rest of the world and for the computation of q_0 and β. In other words, the null optimal solutions (p_0, q_0) and sensitivity coefficients (α, β) move in opposite directions. This makes it likely that $(p_0 - q_0)$ and $(\beta - \alpha)$ be either both positive or both negative. But, then, there is no guarantee for such a condition of equilibrium to exist.

Moreover, $(p_0 - q_0)$ must be great enough or $(\beta - \alpha)$ small enough to make the computation of $(\beta - \alpha)/[\alpha\beta(p_0 - q_0)] \leq 1$. Again, this is possible, though not guaranteed. The sensitivity parameter refers to policy makers' inertia toward adapting to the distance from the optimal solution or to the environment, and this bureaucratic, as well as political, inertia (α, β) does not vary by policy-making units as much as optimal solutions (p_0, q_0) vary by cultures and historical experiences of these policy-making units. This means that $(p_0 - q_0)$ is probably greater than $(\beta - \alpha)$. Finally, the absolute value of α and β must not be too small to permit $[\alpha\beta(p_0 - q_0)] \geq (\beta - \alpha)$. This would mean that all sides remain sensitive to still how far they are away from their own optimal solutions and how others distribute their resources.

Yet, with all the not-so-unreasonable conditions, there appears to be a good chance that the state of equilibrium does not exist.

In reality, in fact, that policy makers alternatively emphasize material national interests in general and spiritual interests such as nationalism across time is a familiar phenomenon. When the state of equilibrium is beyond reach, it is normal to expect policy oscillation between two types of national goals. Thus, a higher proportion for national interests in general in the rest of the world would first lead to a higher spending on the same type of national goals in the nation. This goes on for certain periods until one day the pull away from nationalism incurs a level of grievance dictating both a reverse of the trend and higher spending on nationalism in the following period. The reverse, which is an input to the rest of the world's policy-making, enhances the spending on nationalism there, which then leads to a similar spending in the nation, and so on.

ANTI-IMPERIALISM VS. CIVIC NATIONALISM

There is no doubt that nationalism is a concept difficult to define. To understand nationalism, the contexts that researchers focus on are critical. These contexts include the evolutionary tracks of national identities for the people involved,[19] continuous intellectual reconstruction of their history,[20] and previous policy responses to these constructions.[21] At this moment of entering the postmodern twenty-first century, nationalism may carry religious, ethnic, and biological, as well as political, significance and is very different from the earlier inceptive European nationalisms,[22] which prepared those countries for entry into modernity in Europe. However their origins and whatever their forms, European nationalisms undoubtedly contributed to colonial activities in the rest of the world and created in the present time a different kind of anti-imperialist nationalism throughout what we call the Third World. There are, in a sense, two kinds of nationalisms today; one was formed earlier from within the constructed European nations themselves,[23] and the other, from these nations' Othering policies.[24]

These colonial Othering projects and the diaspora to which colonial nations contributed have hybridized nationalism everywhere in the world.[25] Nonetheless, the universal pursuit of superiority in capital, technology, and management, which has been promoted by the discourses of sovereign competition, has been successful in camouflaging the hybrid nature of all national identities. Not until the end of the Cold War, has the realization of this hybrid nature been brought about by a globalizing trend.[26] Ironically, globalization incurs anxiety in those who have always been absorbed with the discourse of sovereign national identity. Their delusions of being penetrated or contaminated by cross-sovereign activities has led to nationalist revitalizing campaigns all over the world, typically involving quests for a "pure" identity and a concomitant external enemy.[27]

Among the world countries, two civilizer states survived,[28] and have become competitors: China and the United States. They are civilizer states because the elite strata, acting in the name of the nation, regard their own civilizations highly, believe themselves to be models for the rest of the world to follow, and have a tendency to mold the world into their ideal. Nevertheless, neither of them is the nation they claim to be.

China, for example, has suffered the intrusions of imperialism, as almost all Chinese will tell us,[29] since the Opium War of 1842, a time, though, when there was no such concept as sovereignty and thus no possibility of being intruded upon in the contemporary sense.[30] In fact, to revitalize the Chinese nation did not become a national goal until the May Fourth Movement in 1919. And the notion of "nation" has since then been imbedded nearly exclusively in anti-imperialism.[31] It is not an exaggeration to say that, to reiterate chapter 3, imperialism has defined Chinese nationalism and, lately, state patriotism. However, national revitalization in China has always depended on Western technology, capital, markets, and, most importantly, intellectuals and compradors well connected with the West and well versed in its values. Nationalism is self-defeating, in that all such campaigns serve as reminders of China's ultimate dependence on the West.[32] All the more-developed areas inside Chinese spheres today have experienced colonialism of some sort, such as Shanghai, Canton, Hong Kong, Qingdao, Taiwan, and the like. China would no longer be China if not for anti-imperialism, yet anti-imperialism is in actuality anti-Chinese to the extent that Chinese culture has become hybridized since the Opium Wars and increasingly so after the end of the Cold War.

The United States, in comparison, is no better off. As a model of civic nationalism, the United States became a true nation of its own making after the end of the Civil War. The collectivist claim to national identity combined paradoxically with the individualist oath to human freedom.[33] With the rise of U.S. power in the world, increasing numbers of immigrants arrived with various nationalities, threatening the American national identity. As the slogan "America first" emerged to consolidate people of dual identities, U.S. intervention all over the world has prompted citizens with relevant country origins to speak from positions of their original identities, rendering the America-first stand obsolete. Yet, the right to articulate these origins is itself the foundation of American civic nationalism. The anxiety caused by the coexistence of one civic identity and many original identities finds one outlet in human rights policy toward the rest of the world, as if civic nationalism could have an universal appeal.[34] This civic nationalism often offsets the efforts to maintain dominant American power in the short run by upsetting potential strategic allies, market opportunities, and information exchanges, itself making a folly of idealism.[35]

It has so happened that Chinese anti-imperialism and U.S. civic nationalism met in an unpleasant manner after World War II. For complex reasons we cannot detail here, the Sino-U.S. confrontation has been acute on the one hand and absentminded on the other. Apparently, there is more than one perspective in each country as to how to conceptualize oneself and the other.[36] The end of the Cold War vividly reveals this ambivalence of each toward the other. On the Chinese side, U.S. human rights policy has proceded with an unequivocal imperialist intent,[37] yet all-round bilateral relations are considered critical to the strengthening of the Chinese nation.[38] On the U.S. side, China's human rights anomalies are the most convenient targets of the American liberal identity,[39] yet China's all-round cooperation is equally essential to a world order, which a superpower such as the United States must maintain to its own advantage.[40]

Chinese familiar with American civic nationalism and Chinese Americans accustomed to Chinese anti-imperialism are divided in each country as to how to formulate their mutual policies; similarly, Americans, intellectuals in particular, involved in China policy are torn between asserting American civic ideals and doing secular business.[41] This is an issue of self-identity. The hybrid nature of both nationalisms do not permit one single answer. This is where our model fits in.

There have been cycles in China's U.S. policy and in the China policy of the United States. The twist reflects an inability on both sides to reach the state of equilibrium for the two reasons mentioned in previous sections. First, there are some exogenous changes that affect the mood of forgiveness and that recall remote bitter/glory history or enhance/reduce sensitivity toward each other's spending patterns. Second, there are endogenous constraints that do not allow the state of equilibrium to develop, perhaps due to equally high values of amnesia and forgiveness coefficients in both countries (meaning that they do remember well, and do not forgive easily), rendering the equilibrium solution outside of the mathematically available range.

One can recall China's human rights position in four phases: first denying the individualist human rights argument, then releasing some of the more famous political "criminals" from prison (e.g., Liu Xiaobo, Hou Dejian, Wei Jingsheng, Wang Dan), then re-arresting some of them (e.g., Wang Dan, Wei Jingsheng) and others simultaneously or later on, and then sending the most famous to the United States in exile (e.g., Fang Lizhi, Wang Juntao, Harry Wu, Wei Jingsheng, Wang Dan). In comparison, the U.S. human rights policy toward China has witnessed a cycle of two positions. One of them is to monitor, to condemn, and to sanction, and the other, to take notes, to discuss, and to engage. Traditional wisdom would consider these oscillations as a tug of war between an essential realism and an essential idealism. The insight introduced by the model in the previous sections is that as long as civic nationalism or anti-imperialism is a built-in affect in foreign policy, as they must be, then cycles, ambivalence,[42] and inconsistencies can be explained by the hybrid nature of nationalism in both countries and presented mathematically. Nationalism is both an internal identity[43] and an interaction-based construction.[44]

A Response to Cultural Studies

To scholars of cultural studies, the neorealist emphasis on the scientific study of national interests, especially power distribution, and the neoliberal proclivity to institutionalize hegemonic norms are both flawed for treating sovereignty as an essential, authentic being. Once sovereignty is problematized, scholars of cultural studies are able to historicize international relations in terms of practice, instead of theory. In this regard, though, a part of this interpretive literature shares with neorealism and neoliberalism one important epistemological hiatus: neither treats seriously the fact that human affection constrains behavior and that, hence, selected reinterpretations of history are not culpable sins, but psychological necessities. We do not have space here to present support for this necessity, except by saying that some cultural studies have likewise recognized it.[45]

It does not matter if nationalism is authentic (it probably is not); nationalism constrains foreign policy anyway. It does not matter, either, whether there is a universally true definition of "nationalism," for people who act in the name of and respond to the call of nationalism affect resource allocation and consumption. Nonetheless, the formulation we present here acknowledges the hybrid nature of foreign policy, as most postcolonial writers would probably agree.

Objective national interests in the name of sovereignty are implicitly problematized in the model, first by denying that there can be a national consensus on state interests and second by imposing a penalty whenever affective needs are not handled properly. Interpretive literature's concern for the neorealist, neoliberal obsession with one all-encompassing logic of international politics and the lack of a temporal dimension in their research is reflected well in our model. Both the epistemological indifference to equilibrium or optimality and the emphasis on cycles demonstrate this point.

Perhaps mathematical modeling is not in line with interpretive methodology (or, as some would prefer, the refusal of any methodology), which encourages repeated readings of texts and intertexts to dissect unstated assumptions.[46] These assumptions may reveal historical contexts that are unknown even to the writers of contemporary texts. Our model accepts nationalism as a text, including anti-imperialist as well as civic nationalist texts. Compared with the all-are-only-texts perspective, which can establish no dialogue with neorealist or neoliberal analysis, mathematical modeling is perhaps one way to pin down an intertext for conversation. Without an intertext such as this one, interpretive scholarship would become essential and unproblematic. Our model thus asks interpretive scholars to treat seriously the binding forces of nationalist affect in those who are unable to enjoy the hybridity of their own making. The model also urges the neorealist, neoliberal camp to pay more attention to the temporal dimension, as well as to intra-national conditions, which the current approach to power and institution has yet to tackle systematically.

Finally, the model obviously has its limitations for in the real world it is unlikely that one could accurately determine to what degree a policy serves nationalist purposes and to what degree it promotes national interests in general. The point, though, is not the technicality of foreign policy resource distribution, but that nationalism and national interests in general are two kinds of concerns, with the former a matter of affect, and the latter, of cognition. Unlike nationalism, national interests in general are secular interests, which do not increasingly accrue grievances if not met. The model thus denies that a national interest policy, which can serve nationalism only indirectly and in the long run, could be nationalist policy. For example, either growth for China or engagement for the United States requires both to control the immediate nationalist appeals while in the long run Chinese nationalism could actually gain by becoming strong enough to fight imperialism or, potentially, the United States. Likewise, American civic nationalists may be able to spread the gospel of human rights deeper into China. Either growth or engagement can be justified by a long-term nationalist argument. Our model is practical in the sense that real-world nationalists do not feel like waiting. Therefore, policies that serve both nationalist and national-interest purposes are few indeed.

Thus, it should be alright to further claim that epistemological amnesia in contemporary international politics needs a constructive remedy. Although critical literature successfully deconstructs the myth of the state of nature and the norms of market and capitalism, there is no guarantee that the real world will not proceed within the parameters of the intellectually bankrupt notion of sovereign orders. Before any reconstruction can begin we call for some sort of dialogue to recognize that the forces of the status quo are still enormous. Scholars of cultural studies would otherwise find that nationalism would continue to suffer misconceptions well into the next century.

5

THE POSTCOLONIAL CLUE:
BRINGING JAPAN BACK IN

INTRODUCTION

Most of the discussions of China's Japan policy are focused on economic trade and investment, armament and disarmament, and Japan's potential role in facilitating or hindering China's reunification with Taiwan. Focus on these issues indicates (although not without some unstated assumptions) that one would interpret Sino-Japanese relations in light of a predetermined set of national interests, presumably including China's economic development, national security, and nationalism. It is not difficult, however, to observe certain contradictions among these interests, for example, between China's economic need to attract more investment and aid from Japan and the political need to act independently from the seeming surge of Japan's overseas ambition or, for another, between the nationalist need to punish those Japanese politicians interested in rewriting Japan's role in World War II and the political–economic need to maintain an amiable East Asian environment.

The problem is that when nationalism is treated as a plurality of interests guiding China's foreign policy (and perhaps an inferior one from the *realpolitik* standpoint), the psychological foundation upon which Chinese leaders must make sense of their foreign policy options is difficult to identify. In short, nationalism is not a policy goal per se; rather, following chapter 4, it is a first-order screen that often affects sensible second-order policy goals. Nationalism reflects the psychological necessity to draw a boundary between the Chinese and those who are accused of imperialism, colonialism, and hegemonism.[1] What is interesting is that no matter how the labels have changed throughout contemporary history, the main threat to China's sovereignty is thought to have come from those who have remained closest to it, namely Russia, America, and Japan. This symbolic relationship of closeness and threat indicates a ubiquitous and profound sense of uncertainty about China's identity, because, without the threat, the closeness would obscure the boundaries between China and others. If this is true, it is not difficult to appreciate the embarrassing position that Japan faces, compared with Russia and America, as it is racially, culturally, as well as geographically closer to China, yet more than the others it threatens China's sense of boundary.

Whether Japan, the United States, or Russia is in fact more of a threat to China does not really have an easy answer and history has not left much time to give Japan a fair trial in China in any event. The fact is, and will continue to be, that China has up to now perceived Japan as being ambitious; it has acted upon this perception, and has reproduced this image of Japan through its Japan policy.[2] Indeed it would be a painful exercise to find any substantive base for China's suspicion toward the new Japanese generations as a whole today. Fortunately, such an exercise has never been attempted and this perception of a threatening Japan serves to differentiate China from Japan and consolidate an otherwise shaky national identity in China.

Unlike other modes of foreign policy analysis, this chapter will examine three cases wherein Japan is not the major actor, but a critical vehicle through which Chinese leaders interpret their oppositions' intention. Examination of Japan's seemingly auxiliary position in these cases accurately reveals the Chinese leaders' deeply held assumptions of Japan. The first case describes China's critique of Taiwan President Lee Teng-hui as being non-Chinese because of the intimacy and affection he has expressed toward Japanese culture in a quasi-private interview with a Japanese journalist published in May 1994. The second case outlines Lee's attempt to participate in the 1994 Asian Games in Yokohama, Japan, which irritated the Chinese delegation who threatened to boycott the games over the issue. The last case describes China's condemnation of a former Chinese table tennis player, who was a political outcast in China but went on to represent Japan and won her event in the Asian Games in October 1994. These three cases suggest that there is an affective element in China's Japan policy, which is often overlooked, and yet constitutes a deeply rooted element of China's quest for national identity.

JAPAN AS AN OTHER

There is no doubt that China and Japan encountered and dealt with the Western civilization in different ways. In 1887, while Japan's Meiji Restoration launched a successful Westernization campaign, China was still struggling with a conflict between tradition and modernization. Back in the dynastic periods, as argued repeatedly in previous chapters, there was simply no concept of "state" unlike modern Western history. For generations of celestial rulers, the only problem was how to pose as a benevolent example for their subjects, not how to protect themselves from "outside intrusion." They understood "outside," a premise in the notion of modern sovereignty, in purely social and cultural terms. As late as the Qing dynasty (from which the Republic of China ensued), the acceptance by non-Chinese of these Chinese norms were reflected institutionally through a tribute system. Yet, the Chinese were simply psychologically and militarily unprepared to handle their encounter with the approaching Western powers during the second half of the nineteenth century.

In contrast, coming out of the Meiji Restoration, Japan not only defeated China in 1895, but also joined the Western powers by projecting its own colonial interests in China.[3] In fact, Japan was more effective in doing so than other Western powers. Japan was geographically adjacent to its colonial territory in Formosa, and though to a much lesser degree, Manchuria, and culturally assimilated the socially higher Chinese residents on Formosa.

China's colonial experiences diverge from those under the European nations in the Middle East and Africa in three major ways. First, there was more than one colonial power in "China," so Japan's status as a late arrival did not broadly challenge a single established colonial power although it might have produced threats on a smaller scale. Japan's defeat of China in 1895 thus only led to conflict with Russia (which Japan defeated in 1905 without arousing much alarm among other colonial powers). Second, there were places within China that actually witnessed consecutive colonial occupations by different colonial forces. The most notable perhaps being Taiwan with Dutch, Spanish, and Japanese (and some would add Chinese) experiences. Multiple colonialism reinforced the extant notion of "outside" as cultural rather than geographical.

Third, often the same colonial power generated dramatically different images in different places within the same Chinese state. Here, Japan presents a useful illustration again. Japan's colonial rule in Manchuria and Taiwan actually developed a certain level of local support, particularly in Taiwan, where a comparison of Japanese rule with the previous Chinese rule easily gave the impression of an efficient Japan versus a Corrupt China. However, the Nanjing Massacre in which the Japanese military executed tens of thousands during World War II left behind an image of barbarism that has yet to be erased. The Nanjing regime after losing the Chinese Civil War later fled to Taiwan in 1949 naturally carried with them this memory of Japan. As a result, former Dalian residents and Nanjing residents would understandably see Japan from somewhat different angles; similarly, the defeated KMT regime in Taipei would inevitably interpret all Japanese moves very differently than long-time Kaohsiung (the largest city in southern Taiwan) residents. Such dichotomy has seriously impacted identity politics in China, especially as the notion of sovereignty has increasingly become a key to defining China after World War II.

Yet it was not without struggle that China learned to play the Western game of state sovereignty.[4] The establishment of a sovereign Republic of China subsequently brought about numerous attempts to reinstate an imperial system. Thus in order to explain democracy, the founding father of the Republic, Sun Yatsen, made an ironic appeal: in the Republic, he stated, all 400 million citizens can be emperors. The driving force behind Sun's revolutionary movement, which led to the founding of the Republic, was nationalism, a cultural concept that motivated the quest for an anti-imperialist Chinese state. Anti-foreignism and anti-imperialism prompted the adoption of the state as a shield against Western encroachment. I call this Chinese state "counter-state" in chapter 2. Patriotism became the new code word for nationalism. Nevertheless, Chinese people expected this patriotism to protect Chinese civilization instead of Chinese territory, hence dependent nationalism discussed in chapter 3. Indeed it was not clear whether this patriotism was really one of state or culture. Nonetheless, thanks to the rise of Japanese militarism, state patriotism began to prevail.

Yet the Chinese have never really seen Japanese as foreigners. In Mandarin, "Japanese" are called *ribenren*, while "foreigners" are *waiguoren* (literally alien state people). The early version of *waiguoren* was first *yiren* (literally barbarian) and then *yangren* (literally ocean people, for they came in from the ocean). Even today, the Japanese are not *yangren* or *waiguoren*, but continue to be *ribenren*. In other words, there is a deep-rooted, cultural differentiation between the Japanese and foreigners in the Chinese mind-set. In fact, the high expectations of Sun Yatsen and other Chinese revolutionaries toward

Japan and their Japanese supporters helped forge an atmosphere of Sino-Japanese brotherhood in resisting Western colonialism at the beginning of the twentieth century.[5]

In Japan, this we-group mentality actually helped produce Japanese plans for the Great East Asian Co-prosperity Sphere which was to include China and was designed to counter Western dominance in Asia. However, Japan in a certain respect wanted to be a part of the West by colonizing an Eastern country, but realized that the West would not accept it as a member. This sense of Otherness ultimately led to a turbulent domestic debate within Japan on the direction the country should take and eventually produced a decision to assert its leadership throughout the Far East.[6] The impacts of Japan's identity puzzle on China's state building is given in chapter 1.

From the Chinese point of view, this surge of Japanese anti-Westernism became a threat to China's own sovereignty, which itself was rooted in anti-foreignism. The threat from Japan was simply that Japan denied China its sovereignty, something the Republic considered essential to resist Western imperialism. With Japanese incursions China could no longer rely on cultural arguments to keep imperialism at bay. In order to make sense of the challenge from Japan, patriotic statism had replaced anti-foreignism in China to become the key slogan. Thus China's previous ally in the anti-foreign camp had now become an enemy in the interstate world. Base upon this image of Japan, China fought World War II and secured its claim of being a sovereign state. Nevertheless, the fact is China did not adjust its image of Japan by recategorizing Japan as a *waiguoren* state but rather saw itself as an "un-Japanese" state. Therefore, a Japanese threat must precede the Chinese state. The implications of this view are twofold. First, China persists in seeing the state in largely cultural terms so that "Chinese" and "*waiguoren*" are still culturally antagonistic terms. Second, the development of state patriotism as a product of conflict with Japan may have left a permanent mark in later Sino-Japanese exchanges. For Chinese, familiar cultural terms were not sufficient to explain Japan's "betrayal" during World War II. Moreover, China's eventual understanding of sovereignty became rooted in newly drawn geographic boundaries, which were shaped primarily by Japan's challenge.

The emergence of sovereignty as part of China's self-identification unavoidably created tension between cross-boundary and boundary-directed thinking. This tension required continuous external threats to reproduce and consolidate the culturally unfamiliar notion of sovereignty, rooted in anti-foreignism. Yet now acting in the name of "the Chinese State," all those threats previously regarded as "purely" cultural made additional sense. This notion of sovereignty validated China's right to defend its civilization and culture on the grounds of territorial integrity. Consequently, psychological shields against foreign as well as Japanese cultures became redundant. One did not have to bother with what China specifically stood for beyond a few buoyant slogans of anti-foreignism, knowing that the answer by definition lay right on the sovereign borders.

With this understanding of sovereignty, an external enemy replaced the need for a clear identity. China avoided the identity question simply by identifying the opposing Other; first capitalist America, then revisionist Russia, and potentially neocolonialist Japan. During the Cold War interlude, in fact, China did not forget about Japan. For when the enmity with America and Russia was over, the original anti-Japanese character of Chinese sovereignty reemerged and it is thus Japan again who came to be seen as a threat to Chinese civilization and culture. Japan's case is more complicated than the case of the United States because the former carries a much higher level of relative deprivation in terms of China's unfulfilled expectation of Japan's cultural proximity. The emotion against Japan is long-standing unlike that against the United States, which is only issue-contingent.

After the Cold War, Japan became a focal point for Chinese expressions of sovereignty and self-discovery. This was not only a result of Japan's own confusion over what role it should play in the post–Cold War era, but was also a matter of China's own response to the devastating epoch of the Cultural Revolution. At the same time, Japanese leaders increasingly expressed their desire to confirm Japan as yet another victim of White colonialism in Asia before World War II.[7] This way, Japan and China would have again been on the same boat and the last Japanese intrusion of China could be justified. This, however, was not the case. As the Cultural Revolution demoralized Chinese socialism, Japan became a new focal point to shift people's attention away from China's ideological disarray. The occasional attempts to rewrite history in Japan and revoke its responsibility for initiating the Sino-Japanese war in 1937 had aptly met the enemy-searching mind-set of China. What was psychologically soothing as well as simultaneously alarming to China was Japan's investment and business interests in China, which were reminiscent of colonial powers actions during China's Republican period. Alarming because such heavy investment implied that Japan might want to again establish the Co-prosperity sphere; soothing because the Chinese felt that they, in an almost omniscient position and with a sense of certainty, could claim historical knowledge of the Japanese intention.

Assumed knowledge of Japan's intention helped China escape from a more fundamental puzzle about its own identity. This position of knowledge and certainty similarly became a screen through which China came to examine intentions of others when they inadvertently developed a relationship with Japan. Praising or denouncing others based on their relationship with Japan reproduced China's self-image as an un-Japanese state. Japan, of course, has no position to speak for itself in this process. A vicious circle was thus formed. In the past 20 years, more and more Japanese politicians uttered their nationalist wish to reinterpret Sino-Japanese history; yet, one after another resigned to repay their politically inappropriate honesty. It seems that Japanese politicians could not respond to China's problematique, and growing frustration only made the next similar verbalization of Japan's nationalist perspective more difficult for China to tolerate. This vicious circle did not reveal itself more clearly than in 1994. This was a year that would be of no significance from a realist perspective, but was a dramatic year of identity politics, to which this chapter turns to.

THE PITY OF BEING BORN TAIWANESE

In the May 5, 1994 issue of the Japanese language journal, *Asahi Weekly*, an illuminating interview with President Lee Teng-hui of the Republic of China (known as Taiwan) was published. Shiba Ryotaro, a late Japanese reporter conducted the interview in the president's residence and the interviewee professed that he would very much like to have this interview read by the Chinese on the Mainland. However, those who did read it felt deeply insulted. In fact, a director of the leading institute of Taiwan studies in Beijing told me on a private occasion that his interview had unified ("unified" is a touchy word in China today for it signals China's determination to reunite with Taiwan) previously contending views of Lee Teng-hui. All agree that he identifies himself as a Japanese and thus would naturally resist unification of the People's Republic on the Mainland and Taiwan— long held to be a Chinese territory—and advocate the separation of Taiwan from China.

What annoyed the Mainland readers, and in particular scholars of Taiwan studies, were both Lee's words in the interview and his view of the Japanese. "The Pity of Being Born Taiwanese," the title of the interview (suggested incidentally by Lee's wife) precisely expressed Lee's perspective and his understanding of postcolonial Taiwan history.[8] Shiba began the interview by claiming that Taiwan used to be an island without clear national ties. Lee concurred. Moreover, Lee asserted that the fact that China conceded Taiwan to Japan in the aftermath of the 1894–95 Sino-Japanese war indicated that the Qing court viewed Taiwan as an uncivilized land that China did not wish to possess. Further, he continued to argue that the only thing that can be certain today is that Taiwan was once Japan's territory and that if it were not for Japan's education of the Taiwanese during the 50 years of colonial rule, Taiwan would be just like Hainan Island in China with a comparatively low level of economic development. According to Shiba, Japan became a multi-nation state during that period due to its acquisition of Chinese-residing Taiwan, suggesting that the Chinese people were within the Japanese state. Although people may have forgotten this, the Taiwanese were once thoroughly Japanese. At the same time, Shiba pointed out in the article that Lee was Japanese before he was 22.

According to the article, history shows that Han immigrants originally came to Taiwan from Fukan (Fujian) and Guangdong provinces in the seventeenth Century, and thus "no one else" (presumably meaning no one sovereign state) can legitimately claim Taiwan. Yet, according to Lee, those who lived in Taiwan during the period of Japanese colonial rule actually wanted to legally become Japanese. Such comments seem to explain Shiba's confusion regarding the meaning of the word "Chinese," "which is the vaguest word in the world." Lee added that "even the word 'China' is vague and that indeed the words 'Chinese people' are also vague." Lee then said,

> If I have the opportunity to see Mr. Jiang Zemin [the Chair of the People's Republic of China], I want to tell him, prior to any discussion of Taiwan policy or the issues of China reunification, that [he] should first study what "Taiwan" means. If antiquated thoughts of ruling Taiwan remain, there would be another 2–28 incident. [An incident of massive killing occurring in 1947, between earlier Chinese immigrants to Taiwan and late-comers.]

Following this perspective, Taiwan is actually a new state, "a place that must belong to the Taiwanese people." Moreover, Lee charged his own party, the KMT of which he was the chair, being an "alien regime." He added, however, that he believed he had successfully transformed the Chinese KMT into a Taiwanese KMT during his term of office. Lee declared that his Taiwanese citizens resembled Moses's Jewish subjects and that Taiwan should march outward as the Israelites did in their exdous. Lee claimed that Taiwan was already on its way and that Moses's vision was also Taiwan's destiny. Deeply moved, Shiba provided a similar Japanese example, which revealed how the Japanese looked at the role of Taiwan in Chinese history. Close to the end of the Tokugawa Period, the Nagaoka domain struggled to become the first to model itself on Europe. Its leader Kawai Tsugunosuke looked desperately for a teacher and found one in the mountains. The teacher developed a vision of an unarmed, separate domain. Impressed, Kawai went back to reform his government making his domain the only blueprint of a modern state independent of the Tokugawa government. Unfortunately, he could not fend off his neighbors and was thoroughly defeated. This, Shiba believed, was a monumental loss in Japanese history, and he expressed his worry that Taiwan might indeed become a second Nagaoka, thus implying that a violent China would disallow a progressive Taiwan from becoming a model in Chinese history.

While Lee suggested that it is important to scientifically interpret the Japanese legacy in Taiwan in a more positive way, Shiba openly wondered why an anti-Japanese Chiang family would have chosen Lee as a successor.[9] Lee denied that he was the heir apparent for late President Chiang Ching-kuo. Indeed, contrary to popular belief, Lee stated that it was not clear that Chiang really considered Lee as the designated successor. Moreover, Lee suspects that if Chiang had decided to disclose his true feelings about him, Lee would have been "destroyed." The implication is that Chiang did not take Lee seriously in making him the vice president of the Republic of China and simply did not dispose of him in time. Interestingly, Lee then cautioned himself not to uncover whom he personally favors to be the next president. Lee's confident showing of leadership clearly won respect from his Japanese visitor who commended his eventual transformation of the Chinese KMT into a Taiwanese KMT, which he suggests shows a "capacity for quintessential political play." Lee reacted quickly, noting: "I have been very observant since I was young," and his youth doubtlessly bore a Japanese legacy.

Five weeks passed before a Chinese scholar fired the first shot on June 10, 1994.[10] The author asserted that Lee's remarks revealed his Japanese identity, and was disappointed that Lee showed absolutely no affection toward China. In fact, Lee seemed to concur using words that honored Japan's previous colonial rule in Taiwan. For Lee's Chinese critic, what the President meant by "the pity of being born Taiwanese" was precisely and alarmingly that China's connection to Taiwan today was through what Lee characterized as an alien regime, the KMT immigrating from China. Among a variety of comments, "shocking" was the major response to Lee's interview. One critic stated:

> Modern Chinese history is a history of being invaded, diced, and raped. Almost all imperial countries in the world have raided China. Located in the periphery, Taiwan suffered most strongly and bitterly and the Mainland Chinese people could feel [it]. The pity of being born Taiwanese should be the same as the pity of being born Chinese, hence [the sense of pity] is shared by the people on both sides of the Taiwan Straits. Chinese on both sides of the Taiwan Straits share the same mind-set; it is backward and biased to see only the pity of being born Taiwanese.

Yet what was perhaps least forgivable to Lee's Chinese critic was that Lee, as the chairman of the KMT, refused to discuss any enmity toward Japan and the Japanese occupation of China and Taiwan. A feeling that might actually be shared across the Taiwan Straits. Rather, he chose to reveal an abiding friendship toward a Japanese (*ribenren*), who recalls with affection the Japanese occupation of Taiwan and expresses open hostility toward China.

To make things worse, Lee's implicit distancing of himself from the "Chinese" KMT regime of Chiang Kaishek and his son Ching-kuo, only further ingratiated him with the Japanese interviewer. His more positive attitude toward the Japanese colonial legacy ultimately led to the revelation of his own suspicion that the Chiang family actually regarded him as an outsider. The fact that the Chiangs certainly could not comment on this suspicion is not the major point. The point is how Lee has read Chiang's intentions and how, in turn, Lee's reading shapes the perceptions of his Chinese critic. Having read that Lee would like "to establish a Taiwanese state," his Chinese critic further concluded that Lee's ultimate intention was to become "Emperor Lee." One must also note that the critic used the word *tianhuang*, which is exclusively used for a Japanese emperor, and not *huangdi*, normally used to indicate a Chinese emperor. The message could not be clearer; the building of an independent Taiwanese state cannot help but be an exercise of "Japanization," and this is a move to draw a line between "the welfare of the 21 million Taiwanese people in opposition to the great unification project of over 1 billion Chinese people."

Others saw Lee's exchange of true feelings with a Japanese interviewer as a "deliberate invitation of foreign force to oppress the Chinese people";[11] the purpose of such invitation was to provide an excuse to split up China. For them, the Qing court's decision to concede Taiwan to Japan in 1895 led to the enslavement of the Taiwanese people for the following 51 years, and "that part of history records a distressing page for all of the Chinese people."[12] These critics further contended that Taiwan's resistance to Japan continued during colonial rule and those people who led the resistance were "Chinese nationalist heroes." What they wanted was Taiwan's return to China; although they failed, they would, according to these critics, live forever in Chinese history. Thus the charges against Lee cannot be more serious; it is not only a charge of betraying a sovereign state, China, but also one betraying his Taiwanese ancestor. The critics asked, bitterly, "how could a person like Lee Teng-hui who professes such a profound knowledge of modern Chinese history count all the historical facts and still leave out the part about his own origin?" (*shu dian wang zhu*). Moreover, they condemned Lee for "feeling honored and not shameful of being one of the conquered people."[13]

In August 1994, the Fourth Annual Conference of Scholarly Exchange between the Two Sides of the Taiwan Straits was held in Beijing. At this meeting, Lee Teng-hui came under a barrage of unprecedented attacks during the oral presentations.[14] (The time was too short for paper writers to include official government positions on Lee's remarks published in May and thus may have softened their criticism.) Among the first few papers put in writing, one writer suggested that the idea of China's reunification with Taiwan is an attempt to establish a Greater Chinese Empire, which, in essence, is a notion derived from Japan. Lee, as a "half Japanese and half Taiwanese," employs this Japanese perspective "to encourage an Asian opposition to the reunification endeavor."[15] Equally annoying, the writer indicated, is Lee's contention that Japan's attempt to assimilate the Chinese on the status of Taiwan during the colonial period was not an oppression but rather an invitation that the people chose to accept. Clearly, critics believed, and still believe that Lee's reinterpretation of history is a factor in Taiwan's independence movement.

Ironically, Lee's classification of the KMT regime as an "alien regime" has brought the Mainland Chinese critics much closer to the KMT, a seemingly irreconciliatory historical enemy of the CCP. These critics have argued that it is immoral to compare Japan's colonial rule with the KMT's rule over Taiwan. However, it is equally wrong to equate the KMT rule over Taiwan with a Chinese rule per se. Thus the reason Lee has done so is to generate the impression that the Japanese and the Chinese are oppressors, and that the Taiwanese are their common victims. In this construction of history, the Chinese people on the Mainland become the cause of "the pity of being born Taiwanese."[16] What is truly the pity of being born Taiwanese is, according to one critic:

> First, Taiwan was dropped into the hands of Japanese imperialists, enduring enslavement for 50 years as a conquered nation; second, Taiwan, after being forcefully occupied by Japan, further served as a stepping stone for Japan's invasion of China through "enlistment of [Taiwan] Chinese to fight [Mainland] Chinese;" third, Taiwan's return to China after Japan's surrender in 1945 brought with it the reactionary KMT regime which not only failed to heal the serious injuries suffered by Taiwanese but also spreaded salt on the wounds....[17]

In short, from a Chinese standpoint, Lee's interview with a Japanese journalist was anathema simply because of Lee's clear attempt to represent Taiwan as a country independent of China. Such a position runs counter to Chinese nationalism; although Japan is only in the background and marginally connected to this interview, it is this background that makes Lee's sin all the more evident to the Chinese observers. Lee's show of intimacy toward his Japanese visitor (not a politician, a social leader, nor a popular writer!), his reconstruction of Japan's colonial rule over Taiwan, and portrayal of China as an alien place all together revived the bitter memories the Chinese nation acquired from Japan's invasion. Two ostensibly inconsistent implications are equally painful. First, the demarcation between the Chinese and the Japanese on Taiwan in Lee's perspective, obscures and threatens the Chinese identification of a China (which includes Taiwan) apart from Japan. Second, the likely incorporation of Taiwan into the greater Japanese sphere again signals the incessant Japanese threat to China, only reinforcing the image of a China apart from Japan. If not for Japan, Lee would probably not appear as such a threat to China. Similarly, however, if not for Lee's remarks and the subsequent Chinese interpretation of it, the notion of Japan as nation apart from China and China as a non-Japanese state would gradually lose significance too.

THE RIGHT TO ATTEND THE ASIAN-GAMES

In October 1994, the twelfth Asian Games was held in Hiroshima. Several months prior to the Games, the Olympic Committee of Asia (OCA) extended its list of invitations, which included President Lee Teng-hui. When the chair of the OCA visited Taipei in April,

Lee and his officials worked diligently to ensure that Lee, as an "honorable guest," would not need to apply for a visa from the host government, and with this assurance, the Chinese Taipei Olympic Committee (CTOC) notified the OCA and the Japanese Olympic Committee (JOC) of Lee's desire to attend. The CTOC then proposed a trade with the Chinese Olympic Committee (COC) to further insure that the COC would not object to Lee's presence in Hiroshima, and involved Taiwan and the CTOC's support of China's bid to host the 2000 Olympic Games. Unfortunately, despite these efforts, there was no explanation from Beijing except an informal response by the general secretary of the COC that the proposal "was not appropriate."[18]

These events reflect President Lee's active diplomatic quest to achieve independent sovereign status for Taiwan, a process that has become much more active after 1994. In the beginning of the year, Lee in a "private" capacity visited several Southeast Asian countries that recognize Beijing as the sole legitimate government of China (which includes Taiwan as one of the provinces). Beijing's reaction was furious, and enormous pressure from Beijing was placed on some of the host countries, which led to the cancellation of a number of Lee's important meetings with local political leaders. (The same story took place again when Vice-President Anita Lyu, a determined independence advocate, visited Indonesia in 2002.) From Beijing's point of view, it was intolerable that Lee, while being the president of the Republic of China, could be allowed to visit abroad. It was this perspective that was in Beijing's mind with regard to Lee's plan to attend the Asian Games. The Beijing authorities asserted that Lee's pretext of going to Japan only to encourage athletes from Taiwan apart from his capacity as president was a blatant show. Beijing's suspicion of Lee, it should be noted, was only exacerbated after publication of Lee's aforementioned interview with *Asahi Weekly* in May.

On August 18, Lee's plan to visit Japan hit the headlines in Tokyo, when Jiang Zemin, the chairman of the People's Republic of China, told a Japanese Diet delegation that China did not appreciate Japan's acceptance of "the person with the highest responsibility in Taiwan" to attend the Asian Games in Hiroshima.[19] The Japanese government, however, stated on August 18 that it was the JOC, not the government, hosting the Asian Games, and therefore the government was in no position to refuse those invited and thus would not intervene. In order to keep the problem from escalating, neither Lee's office nor any Japanese source would confirm that Lee had actually obtained an invitation to the Games. For the Japanese government, a show of innocence was the only means for the government not to intervene; for Taiwan, the assertion that Lee's visit was to be a purely nonpolitical event. It is also noteworthy that the Japanese premier who apparently wanted to visit China but did not wish to jeopardize his personal credit in China chose not to disclose his position in public.

As the debate grew, pro-Taiwan groups in Japan became very active. One Diet member, for example, recommended allowing Lee to attend the Asian Games with specifically stated conditions that Lee could not meet any government officials and would stay only within certain areas for the duration of the Games.[20] On August 19, Japan's Foreign Ministry announced that it expected Lee to decide by himself not to attend; but if Lee indeed wanted to come, the Japanese Ministry was in no position to make such a high-level decision. The pro-Taiwan Diet members felt increasingly dissatisfied and asserted that the Asian Games were nonpolitical in nature, and insisted that the Japanese government deal with President Lee's visit in a nonpolitical manner. Others went on to remind the government that this was "a God-granted opportunity to ameliorate Japan–Taiwan relations."[21] They charged their government with kowtowing to Beijing with regard to foreign policy decisions so that "the Taiwanese people's sense of dependence on Japan would swing [away]...."[22] Even a member of the Socialist Party, which is typically pro-China, expressed his desire for Lee's attendance.

Taiwan's chief representative, Lin Chin-Ching, also believed that most Japanese would welcome Lee because he "is the only head of state in the world that studied in Japan and thus deserves such respect."[23] Interesting, the *Weekly Post* (*Yuho*) later published an ex post analysis, mentioning that Lee's elder brother once served in the Japanese military and died on the battlefield; so, in Lee's mind, his brother was more Japanese than many Japanese themselves. The article cited Lee's heartfelt desire to visit his "homeland." Moreover, since Lee was "pro-Japan," he could help Japan to better understand Taiwan. The article also pointed out that Lee has many friends in Japan and that Lee told the journal that although he was ultimately unable to go to Japan on this occasion, he appreciated the friendship that most Japanese showed and believed that their warm performance would definitely prove to be a significant contribution to the friendship between "the two countries."[24]

On September 3, Japan's position was that it would respect any resolution reached among Beijing, Taipei, and the OCA. However on September 6, the Japanese premier told the media that Lee's visit might not take place. Lee, in response, again declared that he would accept the OCA's invitation and attend the Asian Games. This move naturally made the headlines and a delegation of legislators from Taiwan left for Japan to lobby for Lee's visit. Before leaving Taiwan, one delegate emphasized that if Japan did not cooperate this time, people in Taiwan would file a suit in the international court for redress of Japan's 50-year "crime" in Taiwan (implying that if Japan helped, there would be no need to mention the "crime").[25] On September 9 Japan's former minister of Legal Affairs publicly announced his support for Lee's visit, and on the same day, a few cadres of the Liberal Democratic Party pronounced their support of Lee's visit as a symbol of the peace that the OCA itself exemplifies.[26] Facing mounting pressure from Lee's adamant gesture and the support it mobilized, the OCA finally proclaimed that it would not invite any political leaders to attend the Games. A decision that effectively silenced the issue for a couple of days and handed the ball back to the Taiwanese government.

The problem continued when Hsu Liteh, the vice premier of Taiwan, was named to lead the Taiwanese delegation. Hsu's job, it was said, was to compete for the right to host the 2002 Asian Games. Due to the lack of time available for further maneuvering before the Games, China's response was urgent and direct. Having seen that the Japanese government agreed to accept Hsu, the media in China launched a series of sharp attacks. While in Japan, the worries were somewhat different. Questions were raised; what if the emperor saw Hsu and shook hands with him? What if media all over the world focused on Hsu's visit?[27] More importantly, how was Japan to pursue understanding with the Mainland Chinese, which was now considering a boycott of the games. On September 17, the Japanese premier explained that Hsu's attendance was related only to hosting the 2002 Games; it was not in his capacity as a vice premier, and thus "has no political color."[28] The former Japanese ambassador to Thailand publicly urged China to concentrate on economic development and he advised that China give more room to Taiwan in international society so as to improve relations.[29] After foreign ministers from Beijing and Tokyo met in Washington D.C., Japan confirmed its decision to accept Hsu. Ultimately, a broader crisis was avoided and China did not boycott the Games.

From the beginning, China had recognized the explosiveness of the issue, it had tried to keep a low profile, and only made the first official statement on September 8. The Chinese Foreign Ministry warned that Japan keep Sino-Japanese relations in perspective, and under the Council of State Affairs, the Taiwan Office urged Japan to resolutely reject Lee's visit. The escalation started on September 15 when the Foreign Ministry said that China could not accept Japan's position on Hsu's visit because Hsu obviously had high political status. The following day, the New China News Agency warned Japan that it must shoulder its historical responsibility not to assist Taiwan in becoming an independent country. The commentator suggested that only a few people in Japan were manipulating the issue in order to develop relationships with Taiwan:

> The most urgent issue is that the Japanese government adopt a quick and effective policy to block Lee Teng-hui and Hsu Liteh from entry. It does not matter under which title they appear, their plot should not be allowed to succeed. Otherwise, not only the incoming Asian Games in Hiroshima would suffer, but the relationship between China and Japan would also seriously worsen.[30]

In fact, China canceled the scheduled visit to Hiroshima by Li Tieying, a ministerial-level official. Receiving the international bureau chief of the Liberal Democratic Party, the CCP Secretary Wen Jiabao and its Foreign Liaison Department head, Li Xuzheng, emphasized that China had "no room for further concessions" because this had to do with "Taiwan's independence which is beyond what the affection of the 1.2 billion can tolerate."[31] On September 22, the scheduled visit of Japanese finance minister to Beijing was canceled by Beijing. On the same day, China's vice foreign minister called Japan's ambassador in Beijing to deliver a note of "serious protest."[32] Tang Shubei, in charge of the cultural and economic exchanges with Taiwan, told the media that Beijing could tolerate only officials at or below the municipal level from Taiwan to visit Hiroshima.[33] Moreover, the Chinese ambassador in Tokyo sent the same message to the Japanese Foreign Ministry. On September 26, Chinese Foreign Minister Qian Qichen told his Japanese counterpart:

> On the eve of the opening of the Asian Games in Hiroshima, Taiwanese politicians such as Lee Teng-hui and Hsu Liteh attempted to use the athletic arena to produce "one China, one Taiwan" or "two Chinas," images imposing problems to the long established and well developed Sino-Japanese relations, as well as provoking serious concerns for the Chinese government and people.... That Taiwan goes to Japan and has activities there is fundamentally a political issue and it is impossible for the Japanese government not to understand the political intention behind Taiwan's move, as Taiwan has stated its political intention straightforwardly.[34]

Qian later said that he would record the entire matter (*ji yi bi zhang*), which many took as a threat of later retribution against both Taiwan and Japan. As all athletes prepared to compete on September 30, one Chinese official declared the matter was "not over yet."[35] From the Chinese perspective, the greatest sin of the Japanese government was its tranquility regarding the issue. This passive position roused the pro-Taiwan groups and the whole affair escalated into an international issue whose atmosphere was totally unfavorable to China. It would seem that Japan had to choose between power/ interest and friendship, a scenario where China looked awkward in moral and cultural terms. As Japan chose the more realistic pro-China side in Lee's case, it lost the justification to do so in Hsu's case. The connotation of which, true or not, was clear to China: while Japan is economically closer to China, Japan and Taiwan are emotionally closer. Moreover, while China may regard Taiwan's dependence on Japan for affective support as a source of shame for the Taiwanese people, it cannot avoid a further suggestion that it is also a source of shame that China has failed to win such attachment from the Taiwanese people. Thus if not Japan, who else to blame?

THE IDENTITY QUESTION ABOUT KOYAMA'S GOLD MEDAL

In the 1994 Asian Games, Japanese women's table tennis player Chire Koyama defeated two top-ranked Chinese opponents to win a come-from-behind gold medal. For most of the Chinese audience, this Japanese victory must have aroused complicated feelings. Chire Koyama is the Japanese name of a former Chinese table tennis star He Zhili; she adopted the name after marrying a Japanese and receiving Japanese citizenship. Having won the medal, Koyama then showed respect to her husband in the traditional Japanese fashion, weeping on the winner's platform. However, Chinese cannot help asking who won the medal? A Chinese or a Japanese?

Still another famous women's table tennis star, Gao Min, married an American and won the 1991 Perth World Cup for the United States; and two others, Chen Jing and Xu Jing , who defected to Taiwan at about the same time, went on to represent Taiwan internationally and defeated former Chinese teammates. A more remote case would be Hu Na's defection to the United States in 1983. At that time, Chinese media derided President Ronald Reagan as Hu Na's foreign father and officially the government terminated a number of newly established cultural exchange programs in retaliation for the U.S.

grant of asylum. Yet, rarely did any stories in China condemn Hu herself, for it was the official position that Hu was tricked by a Taiwanese traveling in the United States. In fact, Hu's parents came out to request her return; she even appeared as an innocent victim. However, none of these athletes' victories or defections incurred such hard feelings among a Chinese audience as He Zhili's did during the 1994 Asian Games.

In the case of He Zhili, the reaction was clearly different. In 1988 she was prohibited from participating in the Olympics by her coach for her disobedience during the 1987 New Delhi World Cup. At that time, He defeated her teammate, whom the coach had wanted to play a Korean opponent in the final. Having defied her coach's instructions to throw the match, He then beat the Korean opponent and went on to win the gold medal. While under suspension, He Zhili married a Japanese. Thus, unlike Hu Na's case in 1983, the Chinese could not fault the Japanese government for seducing He Zhili as it had the U.S. government in relation to Hu Na 11 years earlier. Interestingly, since the Hu Na case, there had been no similar attempt by the Chinese to assign blame and this was demonstrated by Gao Min's American naturalization and the lack of serious charges against her. However, He's case witnessed a renewal of China's vehement condemnation of defection. One matter that made things worse was the defection of He's current coach, Zhuang Zedong, a former men's table tennis star who led the first Chinese table tennis team to visit the United States in 1972, but became a political outcast during the Cultural Revolution. Indeed Zhuang and He together made Koyama's gold medal a form of political revenge.

Clearly it was too strong a smell to be ignored. The problem was simply who to blame, the Chinese or the Japanese? The confusion arose because most Chinese critics did not know whether they should treat He Zhili as Chinese or as Japanese. The *Beijing Youth Review* published several articles questioning He Zhili's way of repaying her motherland and her compatriots.[36] They argued that since she was born and raised as Chinese, there was no way she could become Japanese just by defeating her Chinese fellow countrymen in an international tournament. The issue was simply a matter of patriotism in sports, and as such suggested He Zhili is still Chinese, but one who betrayed her homeland. There were, however, others who supported He's decision to represent Japan. For example, one article published by *Beijing Youth News* praised He's determination to assert herself in the games (she was already 30 in 1994) as a show of genuine Chinese national spirit.[37] Still others applauded her unique way of defeating the authoritarianism and collectivism of the Chinese system. Whichever side one takes, He Zhili seemed to be alone in her choice to become a Japanese national. None of the Chinese critics saw her as Japanese. In other words, they viewed Koyama's victory as a Chinese victory, disguised under a Japanese name. For her supporters, she might incidentally trigger a useful reform in Chinese sports-ethics, which would be a contribution to her homeland.

Again, Japan appears to be only in the background of this case. However, when compared with those residing in the United States, Taiwan, and many other places that accommodate Chinese athlete-immigrants, this Japanese background is significant for it may explain the sense of betrayal exclusively registered in this case among the Chinese rank and file, and that is not extant elsewhere. The psychological inability of most Chinese to recognize He Zhili's Japanese legal identity, under the name of Chire Koyama, suggests that sovereignty-related thinking has never effectively alleviated the fear among the Chinese of a Japanese encroachment on the cultural and racial fronts. Most Chinese are still in need of a clear demarcation between China and Japan. Once a Chinese, He Zhili will remain He Zhili for her Chinese compatriots, be they critical or supportive.

CONCLUSION

Scholars have argued, as I discuss further in chapter 6, that there is a lower case "foreign policy" root of all upper case "Foreign Policy." The upper case Foreign Policy refers to those acts that time and again reproduce boundaries for an assumed identity. The lower case foreign policy on the other hand reflects the deep-rooted identity at the national level based on a national identity rooted in more fundamental cultural, racial, religious, class, and gender dimensions.[38] This chapter is a typical study of foreign policy, and an unconventional way of conceptualizing the Foreign Policy China has toward Japan. The emergence of the Chinese state, which is confined within a clear territorial boundary, is incompatible with the traditional all under-heaven worldview, which allowed no physical boundaries. As the Chinese people have come to understand and accept the concept of boundary, they have found the Japanese a useful "Other" for demonstrating the uniqueness of China as a "state" entity. Japan's earlier vision of East Asia sought to vanquish China's claim on uniqueness, and has, despite Japan's defeat at World War II, served as a piece of evidence affirming China's sense of victimization. More importantly, since then, Japan, as a consistent threat, has long been the target of China's foreign policy decisions.

At the end of 1994, a Japanese news agency acquired an internally circulated document from the Chinese Communist Party (CCP).[39] According to the document, the CCP requested that cadres pay special attention to the Japanese government's recent moves to elevate the level of relations with Taiwan. The rationale for the Japanese is to keep China and Taiwan separate so that Japan would not face a strong, united Chinese people. The document uses Lee Teng-hui's attempt to visit Japan and Hsu Li-teh's actual visit as the evidence of a Taiwan–Japan collusion. Moreover, the document continues by stating that pro-Taiwan groups are believed to be gaining more political influence and the authors anticipated more intense conflict between China and Japan arising from possible changes in Japan's Taiwan policy. This Chinese reading of Japan's Taiwan policy interestingly contradicted with Taiwan's reading of Japan's China policy. The entire issue however is not a matter of objective analysis. The contradiction exists between Taiwan's psychological and political need for friendship with Japan to demonstrate its independence from, and China's psychological need for enmity with Japan to reinforce its precarious national identity. Both sides of the Taiwan Straits treat Japan according to their respective historical experiences with Japan, and these historical experiences influence China's Foreign Policy toward Japan. As the new century begins in an atmosphere of globalization, it would be interesting to see how the lower case foreign policy could evolve into a different kind of Chinese identity. This is the focus of chapter 6.

6

THE GLOBALIZATION CLUE: ESTRANGING THE PARTTIME SELF

INTRODUCTION

In his rewriting of American national security history, David Campbell once made a distinction between two kinds of foreign policy, "Foreign Policy" in the upper case and "foreign policy" in the lower case.[1] Foreign policy, made in the name of the state, in realist and idealist perspectives is the upper case Foreign Policy, which presumes as well as reproduces the ontology of anarchy where epistemologically uncritical states traffic with each other in threat. Campbell is interested in tracing those boundary-drawing practices in the cultural sphere that makes the imagination of the American state into a hegemony to support Foreign Policy. These practices he calls the lower case foreign policy, which provide the discursive economy to produce an enemy, as an Other, upon which the identity of the state rests. Othering practices are also key to James Der Derian's reconceptualization of diplomacy in terms of mutual estrangement.[2] For Der Derian, diplomacy is possible only if the "states" in question are foreign to one another, despite the fact that (or because) diplomacy aims at mutual understanding and mediation.

Postmodern writers' creative deconstruction contributes to the analysis of international relations to the extent that foreign policy defines external enemies;[3] external enemies create international relations; international relations necessitate Foreign Policy; and Foreign Policy reproduces states. However, Foreign Policy is not always made in the name of countering an enemy or with the aim of estranging an Other. Alexander Wendt, for example, summarizes three types of international relations (and he is far from exhausting all likelihoods), whereas both the "Hobbsian" and the "Lockean" versions correspond to Campbell's boundary-drawing while the "Kantian" does not indisputably lead to mutually estranging identities.[4] The prevailing mood of globalization seems to be just one of de-estrangement or, as perhaps Der Derian prefers, anti-diplomacy.[5] Mutual estrangement is nonetheless the foundation of international relations or the ontology of the state. If Othering an "Other" is no longer discursively popular, perhaps one way out of the increasingly murky condition of state under globalization is to Other the self, or self-estrangement.

China, sometimes an estranged state in the "China threat" or "the clash of civilizations" clichés, and, at some other times, a welcomed state in the creation of an undiscriminating global society,[6] is a typical example in terms of the lower case foreign policy confusion. Is China a state sharing the same teleology with those leading the way into globalization?[7] Or is China different from them, since it has a unique cultural combination of Confucianism, Daoism, or Buddhism?[8] If Chinese Foreign Policy is to continue enjoying legitimacy, one must not allow globalization to overwhelm, penetrate, or obscure the boundary of the Chinese state. However, if the contemporary goal of Chinese Foreign Policy is to globalize, the process of integrating unavoidably questions the very foundation of Chinese Foreign Policy. By reinterpreting China's lower case foreign policy, this chapter tackles the discursive strategy, pertaining to nationalism, to make China's entry into globalization emotionally more manageable and less felt as a loss of identity.

The Immigrating State

The Chinese state under globalization is like an emigrant who leaves his/her homeland for good. Under globalization, mutual estrangement stops because Foreign Policy makers, who Other foreign countries, lose the distinction between the inside and the outside. The Chinese state enters a sphere that is previously considered culturally dissimilar, if not inferior, by its citizens, who are now prepared to at least tolerate, if not actively utilize, the cultural varieties surrounding them in their quest for higher profits. What is required of Chinese citizens is not necessarily their physical movement into foreign geography, but definitely a psychological movement into a foreign culture. This type of requirement is familiar to modern Chinese history. In fact, early revolutionary leaders who jettisoned the celestial Qing dynasty to accept the modern state system were engaged in cultural emigration. The notion of sovereign state used to be anathema to the Chinese leadership before it later became a home to resist the imperialist Other. Upon becoming a sovereign state, the Chinese within the borders have been able to maintain a sense of homeliness by resorting to shared cultural traditions. The challenge of globalization today is not about any physical movement required of citizens, either, but the loss of homeliness.

For most immigrants, to mediate the estrangement with the homeland is essential to the building of a new home in the new land. The new land is composed of a different physical environment, language, food diet, religious setting, life style, human network, and other changes. All these combine to inflict a sense of trauma that is hard for immigrants to overcome. A nostalgic familiarity of one's social and economic background back home looms after one encounters the new surroundings. The tendency of local residents to demand evidence of contribution or loyalty exacerbates the wound. That said, the home is nevertheless out there, if not immediately accessible. Some imagined connections with the homeland are important in order to support the psychologically wounded immigrants. For example, ancestor worship is among the most popular mechanisms that can mitigate the loss of "original" identity for the Chinese immigrants anywhere. A plate inscribed with the ancestors' names or parents' photographs is often sufficient to produce the feeling that the motherland's protection is still around.

The imagined connection of this sort is particularly therapeutic for the subalterns (in this case, the immigrants) struggling for a fair and equal treatment. Demands to demonstrate loyalty to the new land can be bitter for the new immigrants, who can easily be conceived of as a cultural threat. It is questionable if any first-generation immigrants can ever achieve total assimilation in their limited lifetime. However, symbolic moves to signal the willingness to accept assimilation are politically useful. To hide or suppress one's original identity in the public place makes the private home a political space where symbols representing the motherland are not only legitimate but also spiritually compensatory. In recalling images about the motherland, the possibility of returning would always remain viable, or at least possible in their own minds.

In addition to the wound, there is a sense of guilt, which has two sources. One comes from subjugation to the pressure of the new social environment that demands he/she to declare loyalty to a foreign state or culture—an Other that is supposedly to be suspected, defended, or even confronted in some extreme cases back in the homelands. The subjugation implies betrayal, or the potential of betrayal. The other source of guilt is from the disregard of his/her suffering fellow citizens in the homeland, but one leaves for a better life. In other words, the guilt is due to this seeming disregard for the home folks who remain in the past. It is those who immigrate that wedge the split between the present and the past. Therapy is thus required to mediate or camouflage the split. One popular practice among the first-generation Chinese immigrants is to hope for the preservation of their "original identity" in one's lineage. Another is to return home bringing investments after one succeeded in the new land. This second alternative is psychologically more rewarding because the earlier split can be rendered obsolete as if immigration never affected the relations between the homeland and the immigrants.

Just like Chinese immigrants settled all over the world, the Chinese state in the beginning of the twenty-first century has been in a process of traveling at a global level, going into a place where it does not belong. The global sphere that China travels in appeared in many different forms, the most recent and noticeable one being the sphere created by the WTO. The tedious negotiation concerning China's entry into the WTO paralleled, in almost every aspect, immigrants' immediate arrival in the new land. Coming out of a central planning system and still slowed by a big, but inefficient state-run sector, the Chinese delegation needs to prove that the Chinese government can abide by the principle of free trade. China should open the market, rather than dump cheap goods in other countries. The Chinese government should respect human rights that keep the ruling Communist Party from intervening in the exchange processes. To be precise, China should be a contribution to the global sphere, not a threat. To demonstrate this, the Chinese people are expected to adopt norms and values familiar to the leading members of the WTO.

It is not difficult to see that some kind of trauma is being inflicted upon those loyal to the Chinese state. Not only are the criteria that the Chinese leaders use to judge their own performance insufficient today, there are much more new criteria imposed from the outside waiting to be met. For example, socialism and its concerns over workers' benefit are irrelevant to the WTO, and the state also cannot come to the rescue of the debt-laden state enterprises after its entry. This will render Confucian benevolence obsolete. To make matters worse, Confucianism is one of the two remaining ideologies that the CCP hold tight during the age of reform, a period of ideological void. A sense of loss is inevitable as the Party strives to draw a promising picture of the future for the wondering citizens. Joining the WTO cruelly exposes the intellectual incapability of the Party to continue serving as a guide. In fact, the Party itself chases after a kind of modernity that discursively originated from outside China. Doubtlessly, there are voices of resistance to China's move into the global liberalist market land. Those voices represent a part of the Chinese self that is to be estranged.

Voices of resistance directly disclose that the Party is in ideological disarray—a condition where party leaders would naturally feel upset. In response, state and party apparatuses depict those resisting the entry to the WTO as backward forces.[9] The most embarrassing point to Party leadership is that intellectuals are using socialism to publicly criticize WTO as well as government's reform policies.[10] Many of those critics are said to be the New Left,[11] a term given to them by a number of self-declared liberals. Ironically, because of their constant fights with the liberals for over a decade beginning with the aftermath of the Tiananmen massacre, Party ideologues used to consider New Left critics to be on the Party's side. As soon as the entry into the WTO was secured, Party leaders wanted to silent claims made by the New Left. Consequently, liberalism became the most readily available means for the Party to enlist in the rebuttal of its once-perceived comrade. However, this would be an impossible approach because in China liberals do not support the Communist Party. The most natural result is to resort to nationalism.

Equally embarrassing is the widespread phenomenon of intellectual piracy. First, the notion of intellectual property rights has never been an intelligent sounding concept to the ordinary Chinese. It is not even moral. For those familiar with the Chinese pragmatic culture, violation of intellectual property rights is not a violation at all. On the contrary, the surcharge imposed in the name of the intellectual property is morally questionable. The money made from it is consequently not "righteous" money. People are especially unhappy about the fact that Chinese workers making sneakers or shoes for foreign brands make only a slim salary compared with the large profits made by the stockowners or the trading companies, which are all registered somewhere outside China. However, to join the WTO, the government has to turn around to tell the disbelieving people that intellectual property rights are legal rights. Violations of intellectual property rights are signs of backwardness in the government's rhetoric today.

The predicament of the Chinese government and the Communist Party is that the past strategy distinguishing China from others familiar to them are no longer viable after China becomes an emigrant state. As capitalism begins to open up opportunities for the Chinese, being socialist becomes passé. After Bill Clinton became a strategic partner, being anti-imperialist no longer makes sense. Anything that symbolizes the good of the Communist Party's rule in the past loses significance today. Anything that tells of China's greatness in the past turns into indicators of backwardness today. These changes henceforth, produce a trauma of self-identification that is particularly strong in China's case because the establishment of the new identity depends on how successfully one can treat the past self as an inferior Other. China's future paradoxically lies in a process that promises China will no longer be China. The even more brutal necessity is that Chinese leaders must demonstrate their determination to jettison China's past in order to move into the global domain, and at the same time, treat their nationals cold-bloodedly.

Assimilation into the New Land

One major problem in the current literature on immigration is that there is too much emphasis on process of moving in and too little on moving out.[12] Most writers on immigration seem to worry about the difficulty of diasporas, or latecomers, to mingle with the larger society.[13] From the local residents' point of view, it is just unavoidable that latecomers are evaluated in terms of the extent of cultural threat they represent and the volume of contributions they make to the local community. Model immigrants are those who make contributions to the local development but bring no strange customs that threaten local values. The emphasis on adaptation in the literature overlooks the fact that the ability to adapt must proceed by instances of successful adaptation. This ability is more psychological and social than physical. For immigrants must consider themselves being a part of the local community before they can act and think like a local, and then get treated like a local eventually. In order to enhance the psychological power to facilitate adaptation, immigrants' trauma resulting from the split with the homeland must be attended to.

Local residents look at immigrants suspiciously especially when they come from a place regarded as culturally inferior to the local community. The ranking of the homeland state relative to the state hosting the immigrants in international politics very much affects immigrants regarding their sense of inferiority (or superiority). In general, Anglo-Saxons arriving in China usually live with a sense of superiority while the Chinese immigrants to North America, White Asia,[14] or Western Europe carry a sense of inferiority. However, neither inferior nor superior feeling is conducive to adaptation. The sense of superiority cautions a person against total assimilation unless this person is critical of her or his homeland's culture and consciously wants a new meaning of life. The adaptation nevertheless begins more as an identity strategy than assimilation. More likely the superior immigrants value the local culture in the same sense that Edward Said's Orientalists collect exotic items.[15] There is little pressure from the local community to demand assimilation of a superior immigrant. In short, a superior-minded immigrant feels no major split with the homeland. There is little trauma to be cured or estrangement to be mediated between the immigrant and the homeland.

By contrast, an inferior-minded immigrant faces the pressure to prove her or his value to the local community. This requires a resolute cut from the homeland. The cut could lead to a sense of void that drives a person exclusively toward material gains as if he/she has no root. Since the cut cannot be complete from the hosting society's perception, few immigrants can escape the scrutiny of loyalty. Those who pretend to be complete locals become extremely sensitive toward any lingering signs of his/her own foreign identity. As a result, the attempt to cut off their roots may lead to pathetic behavior such as denouncing parents or acting against the homeland state. The irony is that the conscious attempt to cut off one's roots hurts the ability to adapt in the long run. The lesson appears to be that the preoccupation with assimilation is detrimental to assimilation. The inferior immigrant cannot be a full person, therefore, without preserving her or his homeland's identity while acting like a local in a local situation.

What is required of an immigrant is an agency that enables her or him to adapt. This agency cannot be developed without mediating the estrangement with the homeland due to the act of immigrating. Methods of mediation could unfortunately incur the nightmare of the host society in that immigrants bring with them a dangerous foreign identity. Among these aforementioned methods, the Chinese immigrants usually carry with them their ancestral plates. Also, their festivals, conventions, and surnames are all reminders that they are outsiders. In reality, these methods of mediation are critical to the immigrants when facing uncertainty. To use the analogy of Donald Winnicott's transitional objects,[16] the ancestors' plate to the Chinese immigrants is like a pillow, a quilt, a blanket, or a teddy bear to the youngsters struggling to establish their own identities independent of their mothers. The transitional objects help the immigrants believe that they did not leave their homeland—or, in other words, the homeland and the ancestors are still with them in the new land.

Once the sense of self-estrangement is cured, the agency to act in accordance with the local conditions can arise. What makes the adaptation so difficult is the misfortune that the transitional objects facilitating the development of agency in the immigrant community are often considered by the locals to be the evidence of refusal to adapt.

The best immigrants can achieve is to defeat the locals by local standards. But, the best they can be is to become "model immigrants." A typical example is Chinese professionals staying in the United States after completing their studies and making a great deal of profits for companies they work for; however, they can rarely achieve or even try to assume the top managerial positions. In this case, contributions are made but no threat posed, which wins them the title of being model immigrants. But, they, after all, are considered as merely model "immigrants," and can never be put into the same league as the natives. In other words, the local community continues to draw a fine line between them and the model immigrants that the latter cannot cross. This interaction between the locals' identity strategy and the immigrants' identity strategy determines what is the fair share and whom it should be allocated to. For immigrants, their share is legitimately lower than the locals who contribute equally, if not less.

In the eyes of the local community, immigrants wanting to assimilate yet refusing to acknowledge assimilation are resistant to assimilation. On the other hand, to mediate the estranged relationship between the immigrant community and its homeland and to adapt to the local society are also two sides of one coin for immigrants. Accordingly, immigration studies should not be just about assimilation but also about mediation of estrangement and must also deal with immigrants' preservation of their roots. To evaluate the immigrants solely by how well they adapt to the local conditions either in terms of identity or in terms of contribution can be misleading. More importantly, how successful the process of moving out of the homeland is can determine how smooth the process of moving into the new land is. This implies a mission for the academics to find those strategies of moving out that are conducive to the development of agency in the immigrant group in the process of moving in.

Globalization has provided ample opportunities to reconstruct the norms of immigration although what has occupied headlines is more about killings that result from the mismanagement of diasporic identity. In the long run, globalization will further de-territorialize world politics to an increasingly greater extent. It may be easier for any specific group to maintain its identity in cyberspace and even influence politics by organizing a number of dedicated voters. On the whole, however, the physical element in a nationalist movement may be channeled away. This will change the feeling toward the immigrants as the easier and more frequent contacts with the rest of the world dissolve the sense of solidarity centering on territory. Assimilation may be a lesser issue in the future while at the same time it may be an easier task. Once the immigrant community can have much easier access to the homeland, either through physically traveling back home or exchanging information in cyberspace, the sense of detachment from the homeland can be mediated. Therefore, immigration does not imply self-estrangement, nor does receiving immigrants necessarily connote an identity threat.

There is no doubt that nationalism can benefit from globalization and the Internet. The new information channels they create can spread nationalism much faster; however, the dissemination of nationalist ideas can only take place along with other issues and symbols that are not explicitly about nationalism or even contradictory to nationalism. In addition, de-territorialization of world politics is less threatening if one can easily find a remedy in the web. In other words, solidarity can be simulated under globalization. Conquering can also be achieved in a simulation. Nationalism would become a game for everybody, not just for national leaders. This will produce an interesting result: the masses and the leaders exchange positions. If one can actively drive nationalism in a private room, the traditional practice of passively responding to the call of nationalist leaders would be an awkward act because to respond would reduce one from a practicing agency in the game to a follower that lacks agency.

Agency created under globalization can thus put national leaders in an embarrassing position. This is especially true when citizens appear more aggressive in an event than the government does. Both the U.S. air shelling of the Chinese embassy in Belgrade in 1999 and the collision of U.S. EP-3 with a Chinese fighter in 2001 witnessed nationalistic criticism in that the government looked too weak in its response to the incidents. News columns loved to quote extremist languages from the Bulletin Board Systems to suggest the dangerous potential of the incidents. Interestingly, no collective action against the government or the U.S. embassy was possible under the circumstances. One actually saw debates going on in various BBS sites involving overseas Chinese scholars as well as overseas–China experts. In fact, the famous State-Strengthening Forum derives directly from the Protest Forum, which was created in response to the Belgrade bombardment. As the government loses monopoly over the meaning of nationalism or the representation of nationalist causes, nationalism does not connote the same threat anymore. The implications to the diasporic community are worth future research. For the time being, easier accesses to chat forums composed of Chinese participants all over the world undermine the physical distance that separates these discussants. It is not clear whether this means that domestic participants are becoming more international or that overseas immigrant communities are becoming less international. When Der Derian examines the element of "speed" of any transaction and concludes that a new age of anti-diplomacy has arrived,[17] it is precisely because shrinking distances has destroyed the mutual estrangement between communities of two different countries. Diplomats who used to be the first to deal with the foreign country are less relevant to diplomacy today as they become the last to legitimize the dissolution of national borders.

NATIONALISM AS THERAPY

What appears to be a perfect remedy for the immigrant community, namely, utilizing globalization to reestablish the lost connection with home, is actually the source of problems for an immigrating state like China, which abandons its traditional realm and enters a new sphere: the international economic domain. There is no home for China in this new domain, just like the immigrants of the nineteenth century arriving in a new land. Today, home is about a decision, not about a place. Home is internal to one's psyche, not external. To return home is to make a dramatic turn in foreign policy as well as state identity. Like the early immigrants, for whom it was a permanent move to quest for a new life in a new land, the immigrating state that is aboard the ship of WTO has reached a point of no return.

The effects of self-estrangement are forthcoming. Many productive sectors in China are expected to face lethal competition from global producers. Perhaps what is hard to swallow for most people in China is that protection at home will no longer be legal nor moral under the WTO. China is in a new land and has to play a new game according to new rules, which are not new at all for those multinational firms that have already established themselves in the global sphere for generations. In other words, the immigrating China has entered others' homes. Like many newcomers who moved into a foreign land, China must also face finger pointing from all directions while trying to find ways to disguise its unfamiliarity of the new surrounding and its awkward display of actions. Immigrants in this case lack confidence, network, or identity. They have the pressure to prove that they are not troublemakers. What China faces today is a new situation that it has never experienced in its modern history—this renders the Chinese as a whole into an immigrant finding a way to survive in a new world order. In the past, adjustments made to cope with external pressures was rarely wholehearted. Those changes were only meant to counter external intrusion, not self-transformation.

Remember the United Nations? Many observers had anticipated difficulties China could have brought to the operation of the organization, but the United Nations ran smoothly counter to their predictions.[18] There was no pounding the table, nor blockade of minutes, nor red guards taking over. It was a delegation cautiously and modestly trying to learn the new game. But, China in the United Nations was like an immigrant who never really left home completely. It was more like a student leaving to cities for higher education, a seasonal worker who believes that he/she will return shortly, or a business traveler exploring a new market. Unlike the case of the WTO, China could very well opt for withdrawal in the case of the UN through absent or obsolete voting. Also, China was, in essence, invited to the UN and the UN was not considered a home by any of its major participants. Therefore, to enter the UN was not permanent immigration and there was no sense of loss. On the contrary, there was a sense of elation. China was recognized with honor and respect. Its need for nationalistic assertion was actually reduced by admission into the UN. The normalization of relations with the United States and the signing of the Shanghai Communiqué in the early 1970s are the results of this lessened sentiment.

The case for China's entry into the globalized market system is much more complicated than joining the UN. The march into market system symbolizes a break from socialist orthodoxy. Under such circumstance, the only intelligent question for the state and the Party leaders to ask is what can mediate the estranged relations between future China and past China. The Party has made an effort since the end of the Tiananmen incident. There was the so-called second and third thought liberations, referring to Deng Xiaoping's 1992 trip to Shanghai to reopen the frozen reforms in 1989 and Jiang Zemin's return to the theory of the primary stage of socialism in 1998.[19] Both liberations were meant to justify the use of market in a socialist county and henceforth indicate the departure from socialism. These were no remedy to the ideological void after the collapse of Mao's Cultural Revolution regime in 1976. Today the emphasis on reform moves

China toward a future that indirectly denounces China's socialist past. The formulation of the "Three Represents" theory by Jiang Zemin in 2000 has been equally attentive to mediating the estrangement of China's past self.

Other semi-official attempts have been more to the point in comparison, in terms of constructing the authenticity of China. There was the so-called cultural fever in the mid-1980s. During that period, the role of Confucianism in maintaining political order aroused much interest. Many television programs reintroduced the classic Confucian texts. Toward the mid-1990s, the Chinese Social Science Academy repeatedly scheduled large-scale, international conferences on "Chinese culture at the dawn of the 21st Century."[20] About the same time, a series of polemics between the so-called liberals and the New Left were staged. These debates dealt specifically with the fundamental question of what it means to be Chinese.[21] On another cultural front, the society was deeply involved in the bid to host the Olympic Games 2000 in 1993, the year China failed. When China returned in 2001 and succeeded in beating all the other competitors by a wide margin, the city of Beijing almost exploded. All this suggests that many Chinese people have desired something magnificent to be attached to the notion of China.

The official participation in the construction of self-respect, which is inversely related to globalization, was most clearly shown in the preparation and the celebration of the handover of Hong Kong. Even in the years before the date of handover, almost everywhere in China, be it a mountain village, a wall-torn school, or in a broken cab, one can read slogans announcing the imminent handover of Hong Kong. Most noticeable was the huge clock hanging in the Tiananmen Square that was counting down every second toward July 1, 1997, the scheduled day of the handover. The Hong Kong drama was a particular kind of therapy for those who were anxious over the loss of an authentic China, as Hong Kong represented the quintessence of globalization. Its return to China not only signaled the opening of China, but also the glory of the motherland. The glory came from the cleansing of historical shame symbolized by the giving away of Hong Kong to Britain in 1842, the year the Opium War ended. One only has to remember that Chinese modern history texts typically start in 1840 to appreciate why the handover is psychologically significant for any ordinary Chinese.

Hong Kong was a golden opportunity to bridge the conceptual gap between the seemingly jettisoned old China and the galloping future China. Many in the West were worried at the time that the handover might give the Chinese a false taste of self-glorification.[22] This was the same kind of worry registered among the world's leading countries when Sydney defeated Beijing in 1993 winning the bid for hosting the 2000 Olympic Games, which was regarded as potentially a nationalist leverage of the Chinese government. Western media treated the handover in a quite ambivalent way. On the one hand, no journalist missed the elation on the Chinese side, but most raised some doubts about China's obsession with the details of the ceremony and whether the handover would become an opportunity for the Chinese government to abuse heroism.[23] On the other hand, the only exception was the British papers, which generally took an optimistic view.[24] This was probably because, as the country to hand over Hong Kong, the British public could not afford a pessimistic attitude that could imply a betrayal on the British part. The British public would thus naturally wish for a successful future for Hong Kong.

There was no doubt that the Communist Party scored high on Hong Kong's handover. The ceremony was wonderfully solemn and smooth; the procedure was unprecedentedly sophisticated in human history; and the decoration was truly imperial. However, the government obviously did not even try to cash in on the seeming rise of nationalism in the period leading to July 1, 1997. In contrast, people were relaxed afterward. On hindsight, Hong Kong's handover was more a therapy than leverage. As a therapy, it released the anxiety caused by the loss of self-respect during the age of reform and openness to the outside world. As leverage, on the contrary, one would expect the government to utilize the occasion to make demands on the population that would not normally be made or at least to make up the loss of credit due to the enforcement of capitalist-like reform policy.

In relation to Hong Kong's handover was the publication of the notorious book entitled *China Can Say No.* There were numerous discussions abroad as well as in China if the bestseller indicated the rise of nationalism in China. In this book, the three authors severely criticize the China policy of the United States. It is not just an analysis. The revelation of hatred is vivid and candid. It is worth pondering why a book filled with hatred and contempt was so popular among Chinese readers. Since then, English literature on Chinese nationalism has boomed.[25] Some justify its rise; others worry about its closed-door tendency; still others urge to take it easy. The latter should rethink their position if they have witnessed the spontaneous rise of nationalism immediately after the U.S. bombardment of the Chinese embassy in Belgrade in 1999. The sentiment could not be more real than the furious students marching toward the U.S. embassy. What should interest the bystander is that the police lined up students to wait for their turn to throw stones at the U.S. embassy in Beijing in an orderly manner. The U.S. ambassador could not take it easy as he later recalled. It was a moment of life and death.[26] Indeed the masses all over the country were furious.

Neither the book *China Can Say No* nor the Belgrade bombardment proved detrimental to Sino-U.S. relations in the long run. This was not to say that they could not be detrimental, but just that the relations returned to a manageable level rather quickly after the events. Whether or not there is nationalist sentiment and how long it can last are a contingent matter. What is certain is that the nationalist sentiment is potentially strong and needs an outlet of some sort. What is also obvious is that Chinese under reform do not have to live on nationalism. They cannot get rid of it, though. For if entering the global sphere is almost the same as immigrating to a U.S.-dominated global sphere, nationalism against the United States would be the cheapest outlet for the estranged self to reassert respect. As a result, nationalism is a parttime business that one needs to have, but not a 24-hours-a-day activity.

Opening up Nationalism

Although occasional displays of nationalism are healthy, nationalism is no longer just nationalism under the new circumstances. This is hardly a new phenomenon in domestic politics. In ethnic areas where minorities are struggling to catch up with the tide of reform and openness to the outside world, the shortest route to produce wealth is to utilize ethnic culture or, more precisely, the imagination about ethnic culture by the mainstream society, to promote tourism. This is not to say that domestic ethnic nationalism is spurious. However, to meet the popular impression of ethnic communities, the tourist industry deliberately decorates the tourist site in such a way that ethnic cultures are always associated with the natural, physical, sexual liberation as well as backwardness. The construction can be so successful that those performers would demand tourists to cooperate to reproduce these images. When cooperation is denied, despite the fact that the performance is designed to satisfy tourists, ethnic performers feel offended because the public image of their ethnicity, albeit volatile, is not respected.[27] In other words, the tourist performance can have the effect of changing the self-images of the performers. This is the domestic counterpart of reflexive Orientalism introduced in chapters 1 and 2 with regard to China's identity in world politics.

Ethnic nationalism takes on two meanings, one for tourist consumption and the other for self-respect. Tourists are predominantly from the majority Han population, against whom the local minorities assert their dignity. In the age of reform where profitability is all that matters, the maintenance of ethnic identity faces serious challenges. Children of ethnic villages yearn for a new life in the cities and parents generally want to help them be prepared for urban living. The quickest way to make money in order to achieve that purpose is through tourism. Again and again, the drive for profits arouses anxiety among older generations, who worry about the decline of their traditional identities (which in many cases are quite fresh in fact). Young ethnic peasants navigating along the railroads between home villages and coastal cities undermine the stability that elders in their hometown used to enjoy. It is usual for minority immigrants in the cities celebrating ethnic festivals every year to preserve their roots. Ethnic nationalism of this sort rarely threatens the sense of superiority among city dwellers.

In reality, neither tourism nor symbolic gathering during the festival can monopolize the meanings of being an ethnic citizen. Tourism can even be detrimental to self-respect because the exotic nature of the business usually fixates on some sort of backwardness. The implications are complicated nevertheless. Since tourism cashes in on ethnicity, it sensitizes ethnic issues. This can create repercussions far beyond what the Party leaders, local as well as central, can expect in advance. The anti-Han sentiment is reported in more than a small number of ethnic sites where ethnic–Han relations have generally, and still, been well maintained throughout. This anti-Han sentiment is not political and has little political effects in reality. I suspect that this sentiment has directly to do with the frustration of incapacity to produce a clear self-identity more than with either government policy or daily ethnic–Han relations.

All in all, ethnic nationalism has developed in various directions that are beyond the government's expectation. However, the new identify formation is not likely to attract the attention of the government because this formation does not emerge in the form of resistance. For example, when the local government blames the Yi people in Liangshan, Sichuan, of holding a slave mind-set and keeping children from schooling, local villagers responded by inaction.[28] After all, schools are generally not positive about the Yi identity. The problem is also exacerbated by the failure of the government propaganda to provide sufficient motivation for the parents to enroll their children. Hence, there is little incentive for the Yi people to go to school. A resistance is nevertheless hidden in the lukewarm response to school recruitment. However, since the government hears, sees, and feels no resistance, it then concluded and produced a backward image of the Yi minority. Ironically, this image protects the Yi children from becoming just ordinary citizens, and also turns into a protective shield that, in effect, prevented the Han government from further intervention.

Another interesting case is about the Muslims in Litong, Ningxia. As more young people enter the market economy, less can afford to pray five times a day toward Mecca or be on a religious diet as the occasion requires. In fact, young people no longer go to the Mosque to hear the weekly preaching. This may suggest the decline of religious identity. A longitudinal analysis suggests otherwise. The local leaders report more visits to the Mosque among villagers over 40. People begin to save money to prepare the trip to Mecca in their 50s. The preparation for the trip occupies many over the age of 60. If they have been to Mecca before, they become fervent followers. The state feels no threat as Muslims return to their religious identity. However, if this were among the younger generations, the government may very well worry that the religious identity would collide with loyalty toward the state. It is almost like a tacit understanding between the government and the local Muslims that before the age of 40 Muslims belong to the state; between 40 and 60 there is a transition period; and after 60, they can be pious Muslims without any intervention.[29]

The situation of the ethnic minorities in China is not very different from the Chinese state floating in the global sphere and willingly estranging those citizens who are seemingly trapped in the traditional (socialist as well as Confucian) mode of thinking. As tourism is believed to be an efficient method to get ethnic villagers out of poverty, there is little left for the villagers to claim pride on except their ability to make a profit, an ability that further dampens ethnic identities. Implicit in the process is the philosophy that ethnic nationalism should be more consciously used. It should not be just an emotional response to the loss of identity. It should contribute to the development of the local community in material terms, for example, to raise funds from international organizations, to ensure tax exemption, to acquire permission to manufacture tobacco and alcohol, to secure a quota for higher education, and so on and so forth. Once ethnic nationalism and pragmatism are linked, it cannot be the same ethnic nationalism as it started with. Ethnic nationalism is interestingly relevant to the reform era now not only because it can resist reform, but because it thrives on reform. Resisting reform and thriving on reform are ironically symbiotic trends with the former mediating the estranged relationship between one and oneself, the latter restraining the extent that ethnic nationalism can go in resisting reform.

The Chinese nationalism that escorts the Communist leaders in the global sphere similarly bifurcates in different directions. While Party leaders definitely need nationalism to sooth anxiety caused by self-estrangement during the state's immigration, they necessarily lose control over the meaning of nationalism both at home and abroad. Nationalism at home is beyond control for several reasons. One reason is that any attempt at domestic ideological control in the name of the state may arouse suspicion of backwardness from the global society although at the same time failure to control the nationalistic sentiment may lead to the same suspicion. National leaders are simply not capable of a clear policy on nationalism, not to mention monopoly over the meaning of nationalism. Another reason is that when people cash in on nationalism for the sake of making money, this is compatible with the purpose of reform and there seems little justification for the state to intervene. In addition, bifurcated meanings of nationalism reduce the extremity of political nationalism, which mediates estrangement and dialectically backs up the move toward globalization. Finally, symbols that represent nationalism become wildly varied in the new age. It is virtually impossible for Party leaders to interpret all the representations for the audience, who are not dependent on the Party for information.

In fact, the Party itself is guilty of bifurcating nationalism into unlimited meanings because it is the Party that sensitizes nationalism among citizens. The first case is again the aforementioned book, *China Can Say No*. This is a strongly anti-American reading, which reflects the attitude of a large portion of the Chinese population. The book sells extremely well but the official position is embarrassingly unclear. This is both because the book speaks the sentiment of many high-level government officials and because the book exposes the government's vulnerability in the face of international pressure. In a very brief time, numerous books carrying similar titles, such as *China Can Still Say No, China Is Not Mr. No*, and so on,[30] appeared on the shelf for sale. The publication of these books is obviously business-oriented, not nationalistically oriented. However, nationalism must be alive in order for this business to make sense. This is an archetypal example of commercialized nationalism.

NATIONALISM FOR SALE

Nationalism can attach to almost anything that has publicity. *China Can Say No* is not unique in its combination of nationalism and market profit. In a study on Basque nationalism in Spain, for example, the radio station that helps to forge the nationalist spirit among nationals in random residences takes on new business as soon as commercial interests sneak into the programs.[31] Since nationalists must appeal to all in China, the more successful the appeal, the higher the potential for profit. When nationalistic education ranks high on the government's priority list, nationalism is more profitable. For example, if the Ministry of Civil Affairs decides to print a textbook on anti-spiritual pollution, it may easily require all villages in China to buy one copy. This may very well result in the selling of the text in over half of the villages, which would mean over 460,000 copies in 1990. Similarly a provincial government would want to compete and order the villages in its jurisdiction to purchase a copy from the publisher affiliated with the provincial government. Some sort of competition over a monopolized market then takes place. This sort of competition probably happens every time there is a propaganda drive.

In the beginning of the 1990s, textbooks on spiritual civilization, anti-peaceful evolution, and China's national conditions were able to ride on the international sanctions of the government's policy during the 1989 pro-democracy movement. Except for a few that appeal to name calling and red labeling (which are sometimes horrifying), the majority of these textbooks are extremely dry readings. Once it becomes a reading for propaganda purpose, it would be mandatory reading for state employees, which includes almost all citizens in the cities. These textbooks compete with one another for a huge market. Each publisher has her or his network. Profit sharing mechanisms motivate the leaders to order the subordinate agencies to purchase a book. The rationale of the purchase is for patriotic education, but making money is definitely also a part of the active participation in patriotism.

Profiting from selling textbooks does not change the message of nationalistic education in general, but it does affect the style of writing since there are always writers trying to appeal to the residual market for textbooks. How to make nationalism writings more attractive is an art. *China Can Say No* represents a successful case. However, as long as these are textbooks, they cannot really attract readers. The fast turnaround in spring 1992 of the antibourgeois liberalization campaign into an unlimited open-door policy indicated how strong the need for openness is. Within a very short period of time, coastal cities completely changed, with Shanghai being the often-cited example. The profitability of nationalism based on the content of textbooks is therefore volatile, depending on how anti-American the government appears to be at a particular time. Under this circumstance, *China Can Say No*, which was published three to five years after the end of the antibourgeois campaign, made big money purely on its own promotion. Its profitability arose from its ability to provide an outlet to the accumulated frustration caused by the mismanaged Sino-U.S. relations in the previous few years.

Other forms of nationalism can also generate revenue, sometimes for the government, at other times for the individuals. In the case of the individual, no one can miss the movie industry that thrives on action heroes such as the late Bruce Lee as well as the more contemporary Jacky Chen and Li Lianjie. No remedy to the loss of identity is better than the projection of a frustrated self-image in real life onto a foreign enemy in the movie, who is defeated by a Chinese hero. Nostalgia, which brought back old times, in good or bitter memories, is a perfect subject for movie making that associates the contemporary with the past and mediates the estranged relationship between the future and the past. Some kind of soft nationalism is always hidden in movies or soap operas of this sort. The deliberate connection that enables the audience of Yongzheng Dynasty (a television series about the fourth emperor of the Qing dynasty) to allude to reform undergone today increases, not decreases, its popularity because of, in my opinion, the program's therapeutic function. It is the common concern over the welfare of all Chinese nationals that brings together the heroes in the movies and the audience.

Outside the theater, the real heroes that defeat the foreigners can also be found in the Olympic Games. Olympic Games are much more conspicuous than Asian Games because Chinese athletes generally compete with the White race in the former. It is not a secret that a gold medal means money in China. Not only does the winner of a medal receive a financial award, but also the person can sell his/her fame. Most of those business practices of selling the faces or logos of Olympic heroes in a capitalist society can also be seen in China. The difference is that the Chinese worship their heroes both because of their personal performance and because of the honor they bring for China. While worshiping heroes is not a typical Chinese custom, it stresses the importance of the great self, not the capability of the little self. Will contemporary Olympic heroes cause anxiety among the Chinese population because heroes in historical novels were typically rebellious. Today heroes are nationalistic instead. This appreciation of China's nationalism cannot be easily proved, but an opposing case can indirectly demonstrate the extent to which the nationals view their heroes in a nationalist way.

One good example of this was the case of He Zhili or Chire Koyama in chapter 5. Koyama's experience suggests that the Chinese nationals contribute to the commercialization of Olympic Gold medals not least because of their patriotism. Gold medals, which imply authenticity in China, bring better healing effects. The ordinary people's faddish collection of heroes' fan merchandise reflects appreciation for the effort made by medal winners, and this act can be viewed as a monetary retribution to the heroes. Worries about Chinese nationalism rising due to the Olympic Games echo the historical memory that Adolph Hitler promoted Fascism by holding the Olympics. This increased the difficulty for the city of Beijing to win trust for its bid to host the 2000 Olympic Games. But, these worries were unfounded. The Chinese need for nationalism in order to produce self-respect during their opening to the outside world is not likely be a cause of hyper nationalism in China. Once nationalism has a shadow price,[32] the value of nationalism is limited.

The meaning of nationalism begin to diverge as the ways to present nationalism multiply. Officially promoted nationalism is still the dominant voice in interpreting the contents and the direction of nationalism. However, the government cannot monopolize nationalism. Citizens have created agency in expressing their need for nationalism at a time when the government was been well prepared. The bombardment of the Chinese embassy in Belgrade demonstrated the quickness of the students' response to the incident. The agency in practicing and interpreting nationalism is directly related to the policy of reform, which un-roots the conventional Chinese identities, to the nascent market, which prices nationalism in various ways, and to the Olympic Games, which instills in the masses a sense of confidence in articulating their demand for nationalist performance by the government.

On the other hand, when the government goes out to meet this sporadic demand contingent upon unexpected events, the social mood, and the government's own propaganda, there is no guarantee that the government can easily maintain firm control. Reconsider the Belgrade case. The expectation that this incident would create another May Fourth Movement—that devoted intellectuals would reverse their obsession with money making in the contemporary academic circle—seems to have dwindled quickly in the aftermath. Even the crash of the U.S. EP-3 with the Chinese air fighter in 2001 did not effectively trigger the patriotic tide worrisome to many liberals in China. The tide was high indeed during the first few weeks of both events. Although in the eyes of America, the tide of nationalism was a result of government manipulation,[33] in reality it was not. In fact, the government wanted the nationalist tide to continue for a while, to satisfy the masses although not too much of a tide as to risk the government's credit in handling Sino-U.S. relations.

There are simply too many outlets for nationalism; people can even express a feeling of superiority when Chinese nationals beat the United States on a video game or they could watch Wang Zhizhi, the first Chinese NBA player, being welcomed by fans in Dallas. Wang's first play incidentally took place at about the same time as the EP-3 incident. The coincidence reminds one of Milan Kundera's *The Book of Laughter and Forgetting*, for the Chinese nationals wanted to cheer Wang yet felt restrained in order to avoid behaving incorrectly during the political confrontation. Both the self-restraint and the pleasure of watching Wang are related to nationalism—but the two seem to be mutually exclusive. This impossible combination of two different types of emotion could lead to Kundera's cynicism in the long run.[34] This does not mean that nationalism will be idle in the long run. On the contrary, the surge of nationalism, its form, length, effect, and meanings are not in the hands of the Party leaders. There is little sense of citizen's rebellion. What is at work is the unnoticed agency that interprets and reinterprets nationalism.

FOREIGN POLICY ON THE SLIDE

The literature in the studies of political science looks at nationalism as an outdated ideology, to be eventually jettisoned by rational society.[35] Those societies, such as Chinese society, which occasionally appeal to the nationalistic sentiment in coping with international affairs, are typically suspected of being dragged down by backward elements in their past history. Even if they attempt to enter the global sphere and institutionally become a formal member, those who usually come from Western Europe or North America seem to enjoy legitimacy among those in charge of global governing. China accepted the global governing mechanism only very recently. Its entry has been met with obstacles inside as well as outside of China. Like an early White settler in America facing a late-coming Chinese immigrant arriving in the late nineteenth century, other global actors examined China by assessing its potential contribution and possible threats.

They frequently resort to some sort of value test in order to determine how far China still is from the standards they set up for latecomers. These tests almost guarantee that China will not be accepted as a normal participant in global governing.

The reason is simple, any immigrant, be it an individual Chinese peasant or the Chinese state, needs certain methods to mediate the estranged relationships between the new immigrant identity and the past identity. The most convenient method is to bring the ancestor along in the form of a plate, souvenir, diet habit, or life style in the case of an individual and nationalism in the form of nostalgia, renaissance, resistance, sacrifice, and so on in the case of the Chinese state. These mediating mechanisms easily beget the sense of being threatened in the local community. It is unfortunate that mediation, which assists in adaptation and assimilation in the long run, often becomes a proof of cultural alterity or refusal to adapt. Indeed the distrust toward the latecomers is so strong that the immigrating state may fall back to a longer cycle of nationalistic resistance. Testing China's capacity to enter the global sphere is increasingly a simple, or simplified, task. Basically, one only needs to look at what one considers the key self-identities and check how far China's image is from them.

One of these standards is about the degree of democratization as well as human rights protection. Observers should look at how many political criminals are still imprisoned in China, how well criminals are treated, how much the Party can tolerate political dissidents forming their own organizations, and so on. The U.S. State Department issues human rights reports every year to deal with these and other related questions. In contrast, Chinese nationalism means that in China a patriot will not use these indicators to evaluate its government. In addition, a more nationalistically correct schema including the rights to economic development, freedom from imperialist invasion, learning one's own culture, egalitarian sovereign status, and so on emerges to counter U.S. human rights standards. If the polemics save enough face for the government in China, the installation of reform that leads to further globalization will probably continue. The same therapeutic effect is also desired by the U.S. government in the sense that the policy to drag China into the global sphere can win the support of Congress only after the U.S. government raises some serious concerns regarding human rights violations to the Chinese government.

A slightly sophisticated and academic standard is to look at a civil society in the making, a base that is said to allow the development of democracy to take place. There is always some wishful observation in this respect. Civil society formation is a long process and observers from this perspective are relatively patient even though the tendency does exist to over-read the conditions for a Western-styled civil society in China to have improved. Cautioning the U.S. government not to push too hard, the civil society approach is implicitly, yet very much, wary of the nationalistic solution that easily arises to support the reversal of the open-door policy if a polemic resumes. From the Chinese side, there is the argument for a Chinese-styled civil society that does not necessarily deny the collectivistic tradition in socialist work units or collectivistic villages.[36] There is in addition criticism taking neo-Marxist as well as postcolonial perspectives that warn against the exploitative potential of the new global environment.

Contrary to the realist prescription, the Chinese government rarely tries to take advantage of a crisis that involves the United States in order to advance China's so-called national interests—which are seemingly at odds with the interests of the United States. As the mathematic model of chapter 4 asserts, national interests are claimed for the sake of confrontation, which in turn preserve nationalism as a remedy to the estranged past self. The process of confrontation and the feeling of pursuing national interests in defiance of U.S. expectations bring more psychological satisfaction than achieving those interests. If the Chinese government is determined that China needs to immigrate to the global sphere, the so-called national interests that may complicate entry are not the most concerning issues. This is why during both the Persian Gulf War in 1991 and the antiterrorist alliance formation in 2001, the Chinese government either released political criminals or cooperated considerably without forcing its own so-called interests ostentatiously. As long as the gatekeeper of the global sphere appears to be weak, the need for nationalistic demonstration drops.

On the other hand, when there is a perceived test for the Chinese government's resolve, the response will likely be higher than the anticipated range of expectation. A case in political and economic areas respectively is useful here. The political case was in the Taiwan Straits missile crises of 1995–96, which was initiated by the Chinese government to bluff the United States from showing support for the Taiwan independence movement. The Chinese government obviously was not able to take over Taiwan, but nationalistic sensitivity compelled it to act in a strong way that would not have been the case if Taiwan's independence-inclined leader Lee Tenghui had not obtained U.S. approval to make an unprecedented visit the United States as an incumbent president from Taiwan. The economic example refers to the war against speculators during the Asian Financial Crisis. The decision to fight until the last minute was not as obviously rational as it may have appeared after the victory. The government frequently appealed to "China's fight" or "China's decision" in its dedicated support to the Hong Kong stock market. This was a sensitive issue especially at the time of Hong Kong's return to China. If Hong Kong fell to the predating speculators, China's rationale to enter the global sphere could have been completely ruined. Nationalism therefore played a critical role in prompting the government to be in a combative position right away, paving the way for further openness.

It is noteworthy that economic nationalism works in both directions. In addition to the war against speculators, there has been the policy of alluring Taiwanese businessmen to China. Despite various harassments that each individual Taiwanese business may encounter in any specific locations, flexibility and concessions are clearly shown at the national level in the regulation of Taiwan business investment. The concessions given are for the sake of prompting reunification between China and Taiwan. Interestingly, the government in Taiwan engages in the same mediating game as does the Chinese government. Taipei authorities' persisting disapproval of its citizens to invest, marry, immigrate, or study in China is met with an enthusiastic Westward movement. It is almost as if the Taiwanese government's refusal to enter reunification negotiations with the Chinese government mediates the estranged relationship between those Taiwanese businessmen participating in the marketization of China and their fellow citizens staying home in Taiwan. Nationalistic anti-China slogans at home in Taiwan sensitize the Chinese to Taiwanese businessmen's identity and therefore serve to maintain that identity.

While there is worry that Chinese nationalism, if mismanaged, may lead to confrontation with the United States, nationalism today is no longer the same nationalism as before. Most importantly, the commercialization of nationalism and the bifurcation of its meanings have granted some agency to individual Chinese to interpret and practice nationalism as each sees proper. This citizen agency coexists in various forms with those in the countryside ready to answer the call by the government and those in the cities acting more spontaneously. Nationalism has a shadow price now. Even though the occasional call for nationalistic action by the government, situations, the New Left writers, or nationalist fundamentalists is hard to resist, as the Chinese state is further involved in the global sphere, the agency to practice and interpret nationalism by themselves slowly grows in each individual. These individuals can together, without necessarily planning collectively, bring out interpretations and carry on practices that are hard for anyone to anticipate.

THE CONFUCIAN CLUE:
PRACTICING ANTI-NEGOTIATION
TOWARD TAIWAN

BRINGING BACK CULTURAL INTERPRETATION

Studies of state behavior often face the difficult choice between "motivational analysis" and "structural analysis." If the state is a unity of human beings with a distinct disposition and character,[1] state behavior should be understood from perspectives that acknowledge the importance of history, culture, and personality. If, on the other hand, the state is a matter of structure[2] or arena,[3] its behavior is then a reflection of some perpetuating foundations or principles. The same question can be addressed to China scholars concerning how cultural Chinese foreign policy making really is, or, to put it in academic terms, to what extent international systemic structures constrain China's external behavior.[4]

Chapter 4 demonstrates that the two modes of analysis need not be in conflict with each other. Although motivation and structures are possibly contradictory in terms of the direction of influence on behavior, they do not necessarily involve irreconcilable epistemologies. A motivational analysis would look to the historical experiences, cultural backgrounds, and life concerns of various Chinese leaders, while a structural analysis would emphasize the principles of capacity, development rationality, and so on.[5] Obviously, motivations and structures interact in such a way that no structures are meaningful without individual politicians actualizing them, and no motivation can develop without some principle conditioning it.[6] This process of structuration can be both long or short term, subjective as well as inter-subjective, with structures practiced in earlier historical periods becoming determinants of latecomers' motivation.[7]

Nonetheless, prevailing social science methods systematically exclude historical, cultural interpretations of state behavior and thus discriminate against motivational analysis.[8] Empathy seems to be anathema for anyone who shows it in a science of detachment;[9] international politics research cannot help but suppress all those texts or intertexts that undermine rationalization based upon a unitary statist position.[10] This bias thus creates misinterpretation and misperception of the meaning of policy for Chinese policy-makers and led the late Kuo Hua-lun,[11] who was able to "feel" Zhou Enlai, to deplore the dearth of Sinology.

Indeed Chinese scholars trained in the West who have returned to their lands are now among the most faithful social science practitioners in China studies.[12] This is particularly the case in the analysis of cross–Taiwan Straits relations.[13] While social scientific epistemology enables Taiwanese (and even Chinese) analysts to treat China as an objective "Other" and provides them with a position outside of China, historical and cultural analysis brings them closer to it. It is perhaps the enjoyment of this sense of distancing that differentiates them from Western psycho-culturalists such as Pye, Solomon, or, last but not least, Lifton,[14] who shortens the epistemological distance confidently by "feeling" that Chinese politicians were just like their psychotic patients in the West.

Distancing from China is important for many Chinese and Taiwanese China scholars because it enables them to feel closer to a superior Western mind-set. Empathy, on the contrary, would induce them to use their intuition in research to which their Western colleagues generally have no access. The danger for them is that the presentation of cultural arguments becomes the evidence that they are essentially Chinese rather than social scientists. Unless they can speak of Chinese culture from a Western psychoanalytical tradition, which is not only unfamiliar but even counterintuitive to them, they would be unable to adopt the rare "Pyescian" analysis, which treats China both as an inferior Other and an empathized subject of study.[15]

The resulting disproportionate stress on national capacity in terms of military strength, economic need, and international alliance disallows us from appreciating the genuine motivation behind each message Chinese leaders in Beijing intend to send across.[16] Beijing's frustration, thus bred and subsequently conveyed in the form of distrust and polemics, can ironically fit into the familiar language of international politics as a typical statist expression of competitive mood. As a result, we may misconceptualize the meaning of those messages to the effect of exacerbating frustration on all sides and provoking the conflict to an irrevocable level.

The following discussion offers a psycho-cultural interpretation of the Chinese communication style, reactivating the relevance of motivational analysis for a deeper comprehension of cross–Taiwan Straits interactions. This piece of work is not an empirical attempt (which is available elsewhere),[17] since it aims at reinterpretation. In short, the cultural interpretation argues that Chinese communication serves the function of moral positioning. This is done by presenting China as a potential victim of malicious politics and inviting the other side to clear China's suspicion. Failure of the opponent to respond incurs anxiety that would in turn determine the tempo of conflict, and transforms negotiation into anti-negotiation of mutual alienation. The extent of mutual alienation may affect how much need the Chinese leaders feel inside to test a particular foreign Other, while a culture of selfless pretension motivates repeated testing in order to control anti-negotiation that denies the legitimacy of any self-interest.

SELFLESS PRETENSION

The practice of Chinese political leaders to avoid giving an appearance of promoting interests for any specific social strata is Confucian in nature. Leaders pursuing self-interests are no different from an invitation for its people to consider them as competitors for resources and treat them as targets of revolt. Leaders would be in the most insecure situation if this competition between followers and themselves occurs. Only when leaders are selfless can politics remain harmonious and people felicious. Therefore, unsurprisingly, a family-oriented polity such as China has stressed the harmony among all nationals each of whom is conceived of as part of one great national family.[18] Interest competition among family members connotes the breakdown of social relations and a return to solitude, a source of fear few could bear.

This selfless requirement has been so pervasive and deep that signs of self-centering behavior, especially in the higher echelons, would incur anxiety among the people, as if losing trustworthy human relations. This is why political battles that exist almost all the time must be camouflaged with selfless dramas, which typically portray one as either a victim of a dirty power play, a volunteer sacrificed for the benefit of the whole, or a willing compromiser for the sake of harmony. However, Confucian politics is not always in harmony. In fact, people consciously know that it is not; still, the pretension of harmony suffices most of the time for the maintenance of minimum peace of mind.[19]

Political communication under this circumstance has three characteristics. First, there is a need to expose one's good intentions and uncover the rest, resulting in a pressure on all sides to demonstrate they all have well-intended goals. If the intention is good, that is selfless, policy conflict can be eventually pardoned no matter how serious it may have once seemed. Apparently it is not easy to know whether or not one's true intention is good, therefore there has been the politics of marriage (*heqin*), hostaging (*dianzhi*), self-revelation (*jiaoxin*), and so on,[20] all of which purport to be a show of selflessness.

Making public statements or a show of self-sacrifice is essential to rescuing one's reputation from an open conflict wherein politicians are compelled to oppose one another for expedient reasons. After demonstrating good intentions on all sides, parties involved in a conflict or potential conflict can save face from having appeared self-centered. If such a selfless show is not convincing, conflict eventually engulfs all, for when harmony breaks down no one is believed to be selfless. Politicians cannot help but become enemies of one another, and, most importantly, the public expectation of them being so. As a result, they accordingly resort to self-defense preparation making conflict more inevitable.

To resolve such conflict, it would be useful for those involved in the core of the conflict to replay the scenario that has incurred the perception of conflict, and yet play their roles differently so as to defeat the surmise of conflict. If, therefore, the rumor says that there is a rivalry developing between President Jiang Zemin and Premier Li Peng since they looked away from each other and did not communicate during a conference, they would have to exchange words, embrace each other with a smile, or speak a few nice words at a subsequent public occasion. Unless they effectively change the public perception of rivalry, they would be unable to enjoy the moral credentials that are critical to their power position.

Second, political leaders have difficulties publicly pursuing what they think is best for their factions, families, or identity groups. A selfless image shields political leaders from *ad hominem* attacks. No one can deny them if they never speak from a personal perspective, and few would dare to discredit them if they indeed address issues from a "public" point of view. As a result, while leaders naturally favor some public policies over the others, they must restrain from taking sides in order to protect the selfless credential of leadership.[21] This strategy therefore infers some moral problems for those who take a different policy position. The focus is typically on morality, not resource allocation.

People with moral problems cannot sell their policy. A moral denial is often sufficient to discredit a policy position supported by the morally corrupted. On the other hand, when an alternative policy is adopted after the moral purge of the previous policy line, the implication is that this is not because leaders want it for their interests, but because it is moral. No leaders need to assume responsibility of any subsequent policy failure in this case, for ironically, they never advocated it. This reinforces the tendency of politicians to criticize or jettison a certain policy not for the purpose of rectifying any drawbacks but to discredit the policy advocates. The most effective tactic is to show how a particular policy has benefited only a small portion of the population and socially relates that group to the policy advocates making them appear self-interested.

Another key to maintaining a selfless image is to have subordinates who would spontaneously promote what policy leaders want. It would be ideal if the leaders do not know these subordinates personally and are only remotely related. People who are sensitive enough to detect the ulterior intention of their superiors are the best subordinates. Moral charges against opponents are a sufficient indication of the superior's disposition, and those who formulate policy in accordance with this disposition help the superior avoid taking a position in public. This capacity very likely wins them the heart of their superiors.[22]

Finally, all politicians know how critical it is to show that the policy they promote is good for all people, especially the disadvantaged and those seemingly in conflict with them. Positions in any negotiation must appear to be long term and collectivistic in nature so that the benefits for those who take opposite positions would seem to be considered, even favorably, as well. In other words, although politicians themselves are culturally prohibited to reveal the calculation of material interests for those with whom they are closely associated, they are lauded if they can deliver material interests for the rest of society.

If resources are available, it is also possible to accommodate opponents. There are several ways of co-opting them.[23] For example, one can provide the opponents with an honorable occasion so they would never appear to lose. A more circular way would be to allow them a share of material benefit. This would presumably discredit their political reputation in any future rivalry. It is also possible that co-option costs too much. A sensible strategy would be to invite the opponents to show that they are selfless and willingly cease contention on the current policy issue. Needless to say, to solicit a selfless "drama" from the opponents normally leads to future, under-the-table compensation for them.

In sum, a drama of selfless negotiation contains three elements: a show of good intention, the ability of avoiding clear position taking, and the capacity to accommodate opponents. When none of these work, effective negotiation can never take place or if it does begin it will simply be a stalemate. Most importantly, mutual denial of selflessness inevitably incurs anxiety on all sides. Subsequent emotional arousal in the forms of fury, frustration, and embarrassment would constrain the range of strategic options in the ensuing interaction. It is unfortunate that mainstream research on Chinese political communication has so far neglected this affective aspect of research.

ANTI-NEGOTIATION

International studies continue to be influenced by Cold War scholarship today. The Cold War was partially a product of ideological confrontation and partially one of balance of power.[24] Neither attends to emotional factors and thus, there are little references to notions such as hatred, sense of belonging, or alienation. However, these feelings, once incurred, may redefine the direction of negotiation. In a Chinese context, the emotional factor is most relevant when the selfless pretension of a Chinese participant is denied in one way or another.

In the Confucian context, this redefinition can work through the following process. In the beginning, the negotiating parties may first doubt the selfless position (or lack of position) that each opponent maintains and consider it as a fabrication. If the opponent fails to make a satisfactory clarification, this suspicion will be increasing and the sense of belonging to a common whole will no longer prevail over the mood of confrontation, and opponents' intentions become morally questionable. It will thus be necessary to exclude them from the moral polity represented by one's own selfless partnership. A feeling of mutual estrangement that follows, in a parallel to what Der Derian calls diplomacy and anti-diplomacy,[25] terms signaling construction and deconstruction of subjectivity or identity that makes diplomacy possible, is in a sense anti-negotiation.

For Der Derian, diplomacy begins as a process of mutual estrangement because it presupposes that diplomats represent mutually exclusive sovereignties. Anti-diplomacy refers to the process that undermines the sense of subjectivity within a supposedly sovereign community. In China, in contrast, subjectivity is gained not by excluding others but by being occupied by a greater self, hence by a kind of self-alienation.[26] Since in form, negotiation necessarily begins on the basis of mutual estrangement, as does Der Derianian diplomacy, to gain the feeling of a worthy self, a Confucian negotiator must nonetheless pretend that he or she has no self-specific position when entering the negotiation process. Anti-negotiation emerges as the opponent undermining this relationship between the self and the whole, and forces the negotiator to deny the worthiness of the opponent in return. Therefore, negotiation initiated by self-alienation becomes a tool of mutual exclusion, hence anti-negotiation.

Like anti-diplomacy, anti-negotiation destroys the premised moral polity that enables selfless pretension both necessary and possible. The emergence of a selfhood in the process of anti-negotiation prepares the Confucianist for confrontation. To the extent that negotiation no longer reproduces a selfless atmosphere and it does not lead to compromises and solutions but becomes a tool of mutual exclusion, it is anti-negotiation. For leaders who carry and are occupied by selfless pretension, there first derives a sense of self-hatred in anti-negotiation, since their position is forced to reside in a clear self during anti-negotiation and mutual exclusion. The self-hatred is then projected to the opponents who are responsible for forcing this unwanted sense of selfhood into supposedly selfless public leaders. Consequently, alienation leads to a mood of conquering opponents.

If negotiation means mutual compromise, it would be hard to reach a conclusion without both sides stating their demands. This is precisely why Der Derian considers diplomacy a process of mutual estrangement. The Confucian culture is keenly aware as well as wary of this premised mutual estrangement. This is why during negotiation, the Chinese side often would announce statements or principles implicitly asking the other side to give up its self-position before entering substantive discussion.[27] While this may delay or even prevent substantive discussion from taking place, it is essential for the Chinese to do so, since they are uncomfortable with self-centered bargaining and would not enter substantive discussions before knowing both they and the oppoenent are selfless.

However, negotiation is a cause of anxiety precisely because it often requires the Chinese to take a position. To act selflessly in any negotiation is the most challenging form of political drama for the Chinese to play precisely because they first need to accommodate their opponent's benefits, which is an extremely demanding task to weave, and also that their efforts are sometimes completely disregarded or unappreciated. If the Chinese culture contains this selfless element as portrayed above, it is reasonable to expect that policy behavior in anti-negotiation cannot be fully understood exclusively by any ideological or realist perspectives.[28] In short, selflessness is intrinsically in contradiction to the kind of negotiation that requires the actor to take a clear position.

This implies that producing negative emotional responses is almost inevitable for a Confucian negotiator unless all parties are ready to stress the common interests and do not take sides. Emotional responses would be exacerbated if anti-negotiation takes place in an all-Chinese negotiation where all sides share many cultural similarities, most importantly the maintenance of selflessness. Inability to speak for all Chinese nationals that include the other participants of a negotiation must be politically dangerous for any Confucian leadership because failed selfless drama may beget further challenges to leadership.[29]

Chinese negotiation is therefore unlike Der Derianian diplomacy in the sense that negotiation proceeds upon a pretended and conscious, though possibly indirect, denouncement of mutual estrangement, which presupposes Der Derianian diplomacy. Instead, a common subjectivity encompassing all sides is assumed in the Chinese game. Anti-negotiation that results from mutual suspicion destroys this premised protection against mutual estrangement and compels the Chinese side to deny the other totally. Anti-negotiation then undermines the formation of a greater self, which can enliven the Confucian lesser self, which provides a position for the Chinese to conduct substantive negotiations and make exchanges as well as compromises.

Cold War scholarship understands competition and conflict from a calculated perspective, so emotion is no more than something geared to support an interest position once it is taken. In a selfless drama, enmity is more a result of stimulus–response than one of intellectual calculation. Even if there is a conflict, except when it is already determined that the opponents lack morality, one does not always enter a negotiation with enmity. Instead, enmity is an emotional outcome of anti-negotiation that challenges the value of a Confucian negotiator in a human relational network. The enmity created as a result is therefore very strong, vulnerable to manipulation, probably irrevocable, and beyond the comprehension of Cold War literature.

COMMUNICATION UNDER SELFLESS PRETENSION

The most effective way of showing one's selflessness is to adhere to certain principles, which appear to be constant and universal. These principles are repeated over and over again in Chinese diplomatic rhetoric as it attempts to establish a relatively higher moral ground in relation to the other states when they negotiate.[30] Each time Chinese negotiators face denial of their principled positions, they will explore the incident to see if it is only a misunderstanding, a mistake, or a sign of an emerging trend. While there is not necessarily one single, genuine intention behind an uncooperative opponent, the Chinese side often assumes there is one—a kind of worst-case scenario under Confucianism. To avoid possible embarrassment, the exploration is subtle and indirect. There are three general tactics the Chinese use to serve this purpose.

The first is to expose China's own weakness in material strength: for example, demonstrating the country has many domestic situations waiting to be solved to signal that it has no intention to engage in conflict. This is what China did during the 1962 Sino-Indian war when negotiating the border dispute, and again during the negotiation for the return of Hong Kong in 1994 concerning the issue of direct elections. According to Chinese logic, if the other side does not seek any further advantage, this means that it shows good intention. The opponent's suspected moves earlier can then be safely interpreted as short term, tactical, and practical, and not directed at China's principled positions.

On the other hand, when China makes a concession, it is sometimes an invitation to expose opponent's malicious intentions to abuse China's pretended weakness. For example, facing war, Beijing will typically withdraw unilaterally from the first few contacts to hint at its reluctance to continue.[31] Withdrawal may seem to reflect weakness; however, only if the other side is essentially malicious will it take advantage of Beijing's peace signal. In another example, during negotiations over the return of Hong Kong China's decision to accept a certain scope of direct elections was met by a demand to further enlarge the scope. Once London's malicious intention was considered exposed, Beijing decided to take a confrontational approach.

Similarly, the objective of the Hundred Flowers Campaign of 1957 was reoriented from an invitation of criticism to a movement to get rid of nonconformists (i.e., elements of feudalism) once the campaign begun to jeopardize regime's legitimacy.[32] In fact, when the Confucianists are anxious and feel obliged to demonstrate their dedication to principles, they will first need the other side to act aggressively so they can launch a counterattack response as a victim. In this sense, a move of compromise serves two purposes: to detect the other side's intention, and psychologically prepare a counterstrike.[33]

The second method is called two-hand tactics or "black face–white face—an analogy deriving from Chinese drama" tactics—signifying that the Chinese side is displaying both weakness and strength at the same time. The purpose is to determine who on the other side are doves and who are hawks. Those who urge new demands are the hawks, while those who caution against provocation are the doves. The Chinese often design two different sets of standards in treating these two groups in subsequent encounters.

Equally interesting is the Chinese style of claiming not to accept the other side's violation of certain principled positions while at the same time not doing anything about the perceived violation.[34] This indicates a long-term perspective, which considers that the remedy to the violated principle will eventually come into being when the time is right. It is not always necessary to deal with the violation at the moment of negotiation. Since the Chinese have condemned the violation, they naturally think they have the legitimacy to take actions against it some time in the future. There is additionally the belief that once the principled position is stated outright in the beginning, subsequent practical compromises do not hurt that position.[35] Equally important is that the other side may consider Beijing's self-restraint a show of cooperation, which will strengthen Beijing's bargaining on other issues. The more adamant the Beijing authorities appear on an issue that they disagree on but nonetheless agree to leave aside, the more sincere they will appear about reaching a minimal consensus.

The third method is to inflame the other side with strong words, purposely alluding to a misunderstanding of intentions. Almost everyone who has coped with a Chinese negotiator has suffered accusations of the worst kind, such as being an imperialist, a man of wicked ambition, a hegemonist, a running dog, a betrayer of ancestors, a rascal, a puppet, a defector, a criminal of a thousand generations, the nation's bad element, and so on.[36] These terms may sound terrible in mandarin, but a Confucianist does not really categorize opponents in this way; they serve to warn the other side that the Chinese are wary. Under most instances, people will feel enormous pressure internally when they are labeled with these terms, and naturally will want to prove otherwise. Only those who have lost their care for people will swallow an accusation of this kind without feeling the necessity to clarify. In other words, when the Chinese throw harsh labels on opponents, they are expecting clarification. If the other side clarifies, the Chinese can use this for future reference. Accusations are sometimes so nasty that people with official titles will not use them lest they gravely jeopardize the moral room for compromise. The worst accusations typically show themselves in the name of a commentator, a reader, or a foreign friend.[37] Like the first method, the accusation psychologically prepares the Chinese for a final showdown, without committing to it. As long as the officials in the position of negotiators never spell out these words, there always remains room for repairing the atmosphere.

THE ECOLOGY OF INFLAMING COMMUNICATION

When China is making response to events that do not concern with them directly, Beijing usually resorts to readymade statements such as sovereign independence, anti-hegemonism, or peaceful coexistence to state its position while remaining emotionally unattached. There is no need to test the intention of those parties involved in an event psychologically remote to China. Statements on these events serve to reproduce China's image of being always on the weak side, hence a selfless player. When certain events take place between China and another party on a one-on-one basis, the exposure of an ulterior Chinese self becomes so imminent that selfless dramas are in serious jeopardy. Such scenarios may include territorial disputes, trade disputes, international intervention on issues such as one-child policy, human rights in Tibet or in prison, nuclear tests, and so on, which are obviously China-specific topics only indirectly related to Third World, all-human-being, or proletarian perspectives.

The easiest solution is to portray China as a victim.[38] Inflaming tactics are useful to the extent they help uncover any unspoken intention beneath the other party's rhetoric. The purpose is to determine from the other side's responses if its policy is aimed at undermining China's stated principles. The worry on the Chinese side escalates when evidence suggests so; consequently, the trivial matters that China previously neglected or acquiesced to may suddenly acquire entirely different connotations. How China tests the other side is sometimes contingent upon the perceived relative strength of the parties involved, and this deserves more attention.

Contrary to what a contemporary realist analyst would predict, a Confucian negotiator stresses adherence to principles when facing a stronger opponent. Equally important is that Beijing will disengage to show loathing. Indeed, a stronger opponent would not be subject to Beijing's sanctions. For China to maintain a moral high ground, to disengage shows that China wants nothing from the opponent; hence it is a gesture of contempt. Moreover, to disengage at the moment of stalemate would help prevent the situation from aggravating the disadvantages of the weaker side. In order to avoid appearing weak, disengagement thus only follows certain inflaming initiatives designed to show fearlessness.

For example, at the beginning of the Korean War, Beijing warned against American military movement across the 38th Parallel, which nevertheless took place. The People's Voluntary Troops launched a series of counterstrikes on behalf of North Korea with a number of unilateral cease-fire interludes. Chinese intervention signaled Beijing's readiness to fight the stronger U.S. troops, with the unilateral cease-fires purporting disdain.[39] A realist prescription would be precisely the opposite: to bluff off upcoming attacks yet prevent escalation by avoiding direct engagement. The subsequent exchange of messages, though indirect, soothed Beijing, for the United States stopped at the 38th Parallel when pushing the PVTs northward.

Similarly, the March 2, 1969 Zhenbao Island clashes between China and the former Soviet Union witnessed a surprise Chinese attack and unilateral withdrawal after a limited victory. However, the Soviet Union counterattacked, and China was thrown into preparing for a nuclear confrontation. It was not until Russian Prime Minister Kosygin visited China in November did the war mentality cool off. However, earlier in April, Lin Biao had proudly announced to the Ninth National Party's Congress that only the true revolutionary had the honor of fighting both superpowers at the same time (remember the Vietnam War). Thanks to Kosygin's late response, Lin Biao had enough time to declare China's selfless sacrifice.[40]

If, however, China is stronger than the opponent, as is sometimes the case, Beijing will not easily resort to sanctions to avoid the appearance of being more dictatorial than moral. On the contrary, Beijing will adroitly pretend weakness to induce the opponent to take advantage of it. When it does, Beijing would not lose too much due to its relative superior strength, but enjoy the information concerning the opponent's intentions. Ensuing Chinese voices would change from a compromising tone to a threatening one. The expectation is that the opponent will reevaluate the situation, but reality often shows that opponents have mistaken China's later warnings as mere bluffing.

On the eve of Bejing's attack on the Indian troops in the October 1962 border clashes, Beijing reiterated its priority of handling domestic economic difficulties both to the world in general and to the

Indian embassy in particular. Chinese troops then retreated 20 kilometers from the borderline claimed by Beijing. Yet, New Delhi considered this a sign of weakness and continued to move troops forward. Beijing began to use anti-imperialist propaganda as a reminder to India that it was being used by superpowers, which resulted in no effect. The subsequent Chinese strike pushed the Indian troops away, and before the latter were able to rally again, Beijing disengaged unilaterally.[41]

What is interesting is when the two sides have been considered about equal in national capacity, Beijing's messages have appeared inconsistent. The major task of the Confucian communicator is to make sure Beijing appears to have no desire to dictate, nor fears confrontation. The trick is to let the other side choose between the courses of confrontation and resolution. Which message the opponent opts to act upon enables Beijing to determine what intentions lie beneath it.

Whether U.S. condemnation of Chinese human rights violation is an intended infringement of the principle of sovereignty or a gesture for U.S. domestic consumption bothers Beiijng all the time.[42] In 1993 and 1994, China released a number of political prisoners and yet arrested a number of others. It is up to the United States to decide now whether there has been improvement in China's human rights situation amidst these conflicting messages. In fact, the U.S. decision to de-couple human rights from trade issues proved to be effective in ameliorating the bilateral relations frozen since the 1989 Tiananmen massacre.

Finally, when opponents have included both a weaker country and a stronger supporter, the Chinese have also designed mix messages, some for the weak, others for the strong. Presumably the weaker opponent is granted some compromise to detect its intentions and the stronger opponent should be allowed no ambiguity about China's dedication to principles. If the weaker opponent shows malicious intentions, a clear warning must be sent to both opponents lest either thinks there is maneuvering room for to be gained.

The difficulty lies in the fact that all parties receive all messages. Interpretation is first blocked by the lack of understanding of Beijing's selfless pretension and then by the reception of messages not designed for them. Once the opponents fail the Chinese test, a process of alienation develops inside of the Chinese negotiating team and the ensuing anti-negotiation witnesses Beijing using negotiations exclusively as a means to collect evidence of others' moral decay. Cross–Taiwan Straits negotiation is the best example of this, with

Taiwan weaker than China, but Taipei's American supporter stronger than Beijing. The solution to which Beijing resorts eventually is to deal with each separately and with the stronger United States particularly. We will return to this case later in this chapter. In any case, the more rigid the Confucian negotiator looks, the more fearless and thus selfless Beijing appears.[43] However, it does not help Beijing in discovering the intention of the other side to simply reiterate principles. It is psychologically necessary, though, for the Chinese to raise the issue to such an abstract level that specific issues such as territorial disputes, sovereign integrity, trade privileges, and others are presented in terms of anti-imperialism and anti-hegemonism, alluding to a scope of concern much broader than China's own sphere.[44]

As a result, Beijing accused the United States of imperialism during the Korean War, the USSR of social imperialism during the Zhenbao Island crisis, India of being an imperialist agent in 1962, and the United States again of hegemonism during the human rights dispute. Was it true that Beijing truly intended an anti-imperialist war against the United States or anti-hegemonist war against the USSR? Certainly not. It was probably hoped that the United States and the USSR felt so misrepresented that they clarified their positions. Beijing then would not hesitate to completely change its terms for these opponents and compromise willingly. If the inflaming remarks stimulated no response from the opponent to clarify its intention, could anyone, a Confucian negotiator would ask, not demonstrate determination against it without inviting further imperialist aggression?

THE EMERGING SELF IN ANTI-NEGOTIATION

Most political scientists are not familiar with the Chinese inflammatory technique and are unable to appreciate the anxiety incurred when inflammatory remarks fail to stir the hoped clarification from the other side. Since the inflaming remarks portray China in a victimized light, Beijing's negotiations thus appear unrelated to any desire for material interests. This selfless presentation breaks down once it is clear that the other side will show no self-restraint in response and would, as a result, prompt China to really regard itself as a victim. Hence, the challenge is a twofold one.

The first challenge of which is China not being recognized for its performance of maintaining a higher moral ground, and the corollary, namely that no due respect is given to them. The inability to relate the Chinese to their opponent exposes the Chinese self in a chaotic world, and the Chinese people would perhaps cease their respect for their leaders. Second and more important, any self-defense China adopts in coping with the perceived victimizing or weaker opponent inevitably drives away the Chinese selfless dramas. This will render China to be like everyone else in the world—just another self-centered player, with moral pretensions. As it turns out, China would be unable to express itself internationally, since it would be unable to use interest argumentation lest this exacerbate the moral crisis, or any lofty jargons about China's selflessness since these have already failed. The Chinese self would be void of principles, which can be nightmarish for the Confucians.

When compromising techniques fail to placate a weaker party, Beijing naturally resorts to sanctions. Yet the use of sanctions is obviously not motivated by any calculation of material interests but by anger at the other side's uncooperative stupidity. Only after the disposition toward sanctions is ready to be carried out, would the Chinese begin calculating the pros and cons of the proposed alternatives. In other words, rational calculation is a result of emotional disposition, not a cause that leads to actions. Again, the resort to sanction implies the disappearance of moral appeal on the Chinese side and can thus stir up a stronger negative emotion.

The best-known example is probably China's punitive war against Vietnam in 1979. All the propaganda inside China described Vietnam as a defector, which is consistent with the usual self-victimization logic. Beijing accused Vietnam of asserting regional hegemonism and colluding with Soviet hegemonism. When Deng Xiaoping told his audience while visiting the United States that China was going to punish Vietnam, the host must have tried to figure out what concrete policy goals Beijing was aiming at. It turned out that there were no concrete policy goals—China simply entered Vietnam and returned. This was done with heavy casualties on both sides. The United States for its own reasons was not against Beijing's actions, but China had to talk to the United States before launching the punitive war, which was truly a humiliation because China was soliciting support from an imperialist. The blame was placed on Vietnam. Subsequent negotiations, which were in actuality anti-negotiations, between China and Vietnam went nowhere with each side reiterating their positions over and over again.[45] Vietnam wanted a nonmilitary zone while China wanted Vietnam to withdraw all its troops from neighbor states, most importantly, Cambodia.

Another example of the compromising techniques China employs is the dispute over the agricultural cooperative movement, whether it should be enforced or not (an incident took place during the years of the first five year plan). Mao Zedong understood that peasants were culturally not ready for such radical development and he seemed to agree to a "stop, contraction, development" policy, an alternative to the movement, in January 1955. He was not happy about the move, stating later, "regarding contraction, it could be entire contraction or limited contraction, it could be great contraction or little contraction. What can you do about it if a peasant insists on withdrawing from the cooperative?"[46]

What Mao really wanted was development, noting, "areas of liberation basically need the development [of cooperative movements], not stoppages or contraction. Development should be the basic policy." On March 22, 1955, the government nonetheless decided to stop forming new cooperatives. Mao consulted with the major opponent of the cooperatives, Deng Zihui, who suggested that half the areas could develop cooperatives. Surprisingly Mao allegedly said that one-third would be enough; Deng was too happy to detect Mao's true intentions and launched an anti-adventurist campaign in May. In actuality he disagreed with Mao's cooperative movement. On July 31 he was denounced by Mao as a foot-bound woman, a cadre who bred an extremely dangerous sentiment of passivity in the process of socialist reformation, losing the spirit and passion that had been present during the land reform period. Mao later recalled this period as one filled with "dirty air" and "black clouds."[47] All in all, Deng made a serious mistake when Mao appeared to have compromised on the development position, and it can be said that Mao was merely testing him.

Mao used the technique of false compromise on other occasions. During the 1956 nationalization campaign, he was asked how long capitalists should be allowed to receive an interest as their reimbursement, and Mao replied that the capitalists themselves could decide this and they could receive it as long as they wanted.[48] If capitalists understood this was only a test, they would have voluntarily given up all the interests due to them.

Mao also believed that others were using the same strategy on him. In the drafting of the Constitution in 1954, Mao's remark about business and industry reformation indicated this logic, as he pointed out that the enemy was trying to use inflammatory techniques to trick him into breaking all alliances while he was testing if his true intentions of moving toward socialism could be supported:

> In order to sabotage our socialist development, cunning enemies have employed a number of people like Leon Trosky and Chen Duxiu, who represented a leftist face but attacked the goals of socialist reformation.

They have said that we have not done enough, compromised too much, and deviated from Marxism. They have used this kind of nonsense to confuse people's understanding. They have wanted us to break the alliance with the nationalist capitalist class, and to deprived them immediately. They have even criticized our agricultural policy for being too slow. They have wanted us to break our alliance with the peasants. Has not all this been nonsense? If we followed all this, only imperialists and the betrayer Chiang Kaishek would feel happy.[49]

Negotiations over the return of Hong Kong are another example. As mentioned earlier, when London raised the issue of direct elections, it was welcomed by both Hong Kong and the world public opinion. Beijing swallowed the proposal at the time but when London unilaterally announced the plan of enlarging the scope of direct elections in 1992, Beijing was furious for not being consulted in the first place and was suspicious that London was trying to influence politics in Hong Kong after its return in 1997. This time Beijing mobilized all its media to denounce Governor Chris Patten, who did not respond and continued to remain strong on his new plan of direct elections. Finally, in 1994, Beijing decided to compromise in the fifteenth round of a total of seventeen rounds of negotiation. Patten then wanted to further enlarge the scope of direct elections to include Hong Kong legislators; Beijing decided that this revealed Patten's true intentions and revoked all previous compromises. All the reforms Patten managed to sneak in at the last minute were canceled at the moment of Hong Kong's return.[50]

It is worth noting that Chinese communication is very personal to the extent that most rhetorical attacks are launched against specific individual persons. The focus of pressure on those directly facing the Chinese negotiator is considered a useful psychological mechanism, which shows that they are selfish and also prevents them from looking down on China. All this does not seem to help negotiation; rather, it often alienates the opponent who may similarly misunderstand Chinese intentions as seeking confrontation. This mutual alienation in the process of anti-negotiation explains why the Chinese always look serious, if not angry, during negotiations, for anger camouflages the uneasiness and anxiety begotten by the exposure of self-specific concerns.

TESTING IN CROSS-STRAIT RELATIONS

The Chinese attitude toward Taiwan is controlled by Chinese nationalism. The specific Chinese nationalistic position in the cross-Strait negotiation is clear, which is, of course, the "one China policy" that

Beijing has reiterated again and again.[51] Understanding one China to be Beijing's principled position, Taipei had been struggling to come up with its own footing until later in the 1990s when it decided that they had to leave behind this position in order to achieve equality with Beijing. Nonetheless, Taipei has done this with extreme caution, with an appreciation of the Chinese negotiation style that Taiwan also shares.

Taipei announced its own one China policy in 1990 when the authorities drafted the *National Unification Guidelines*.[52] In responding to Beijing's notion of "one China, two systems," Taipei first formulated a "one China, two regions," and later "one China, two governments," policy. For Beijing, its "two systems" idea presupposed a local status for Taiwan while Taipei's notion of "two governments" implied two central governments. Beijing was thus suspicious of the sovereign one China Taipei had in mind. Taipei's response in the Guideline states that the so-called one China is one historical, cultural China, not one political China.[53] With this clarified, Beijing shifted its emphasis accordingly.

Originally, Beijing's one China was aimed to end the continuing Chinese civil war between the Communists and the Nationalists. From Beijing's point of view, the victory clearly belonged to the former; the task was how to get Taipei back, hence it attempted to show some leniency toward the defeated Nationalists by granting Taipei a status of super autonomy after reunification.[54] Now that it was clear that Taipei was not enthusiastic about reunification, the threatened Beijing authorities decided to stress that the so-called one China had to be a political China, defined in terms of sovereignty, not a historical or cultural notion.

The clarification demanded by Beijing incurred enormous anxiety on the Taipei side, which responded by arguing that the contention should be about which side could develop a political system appropriate for all Chinese, not which side had more power. Beijing was unsure if Taipei was still interested in reunification at this point, since in the past, it was thought that the problem was merely making political arrangements for an incumbent Taiwan, rather than for anti-Chinese nationalism in Taiwan. Indeed, Taiwan leadership was Japanese subjects during the colonial period, and chapter 5 shows that it was natural for them to feel close to Japan and alienated from China. This sense of alienation was then strengthened by Taiwan's total dependence on the United States for survival during the Cold War. When the Chinese and the Japanese recently debated about whether Japan should feel sorry for what the Japanese military did in

China, particularly the Nanjing massacre, Taipei authorities felt alienated from anything Chinese, which baffled, and even threatened Beijing's Chinese nationalism more seriously than anything else. Taiwan's Japanese American "tag" of emotion gives the meaning of selflessness a double mission. On the one hand, its Chinese background taught it the importance of not running counter to the selfless drama that Beijing put on. On the other hand, Taiwan leadership's separatist disposition has its own definition of selflessness, namely, no fear of China and complete loyalty to Japan and the United States.[55] Caught between these two, the Taipei authorities have adopted an obscuring policy, that is, pursuing Taiwan's separate sovereign status by either avoiding the mention of one China or reinterpreting the meaning of one China instead of outright confronting or negating it.

Criticism of Taipei's separatist policy by Beijing has nonetheless been indirect, accusing it of using "tricks" (*huayang*). By initially avoiding calling Taipei separatist, Beijing has left some room for negotiation, otherwise it would have no alternative but war. Taipei has been able to collaborate to the extent that all the separatist statements have either been made through the president's back door or by local or legislative leaders. One thing was certain by 1995, however: Taipei would no longer even mention the term one China no matter how it was going to be interpreted.

As a seemingly last resort, Beijing in the beginning of 1995 announced an eight-point statement, generating a conciliatory atmosphere for further negotiation. However, "the Chinese should not fight amongst themselves" maxim, which China rests the statement on, can ironically be unclear if Taiwan still considered itself to be overseas Chinese. Unfortunately, before this exchange of meanings achieved anything, the United States had agreed to host Taiwanese President Lee Teng-hui during his visit to Cornell University. For Beijing, this indicated that the United States was about to step in to support Taiwan's separation from China.

After Lee's trip, Beijing initiated a series of inflammatory charges. They called the Taipei leadership a group of renegades, betrayers, criminals of a thousand generations, guides to a dead end, clowns, a piece of bondage tying people to a tank, anti-Chinese puppets, beggars, bags of historical trash, and so on.[56] This forced Taipei to announce again that there would be no attempt at Taiwan independence, only that Taiwan was itself a sovereign country. However, this was strong enough evidence of separatism for Beijing, who canceled all ongoing negotiations. Anti-negotiation began at the moment when Beijing decided that

Taipei had unambiguously denied the moral polity of one China, which contained both sides.

However, Beijing's antagonistic response in terms of four missile exercises in the Taiwan Straits in 1995 and 1996 further alienated Taipei, although it effectively warned against any international involvement in Taiwan's potential independence drive. Reassessments went on in Beijing before and after the missile tests at all levels. On the other hand, Taipei also sensed Beijing's success in blockading its diplomatic maneuvering, gaining anxiety from the breakthrough of Sino-U.S., Sino-Russian, and Sino-Japanese relations, which forced Taipei into an increasingly self-centered position. Taiwan claimed to the international media that "Taiwan" (not the Republic of China) was an independent country just like Great Britain,[57] and hence a regime that did not fear Beijing's threat. Surprisingly, there was no vehement attack from Beijing this time; on the contrary, one witnessed a dramatically different approach. Beijing reiterated the one China policy, yet it was also mentioned that anything Taipei considered relevant could be discussed. (This was said before but almost forgotten amidst the four missile exercises.) After the Sino-U.S. strategic relationship was secured in October 1997, a brand new message came from Shanghai that Beijing was ready to accept Taipei's previous interpretation of one China, namely that one China referred to a future reunited China that contained both People's Republic and Republic of China. The name of the future China could well be just "China," and it was also noted that the process of reunification should go on continuously.[58]

The obvious compromise was met with Taipei's aforementioned statement that Taiwan is an independent country. Again, there was no attack from China. In addition, Taipei authorities said to a Japanese newspaper that Japan should not be asked to apologize repeatedly for the Nanjing massacre.[59] This presumably touched the most vulnerable spot of Chinese psychology, yet there has not been a strong response. Most dramatic was Beijing's "wait and see" attitude after the independence advocate Chen Shui-bian's victory in the presidential election in March 2000. In 2002 even when Beijing decided that Chen was a determined independence seeker, the overall policy has continued to be one of self-restraint. It appears that Beijing has adopted a persistent compromising technique, either to shun Taipei's obvious anticipation of Beijing's violent reaction, which would at best fulfill Taipei's fearless drama, or to collect more evidence of betraying Chinese nationalism for use in a final showdown.

MANAGEMENT OF ANTI-NEGOTIATION

The problematiqué for Taipei is how to achieve independent status without causing a disastrous confrontation with China.[60] With its deep appreciation of Confucian culture and moral pretension, Taipei has been able to maintain minimum credit with Beijing to the extent that it has not formally declared independence from the yet-to-come reunited China. Taipei has been moving little by little, undermining the clarity of Beijing's notion of one China. This was achieved by first accepting the one China principle, then by attaching one China with two institutions, two regions, two governments, two jurisdictions, and so on. When Beijing felt more accustomed to and less threatened by these terms, Taipei then moved further to speak of the Republic of China as an independent sovereign country and added the term "on Taiwan." In 1999, there was the official statement of cross-Strait relations being "state-to-state," and in 2002, the further claim that there is "one country on each side." Since 1990, it almost seems that the Republic of China has ceased to exist; it has been replaced with the "Republic of China on Taiwan."

Although Taipei has faced enormous military and international pressures, these pressures have only been periodical and, due to Beijing's own negotiation position, have been tactically restrained. What is clear is that Taipei has managed mutual estrangement by reiterating one China with a combination of different footnotes. The difficulty lies in the fact that Taipei's goal is clearly separatist while being aware of the Chinese obsession with selfless pretension, and open defiance of one China. Even if "Taiwan" is now replacing the "Republic of China" as the discursive focus, Taipei has continued to highlight the importance of Taiwan in providing a model political system that the reunited China should and will eventually adopt.[61] The appreciation of Chinese anxiety toward the breakdown of the one China position has been both a barrier to Taipei's drive for full sovereign status and a contribution to peace across the Taiwan Straits.

For Beijing, the task has been no less complicated. It has had to first manage the relationship with the United States while at the same time deal with Taipei. Taipei has easily interpreted its conciliatory policy toward the United States as a compromise to the latter, and its violent reaction to Taipei's separatist policy such as that in 1995 and 1996 has also been understood as a challenge to the U.S. hegemonic status.[62] In fact, China would like to maintain a selfless image when facing Taipei. The missile exercises have necessarily alienated both Taipei and Washington, but in 1997, 1999, and 2002, during the visits of the two US presidents to China, Beijing's policy shifted to cope first with Washington, leaving Taipei aside. The major message was that China did not seek confrontation. It then compromised on a number of issues such as nuclear proliferation, arms control, and trade practices as well as even human rights. In return, Washington agreed to adhere to a one China policy.[63]

All these compromises have indicated China's self-sacrifice. The most dramatic move was that Jiang Zemin refused to act strongly when Clinton criticized China for taking the wrong side on human rights issues in 1999 and when George Bush refused to mention one China publicly during his visit to China in 2002. Self-restraint of this sort has been shaped by the American awareness of China's emphasis on the Taiwan issue. In other words, strength has been demonstrated, followed by sudden Chinese conciliatory gestures. Facing a stronger opponent such as the United States, this is a sound method to arrive at a reconciliation, and it has worked well so far.

When it comes to Taiwan, Beijing has alternatively used the two familiar techniques: inflammation and compromise. A number of times, Beijing has criticized the Taipei authorities of spreading separatism and giving vague definitions to key terms. Clearly Beijing has not trusted any of these clarifications, but they have served as checkpoints on Taipei's subsequent policies. However, inflammatory techniques have transformed negotiation into anti-negotiation when the other side has been unable to respond as anticipated. The anxiety thus incurred has pushed Beijing toward confrontational policies at this time; for example, the disposition for a sanction approach became extremely strong in mid-1995. Policy makers only calculated how to implement sanctions rather than assess if they were sensible, or rational. The latter type of calculation denied the existence of a moral polity across the Taiwan Straits and therefore exposed Beijing's selfhood vis-à-vis Taipei, a scenario that any cross-Strait negotiations were supposed to avoid.

The compromise technique has been equally important in that it has patched up the distance created by the sanctions approach. In fact, in the 1995 eight-point statement, many of the concepts such as Chinese cultural heritage, shared sovereignty, and a first-step negotiation to end enmity probably originated from Taipei's position. The principle purpose of Beijing's concessions has been to show the Taiwanese people that it has not been doing this for its own interest, but for every Chinese, including Taiwanese. Beijing's compromise approach has also provided Taipei with an opportunity to reevaluate its status in cross-Strait relations as the relationship between Beijing and Washington continue to improve. For how long this compromise approach will continue and to what extent Beijing will tolerate Taipei's provocation are matters dependent on Beijing's perception of Taipei's separatist developments and the stake of the one China position.

CONCLUSION

A selfless drama depends on all sides of negotiation pretending to be morally superior and that they have moved above the mere concern for self-interest to encompass the interests of everyone involved. Only if everyone considers his or her partners of negotiation to be selfless, can substantive discussion ever be possible. Clearly, this is incompatible with Der Derianian diplomacy, wherein mutual estrangement is both a precondition and a reproduced outcome. However, the logic of anti-negotiation is well informed by the process of Der Derianian anti-diplomacy. Both point to a mechanism that undermines the sense of subjectivity of negotiators. For the Chinese, positioning in a selfless drama assumes that China has already achieved a relational niche in a larger whole (i.e., the greater self). The sense of subjectivity thus bred is a dependent subjectivity. When the whole breaks down, China loses its sense of subjectivity and adopts an unwanted subjectivity for a lesser self, which separates it from the opponent, and is hence a blow to selfless pretension. Anxiety and anger are the typical consequences.

Under these circumstances, Beijing has developed a unique style of communication. The inflammatory technique, which was thought to set out to provoke the opponent, actually carries with it the expectation for clarification, and the desire to hide Beijing's lack of confidence. However, after all, it is most importantly a means to reinforce Beijing's selfless position. This is because Beijing cannot tell an opponent what it wants, as it is not supposed to want anything from others. The other side is expected to know what is to be done. Only if the opponent meets Beijing's expectations, can Beijing accept it as a selfless player, and only then substantive bargaining can proceed.

The compromise technique also helps Beijing evade revealing a clear position. All compromises purport a selfless image so that the other side will have no recourse to blame Beijing of being mundanely materialistic. Only after some clearly compromising gestures would the Chinese feel comfortable with the subsequent sanctioning approach, but sanctions are less for real gain than for just retaliation for betrayal. China's punitive war on Vietnam is a case in point.

Cross-Strait negotiation over the interpretation of one China has witnessed both sides understanding the stakes of losing the meaning of the term. Before 2002, Taipei had looked for ways to deconstruct the one China position without jettisoning the term, while Beijing has throughout struggled to keep Taiwan in the one China castle through both inflaming and compromise techniques. To transform negotiation into anti-negotiation, Taipei has acquired a sense of subjectivity outside of the one China position due to Taipei's identification with Japan and the United States. In doing so, though, it risks the explosion of Beijing's frustration caused by the breakdown of the moral principle. As a result, ironically, Beijing's efforts to maintain relatedness to Taiwan is precisely the very reason why Taipei feels increasingly alienated. No substantive negotiation has taken place between them; in fact, for five years ending 1995 they had only negotiated on various trivial issues with almost no achievements and after 1999 no contact has been made whatsoever.

This unique style of demanding a selfless statement before entering substantive discussion has prevented Beijing from comprehending the real needs of the Taiwan people and kept Taipei from adhering to the so-called one China principle in order to take advantage of all the compromises that almost certainly would follow. The impossible task for Taiwan leaders is to prove selflessness to Beijing in the one China scenario and at the same time convince their citizens that as fearless leadership, it dares challenge China. They also need to perform for Japan and the United States that as a selfless post-colony, it deserves unconditional support from them. For Beijing, the task becomes to both co-opt and coerce Taipei into accepting Beijing's compromise. Taipei has hurt Beijing most not only by abusing these compromises, but also by sometimes leaving them aside as if they were worthless.

The vicious circle will probably continue in the near future until Beijing decides that it will not tolerate it any longer. Before the final showdown, it is likely that Beijing will stage another magnificent compromising show as an ultimate invitation to Taipei to return to the one China policy. Equally likely is that Taipei will be unable to tolerate this split among selfless one China for audiences in Beijing, fearless separatism for audiences in Taiwan, and helpless dependence for audiences in Japan and the United States. Taipei may opt for an anti-China campaign, which if not directly aimed at fighting China will at least focus on those Taiwanese who are sympathetic being themselves Chinese. In fact, one purpose of President Chen Shuibian's remark that there is one country on each side of the Taiwan Straits in August 2002 was precisely to coerce the opposition, who consider Taiwanese being Chinese, to come to terms with him. Either Beijing's compromising show or Taipei's anti-China campaign can guarantee that confrontation is inevitable unless the self-split and anti-negotiation phenomenon can be solved.

CONCLUSION

BECOMING AN EAST ASIAN STATE?

East Asia was never a kind of international political system described in the realist or liberal IR literature. No state in the said system was ever unproblematized. China becoming a sovereign state, for example, was the product of a historical process, which began with Japan becoming a sovereign state first. How Japan became a state is not the focus of this book, but it is clear that whether or not China would eventually become a modern state bothered Japanese leaders much more than the Western leaders. Japan's China puzzle proved to be a revelation of Japan being a different kind of state than what the Japanese leaders once desired. Occupation, transformation, and war were natural solutions available to Japanese leaders in the face of a China that exposed Japan's inferior oriental root.

Denying the difference China represented was, therefore, the key to Japan's pretension of a unified Asian front to counter the White race. Accordingly, the fundamental question of the Japanese leaders was not just about China's alterity, but also about Japan's own identity as an alterity—one that Japanese intellectuals camouflaged with a Western and modernist perspective. In other words, it was the undecidability of the nature of the Japanese state that resulted in the indetermination of the nature of the Chinese state.

The result was the coupling of physical violence with discursive East Asia. Violence took place in two forms. Physical violence plagued East Asia as early as in 1894 and through the twentieth century. In 1931, the aborted Pan-Asian ontology resulted in Japan's occupation of Manchuria. China and Japan failed the test of brotherhood as large-scale killing began in 1937 and ended in 1945. Behind this eight-year bloody war and the subsequent mutual disliking lay the shadow of the Western model of the modern state. Both struggled among three ontological levels of a state embedded in one's cultural root, a state connected to a Pan-Asian front, and a state modeled on the West. Believing that only one form of state could survive, intellectuals and leaders resorted to confrontation, which was as fierce within as it was between China and Japan. Politics of alterity did not mature in East Asia. Violence effectively reproduced the "warring state" as the exclusively right model of state. No leaders felt ethically responsible for the possibility of having a different form of sovereignty either in another state or in their own state. This ignorance led to a deeper form of violence.

The second form of violence was discursive in essence. It involved the teleological modern state fixated in a linear philosophy of history. The state thus represented a higher form of civilization with backward images associated with all other pre-state communities, including the most sophisticated cultural systems under the celestial dynasty, such as China and Japan. Violence was so great that other forms of differentiation from the European state were discursively meaningless except that they proved the superiority of Westphalian ontology. It would be justifiable then to physically eliminate these forms of existence for this was supposedly good for the ontologically non-existing people to build a state and achieve recognition. Buying the same modernist discourse, Chinese as well as Japanese leaders found themselves speechless in their own cultural traditions, which then became alterities to be eliminated. In other words, it was the modernist discourse that closed off the space for alterities. No sense could be made out of different forms of state that continued to cherish pre-state legacy. Physical violence quickly escalated to carry out this discursive negation of alterities. Within the state boundary, this violence of negation was apparent in the way minorities were arbitrarily defined and "civilized," class enemies beaten to death, and, after reform started in the 1979, exploited workers and peasants downgraded to backward elements.

East Asia never existed. Geographically as well as temporally, it took on no closed boundaries. Imperialism was widespread in this part of the world at the high tide of Pan-Asianism in the early twentieth century. It was imperialist intrusion that determined the meaning of being an Asian as well as incurring local responses. Countering imperialism, these local responses participated in the form of self-empowering state building. After World War II, the said East Asia was penetrated and divided by the two superpowers. In the aftermath of the cold war, again, globalization continued to obscure the realization of a long deferred East Asian system. This aborted systemic structure could either be a demonstration of East Asian backwardness for not complying with the realist state ideology, or a harbinger for a nascent ontology that might allow coexistence of alterities with the state.

Falling back to the modernist ideology or the realist/liberal frame, one could easily close off the voices of alterities—forms of true difference. However, no East Asians are just East Asian. They are also fluid in imperialist-made, socialist-washed, globally connected, colonially mutually constituted, and nationally split alterities. An East Asian ontology thus looms large in the possibility of breeding moral responsibility to all narrators of alterity. The subaltern struggle for recognition of this kind will be as intense as U.S. leaders will not easily tolerate the recognition of any alterity lest this should threaten the hegemonic ontology of state.

In any case, a nonsystem is now called into being and becomes a system. The politics of "becoming a nonsystem" is a show of fluidity and potentially a statement of the unrecognized. This book thus moves both back and forth. It moves back to the extent that it discloses the nature of the East Asian state as being far from realist/liberal statism. It moves forth in the sense that it willingly accepts East Asia as a system. This calling of a nonsystem into a system points to the explosive potential of an unprecedented East Asian ontology that welcomes alterities. In short, the East Asian system, to be truly substantiated, does not tell how a state must function under the constraint of its systemic paremeters. On the contrary, it tells how a state can have its own form of existence that is completely outside the discursive domain of realism/liberalism.

Once the East Asian nonsystem becomes a recognized system, violence would be redundant in that there is no need to absorb alterities for the purpose of maintaining a totalizing ontology. Voices would then come from refugees, transnational families, as well as national leaders. As national leaders become prepared to recognize alterities, they in turn experience living in all different forms of existence. This would then create a discursive room for all national leaders to develop themselves into different alterities, which were either previously hidden or creatively acquired. Once politics of this sort is legitimate, the politics of alterity would be common. In this regard, even the much dreaded Chinese nationalism may lose its violent connotations. Nationalism that is opened up might be more a therapy than a need.

The East Asia of the twenty-first century will likely be a surprise. Judging from repeated failures of the Chinese state to be modeled after realist statism, the current ambiguity of the state system by the China–Taiwan reunification issue, and the Japanese discursive inability to express a complex of feelings toward China in realist/liberalist terms, the U.S. ubiquitous presence in the area may ironically help spread the East Asian ontology that can eventually rock the omniscience of realism. The East Asian ontology in a sense is no ontology, or is an ontology of flexibility open to interpretations, that recognizes differences, welcomes new possibilities, and embraces surprises. These are the differences in the form of being and in the possibility of becoming, not the differences in national interest that guarantee the closing off of meanings. Closing off would force alterities violently out of our consciousness. Thanks to the tumultuous experiences most geographical East Asians have gone through, the potential for a tolerant ontology must not be overlooked.

Despite the fact that realism and liberalism still occupy the minds of leaders of East Asian states, varied positions emerge to challenge, undermine, and/or even collude with states to achieve transnational alliance. This is done in the name of a city, NGO, firm, new family, worker immigrating, and so on. A new international as well as East Asian discourse should be well timed to bring these positions out of realist/liberal hegemony and bring them into the ontology of alterity.

China has been a unique participant in world politics. The fate of the Chinese state was heatedly debated right from its foundation, but, ironically, the dispute was carried on outside the Chinese territorial boundary. Japanese intellectuals as well as political activists who were most puzzled by the nature of the Chinese state were the ones that first addressed this topic. Unsure of the fate of their own nascent state, the Japanese narrators debated on how the Chinese state could get along with the others on an international level. For the Japanese, the study of China was actually a study about how well they themselves will fare in international politics, since they are also a country with a Confucian legacy. Lucian Pye, who suspected in 1990 that China is a fake state, is truly outdated because the problematization, and hence the deconstruction, of the Chinese sovereign state by the Japanese narratives is at least 100 years old.

On hindsight, the Japanese narratives echoed postmodern skepticism. It was this skepticism that had carried the premodern Chinese dynasty through its transformation into a sovereign state. In the past hundred years, occasionally treating China as a sovereign state by the world leaders did not resolve the difficulty of making China into a sovereign state. Except momentarily complaining about China's awkward displays in world politics, they would rather forget about the alterity that is built into this territorial mass for various expedient purposes. Chapter 1 deliberately traced the initial uneasiness the world felt about China when it became a "sovereign state." In brief, China is a problem for the statist world and the statist identity is also a problem for China. The acknowledgment of the state as a Western-constructed puzzle to the Chinese is where this book begins its journey.

Once locked into the space called China, Chinese leaders responded anxiously by trying to regain the narrating position. They learned to speak of China from a standpoint that regarded China as an inferior Other so that they could pretend control over the meaning of being Chinese. This corresponds to self-Orientalism. To distinguish themselves from the foreign narrators, therefore, the Chinese discourse, while noting the teleology of modern state, emphasized China's uniqueness in pursuing modernity. The combination of anti-foreignism and the preoccupation with modern state building created a mentality of counter-state. Chapter 2 details the psychological processes underneath the irony of compliance with standards of modernity aiming at revenging those states forcing modernity into China.

As a result, the defense of the state was motivated more by anti-foreignism than by territorial integrity. To demonstrate that the state possessed people's hearts is more important than to protect borders. Chapter 3 calls this performance dependent nationalism, meaning that an external imperialist Other that served to unite the Chinese people was the premise on which Western styled national defense depended. Territoriality, which defines sovereign modernity, was reduced to a symbol of nationalism to the effect that a piece of land could be given up to take on an identity that is beyond territoriality after disproportionate sacrifice had been invested in honoring the territorial claim. This partially explains why cycles in Chinese foreign policy appear normal and frequent.

On the one hand, there is the Orientalist pressure to keep up with the world standard about a normal state. In the process of calculating national interests in terms of military power, alliance, economic development, and so on, Chinese leaders are able to pretend statism. On the other hand, there is the internal need for nationalist assertion premised upon an imperialist Other. To occasionally refute the external forces concerning their expectation of China adopting modernist values is no less rational than exclusively focusing on enhancing statist, modernist national interests. Chapter 4 deliberately applies the modernist methodology to the study of the affective process to entertain the possibility that the rational approach does not always have a solution. The notion of the national interest, once coming to mind, simultaneously sensitizes the deep-rooted alienation from the modernist values or the statist world.

The affective constraint on China's adaptation to the sovereign world reached its first height at the point of concession of Taiwan to Japan and, later, the second during the eight-year war of resistance against Japan. Chapter 5 goes back to these most unpleasant experiences, which the Chinese people encountered while building their state, to illustrate how atavistic memory of colonialism has poisoned China's submission to sovereign worldism. China's Taiwan policy is intrinsically a response both to Japan's 51-year occupation of the island and to the two wars, as China yielded and regained it respectively. This atavistic memory is lasting and only reasonable when defense is conceived as being about people's hearts rather than territorial integrity.

Reminders of anti-Japanism, not unlike nationalist cycles in foreign policy or obsession with people's hearts in national defense thinking, can be conducive to China's entry to the sovereign world. Nationalism as a therapy reconstructs the sense of subjectivity possibly to an extent that leaders acting in the name of China no longer feel estranged from Chinese cultural identities. This would make them more comfortable when pressured to constantly adapt to the norms associated with the sovereign world in the past and the global society in the future. Chapter 6 theorizes this postmodern solution to self-hatred, which is caused by hybrid identities of Confucian values, socialist legacy, and global institution. By practicing different identities in accordance with the situations calling upon them, all values appear legitimate in certain occasions, but never universally.

The revival of interest in Confucianism in China since the late 1980s reveals that indeed Confucian values have survived socialism. This revival of Confucianism reconnects Chinese people on the two sides of the Taiwan Straits. It eases the goal of reunification by bringing the two societies together, but complicates the political process needed to facilitate unification. Confucianism, which despises self-centrism, makes the negotiation between Beijing and Taipei dramatically difficult as both sides are torn among discourses on sovereignty, nationalism, Japan, democracy, and the United States, containing both self-centric and self-denying messages. Confucianism as a therapy to smoothen the negotiation disallows positioning required by negotiation. Chapter 7 analyzes how the silenced Confucian values continue to drive Chinese statism in the age of globalization.

The institution of sovereignty is playing a joke on the Chinese leaders who have been suffering from alienation since they adapted to the world of sovereignty only to be told 100 years later that sovereignty is no longer sufficient to win respect. This reversion happens ironically at the exact moment when the Chinese leaders finally feel confident in asserting their statist identity. It is no less true to say that China has been a joke to the sovereign world, which completely refuses to acknowledge China's alterity. China now faces the embarrassing position of vehemently sticking to statism in the age of globlization. Both jokes are seriously enough to make the Chinese leaders believe that the global age is no more than another deceiving mechanism to trap China, and the leaders of world politics at large may feel reconfirmed in their opinion that, after all, China can only be a threat to the world.

NOTES

INTRODUCTION: TAKING CULTURAL STUDIES SERIOUSLY

1. For example, Zheng Yongnian, *Discovering Chinese Nationalism in China* (Cambridge: Cambridge University Press, 1999); Edward Friedman, *National Identity and Democratic Prospects for Socialist China* (Armonk: M. E. Sharpe, 1995); Gongwu Wang, *The Revival of Chinese Nationalism* (Leiden: Leiden University, 1996).
2. See Lowell Dittmer and Samuel Kim (eds.), *China's Quest for National Identity* (Ithaca: Cornell University Press, 1993).
3. See Jonathan Unger, *Chinese Nationalism* (Armonk: M. E. Sharpe, 1996).
4. For example, *The Spirit of Chinese Foreign Policy* (London: Macmillan, 1990); *China's Just World* (Boulder: Lynne Rienner, 1993); *Reform, Identity and Chinese Foreign Policy* (Taipei: Vanguard Institute for Policy Studies, 1999).
5. *Reform, Identity and Chinese Foreign Policy.*

1 THE POSTMODERN CLUE: DEFINING CHINA AS AN ALTERITY

1. Alexander Wendt, "Anarchy is What States Make of It: The Social Construction of Power Politics," *International Organization* 46 (1992): 391–392, 397, 402, 424–426.
2. Michael J. Shapiro, "The Ethics of Encounter: Unreading, Unmapping the Imperium," in D. Campbell and M. J. Shapiro (eds.), *Moral Spaces: Rethinking Ethics and World Politics* (Minneapolis: University of Minnesota Press, 1999), pp. 65–66.
3. See Lucian Pye, "Erratic State, Frustrated Society," *Foreign Affairs* 69, 4 (1990): 56–74.
4. See Samuel Huntington, *Clash of Civilization and the Remaking of World Order* (New York: Simon & Schuster, 1996).
5. See Edward Friedman, *Democratic Prospects for Socialist China* (Armonk: M. E. Sharpe, 1995).
6. See Gordon White, *Riding the Tiger* (Stanford: Stanford University Press, 1993).
7. Merle Goldman, *Sowing the Seeds of Democracy in China* (Cambridge: Harvard University Press, 1994).

8. Andrew Nathan, *China's Crisis: Dilemmas of Reform and Prospect for Democracy* (New York: Columbia University Press, 1990); also his chapter "Chinese Democracy: The Lessons of Failure," and Larry Diamond's "Forward," in L. Diamond (ed.), *China and Democracy: The Prospect for a Democratic China* (New York: Routledge, 2000).

9. See the discussion in Michael J. Shapiro, "The Ethnics of Encounter," in D. Campbell and M. J. Shapiro (eds.), *Moral Spaces: Rethinking Ethics and World Politics* (Minneapolis: University of Minnesota Press, 1999), p. 66.

10. Nomura Koichi, *The China Knowledge in Modern Japan (Jindai riben de zhongguo renshi)*, Zhang Xuefeng, (trans.) (Beijing: Central Translation and Editorial Press, 1999).

11. Ibid., pp. 6–14

12. Ibid., pp. 15–30.

13. Ibid., pp. 31–41, 80–86.

14. Ibid., pp. 52–57.

15. Ibid., pp. 57–67.

16. Ibid., pp. 67–80.

17. Ibid., pp. 87–96

18. Ibid., pp. 97–105.

19. Ibid., pp. 122–169.

20. Ibid., pp. 171–195.

21. Ibid., pp. 200–281.

22. See Mineo Mizoguchi, *Sinology in the Japanese Perspectives (Riben shiye zhong de zhongguoxue)*, Li Suping, Gong Ying, and Xue Tao (trans.) (Chinese People's University Press, 1996).

23. Gu Changsheng, *Missionary and Modern China (Chuanjiaoshi yu jindai zhongguo)* (Shanghai: Shanghai People's Press, 1991).

24. See Richard Madsen, *China and the American Dream* (Berkeley: University of California Press, 1995), p. 30.

25. Ting-yi Li, *Early Sino-American Diplomatic History (Zhong mei zaoqi waijiao shi)* (Taipei: Chuan-chi Literature, 1978), p. 174.

26. See Chih-chi Chen, *Chinese Diplomatic History (Zhongguo waijiao shi)* (Taipei: Nantian, 1993), p. 989.

27. For documents, see, e.g., ibid, pp. 993, 994.

28. Chen, *Chinese Diplomatic History*, p. 998.

29. See Chang, *Cross-Strait Relations*, p. 123.

30. Chi-hsueh Fu, *Chinese Diplomatic History (Zhongguo waijiao shi)* (Taipei: Chi-hsueh Fu, 1957).

31. Ibid., p. 438.

32. See Yan Liu, *Diplomatic History of China*, pp. 304–306.

33. See *PUCK* (New York) Vol. XIX, No. 471 (March 17, 1986).

34. Ibid., p. 262.

35. Hsian-te Hsi, *The Image of the United States Presented in the Chinese Journals During the Late Qing Period (Qing mo zhongwen baokan chengxian de mei guo xing xiang)* (Taipei: Wenzhang Press, 1991), p. 494.

36. Ibid., pp. 495–496.
37. For example, Kenneth Liberthal, "The Background in Chinese Politics," in H. J. Ellison (ed.), *The Sino-Soviet Conflict* (Seattle: University of Washington Press, 1982), p. 5; Dorothy J. Solinger (ed.), *Three Visions of Chinese Socialism* (Boulder: Westview, 1983); Gordon Bennett, "Traditional, Modern and Revolutionary Values on New Social Groups in China," in Richard Wilson et al. (eds.), *Value Change in Chinese Society* (New York: Routledge, 1979), pp. 207–209.
38. For an account of genealogy of state sovereignty, of which the Chinese state has had no experience, see Jens Bartelson, *A Genealogy of Sovereignty* (Cambridge: Cambridge University Press, 1995). Little literature in political science has reflected upon the history of China becoming a sovereign state, for a related discussion, see Chih-yu Shih, "A Postcolonial Reading of the State Question in China," *The Journal of Contemporary China* 17, 7 (1998): 125–139.

2 THE ORIENTALIST CLUE: EQUALIZING THE COUNTER-STATE

1. For example, see Andrew Nathan, "China's Goals in the Taiwan Strait," *The China Journal* 36 (July 1996): 87–93.
2. A recent case has been reported by China News Agency about President Jiang Zemin's warning against a Westernizing campaign targeted at China, see *United Daily* (April 2, 2000): 14.
3. Typical cases include the widely circulated books such as Song Qiang, Zhang Zangzang, and Qiao Bian, *China Can Say No* (*Zhongguo keyi shuo bu*) (Beijing: Chinese Association of Industry and Commerce Press, 1995); Li Xiguang and Liu Kang, *Behind Demonization of China* (*Yaomohua zhongguo de beihou*) (Beijing: Chinese Social Science Press, 1996).
4. For example, Gerald Segal (ed.), *The China Factor* (London: Croom Helm, 1982); Andrew Nathan and Robert Ross, *The Great Wall and Empty Fortress* (New York: W. W. Norton, 1997).
5. Edward Said, *Orientalism* (New York: Random House, 1978).
6. For example, "Provincial China" is now used to replace "China" as a reminder that China is a complicated mass of dynamic phenomena. *Provincial China* is a journal published by Sydney Institute of Technology. Also see Barry Naughton, "The Foreign Policy Implications of China's Economic Development Strategy," in T. Robinson and D. Shambaugh (eds.), *Chinese Foreign Policy* (Oxford: Oxford University, 1994); Gerald Segal and David Goodman, *China Deconstructs* (New York: Routledge, 1994).
7. In literature, there seems to be a disproportionate interest in why and how civil society cannot develop in China or why and how it has begun to develop. Examples of the former perspective include Edward Friedman, *National Identity and the Democratic Prospects for Socialist*

China (Armonk: M. E. Sharpe, 1995); Lucian Pye, "The State and the Individual," *China Quarterly* 127 (1991): 443–466; Chih-yu Shih, *Collective Democracy* (Hong Kong: The Chinese University Press, 1999); Kevin O'Brien, *Reform without Liberalization* (Cambridge: Cambridge University Press, 1990); for examples of the latter perspective, see Gordon White, *Riding the Tiger* (Stanford: Stanford University Press, 1993); Minxin Pei, *From Reform to Revolution* (Cambridge: Harvard University Press, 1994); Merle Goldman, *Sowing the Seeds of Democracy in China* (Cambridge: Harvard University Press, 1994); Peter Van Ness (ed.), *Debating Human Rights* (New York: Routledge, 1999).

8. The terms he used specifically are *fengjian* (feudal), *zhuanzhi* (despotic), *pinqiong* (poor), and *luohou* (backward). He proclaimed that Taiwan was no longer Chinese in the sense that Taiwan has developed out of that tradition. See *China Times* (*Zhongguo shibao*) (May 20, 1996): 2. Interestingly, the Presidential Office deleted this provocative statement in the following days' new release.

9. See, e.g., A. James Gregor and Maria Hsia Chang, *The Iron Triangle* (Stanford: Hoover Institution Press, 1984); Parris Chang and Martin Lasater (eds.), *If China Crosses the Taiwan Strait* (Lanham, MD.: University Press of America, 1993); Andrew Nathan, "China's Goals in the Taiwan Strait," *The China Journal* (July 1999): 87–93; Dennis Van Vranken Hickey, *Taiwan's Security in the Changing International System* (Boulder: Lynne Rienner, 1997); James Lilley and David Shambaugh, *China's Military Faces the Future* (Armonk: M. E. Sharpe, 1999); James H. Anderson, "Tensions Across the Strait," *The Heritage Foundation Backgrounder* 1328 (September 28, 1999).

10. See Allen Whiting, *The Chinese Calculus of Deterrence* (Ann Arbor: University of Michigan Press, 1974); Steven Chan, "Chinese Conflict Calculus and Behavior," *World Politics* 30 (1978): 391–410; Jonathan Adelman and Chih-yu Shih, *Symbolic War* (Taipei: Institute of International Relations, 1993).

11. See, e.g., Robert Ross, *Negotiating Cooperation* (Stanford: Stanford University Press, 1995); and his "China Learns to Compromise," *The China Quarterly* 128 (1991): 742–773.

12. See Dorothy Solinger, *China's Business under Socialism* (Berkeley: University of California, 1984); Peter Van Ness and Satish Raichur, "Dilemmas of Socialist Development," *Bulletin of Concerned Asian Scholars* 15, 1 (1981).

13. See, e.g., Thomas B. Gold, "Taiwan Society at *Fin de Siécle*," in D. Shambaugh (ed.), *Contemporary Taiwan* (Oxford: Oxford University Press, 1998), pp. 47–70; Linda Chao and Ramon Myers, *The First Chinese Democracy* (Baltimore: The Johns Hopkins University Press, 1997). Suspicion about the meaning of democracy finds an outlet in Lily L. H. M. Ling and Chih-yu Shih, "Confucianism with a Liberal Face," *Review of Politics* 60, 1 (1998): 55–82.

14. Examples of advocates for socialism can be Zhang Dongsun and Li Dazho, for liberalism, Hu Shih and Chen Xujin, for empircism, Yan Fu and Jin Yuelin, for humanism, Zhou Zuoren and Chen Duxiu.

15. For example, see Jin Yuelin, *The Outlet for Chinese Culture (Zhongguo wenhua de chulu)* (Shanghai: The Commerce Press, 1934).

16. An archetypal example is Lu Xun, see Zhang Zuo, *Chinese Civilization and Lu Xun's Critique (Zhongguo wenming yu lu xun de piping)* (Taipei: Guiguan, 1993).

17. For a motivation analysis, see Hu Xiwei, "Rationality and Utopia" (*Lixing yu wutuobang*) in Gao Ruiquan (ed.), *Currents of Social Thoughts in Modern China (Zhongguo jindai shehui sichao)* (Shanghai: Eastern China Normal University Press, 1996), pp. 224–250.

18. Sun Yatsen, e.g., treated his nationalism in terms of "freedom" and "of the people." For him, there was no individual freedom without national freedom. The preoccupation with collective freedom was clear right from the beginning when Western thoughts were introduced, see examples in Zhu Zhixin, *Collection of Zhu Zhixin's Writing (Zhu zhixin ji)* (Shanghai: Chinese Bookstore, 1979); Liang Qichao, *Selected Writings of Liang Qichao (Liang qichao xuan ji)* (Shanghai: Shanghai People's Press, 1984).

19. Xie Xialing, "Reinterpreting May Fourth Spirit, Absorbing Confucian Thoughts" (*Chongshi wu si jingshen, xishou luxue sixiang*), *Fudan Xuebao* 3 (1989).

20. Examples include Xu Youyu, Zhu Xueqin, Wang Dingding, Liu Junning, and Jing Yaojin, etc. See literature in journals such as *Ershiyi Shiji* (twenty-first century), *Dushu* (reading), *Tianya* (brink of heaven), *Jintian* (today), and *Zhanlyue yu Guanli* (strategy and management), etc.

21. For a collection of intellectual debates concerning liberalism in the new century, see Li Shitao (ed.), *Positions of Intellectuals: Debates on Liberalism and the Division of Chinese Intellectual Circles (Zhishifenzi lichang: ziyouzhuyi zhi zheng yu zhongguo sixiang jie de fenhua)* (Changchuen: Times Art, 2000).

22. Scholars in this stream trace their work back to Hayek, see, e.g., Deng Zhenglai, *Rationality and Reflections (Lixing yu fansi)* (Shenyang: Shenyang People's Press, 1998).

23. One extreme argument about national dignity in this stream is that genuine dignity lies in the acknowledgment of national backwardness, see Fan Qinlin, "Caveats of National Dignity and the Choice of Modern Culture" (*Minzu zizun de wuqu yu xiandai wenhua de xuanze*) in Li Shitao (ed.), *Positions of Intellectuals: Turbulence between Radicalism and Conservatism (Jijin yu baoshou zhijian de dongdang)* (Changchuen: Times Art, 2000), pp. 336–342.

24. Reports on her trip to the United States often used "return," "homecoming," and "back" to suggest that she is American and she responded by constantly mentioning "home" in her speeches while in the United States. See Chih-yu Shih, "The Eros of International Politics: Madame

Chiang Kaishek and the State Question in China," *Comparative Civilizations Review* 46 (Spring 2002): 91–119.

25. Generalissimo himself converted to Christianity after marrying her.

26. One justification for his nomination for the Nobel Peace Prize is that he had led Taiwan out of 5,000 years of authoritarian tradition.

27. Lee was able to receive a visa from the Untied States in 1995 and visited his Alma Mater in Ithaca, Connecticut. Beijing responded furiously, as if Washington would support Taiwan independence, by launching missiles at offshore Taiwan. Washington sent two aircraft carriers to nearby waters as a show of support to Taiwan.

28. Famous examples of indigenizers include Zhang Junmai, Wang Xinmin, Wang Guowei, Zhang Foquan, Liang Suming, etc.

29. For example, Tan Sitong, Chen Tianhua, and Zhang Taiyan.

30. While progressionists typically denounce Confucianism, one interesting revision done by the indigenizers is "to destroy all the Confucian stores in order to save Confucius."

31. This is called neo-Confucianism, represented by Xiong Shili, Mou Zongshan, Du Weiming, etc. See n.e. (eds.), *Contemporary Neo-Confucianists* (*Dangdai xin lujia*) (Shanghai: Sanlian, 1989).

32. Mao was an indigenizer as he stressed the importance of Sinifying Marxism. On the other hand, the Cultural Revolution was anti-tradition as well as anti-Western. It could represent a move toward reflexive Orientalism in the sense that China's cultural backwardness was acknowledged and the meaning of revolution was left open-ended. He remained an indigenizer to the extent that he would use permanent revolution as retaliation on the imperialist forces and as a solution to China's backwardness.

33. This involves a counter-demonization of the so-called West. See Chen Xiaomei, *Occidentalism* (Oxford: Oxford University Press, 1995).

34. Homi K. Bhabha, "The World and the Home," *Social Text* 31–32 (Summer 1993): 141–153.

35. Wang Hui, "The Situation of Contemporary Chinese Thoughts and the Issue of Modernity" (*Dangdai zhongguo de sixiang zhuangkuang yu xiandaixing wenti*), in Li Shitao (ed.), *Debates on Liberalism*, pp. 83–123.

36. Chinese scholars taking this view are nicknamed "Neo-authoritarian scholars," see Xiao Gongqin, *History has Refused Romanticism* (*Lishi jujue langman*) (Taipei: Zhiliang, 1998), chapter 1.

37. Chih-yu Shih, "How Flexible Is Peking's Foreign Policy?" in B. Lin and J. Myers (eds.), *Contemporary China in the Post-Cold War Era* (University of South Carolina Press, 1996), pp. 306–327.

38. Deng Xiaoping was a follower of Zhou. Deng accepted standards set according to the sovereign paradigm and considered China a backward country. Similarly, Deng also showed an almost obsessive concern with symbols of sovereign independence. In contrast, Mao Zedong was indisputably the most important indigenizer.

39. Almost all the celebrities in Chinese diplomacy contributed to a book in memory of Zhou, Pei Jianzhang (ed.), *Studying Zhou Enlai* (*Yanjiu zhou enlai*) (Beijing: World Knowledge Press, 1989).

40. Zhou Enlai, "Struggling for the Sake of Consolidating and Developing People's Victory" (*Wei gonggu he fazhan renmin de shengli er fendou*) a lecture given to All-nation Commission, National Political Consultative Conference, published by Renmin Ribao (October 1, 1950), see *Selected Works by Zhou Enlai* (*Zhou enlai xuan ji*) (Beijing: People's Press, 1984), p. 43.

41. Zhou Enlai, "On Current Financial Situations and the Few Relationships in New China's Economy" (*Dangqian caijing xingshi he xin zhongguo jinji de jizhong guanxi*), in *Selected Works*, pp. 10–11.

42. Zhou Enlai, "Construction and Unity" (*Jianshe yu tuanjie*), in *Selected Works*, p. 23.

43. Ibid., p. 23.

44. Ibid., p. 25.

45. Zhou Enlai, "About the Issue of Chinese National Bourgeoisie" (*Guanyu zhongguo deminzu zichanjieji wenti*), a lecture given on June 19, 1952 at a United Front Conference, in *Selected Works*, p. 95.

46. Zhou Enlai, "To Build Our Country into a Strong, Modern Socialist State" (*Ba woguo jianshe chengwei qiangdade shehuizhuyide xiandai-huade gonye guojia*), *Selected Works*, pp. 132, 133.

47. Zhou Enlai, "Construction and Unity," p. 27.

48. Ibid., p. 30.

49. Zhou Enlai, "On the Intellectual Rectification Issue" (*Guanyu zhishifenzi gaizao de wenti*), *Selected Works*, p. 53.

50. For example, Zhou Enlai, "Struggling," p. 33.

51. Zhou Enlai, "Principles and Missions of Our Diplomacy" (*Womende waijiao fangzhen he renwu*), in *Selected Works*, p. 87.

52. Ibid., p. 91.

53. Zhou Enlai, "Speak Only on International Situations and Foreign Policy" (*Zhi jiang guoji xingshi he waijiao zhengce*), in *Selected Letters of Zhou Enlai* (*Zhou enlai shuxin ji*) (Beijing: Central Literature Press, 1988), p. 520.

54. Zhou Enlai's speech during the Asian-African Conference, in *Selected Works*, p. 154.

55. Ibid., p. 155.

56. Zhou Enlai's note to Li Kenong and Qiao Guanhua, in *Selected Letters*, p. 470.

57. For the development of Chinese foreign policy themes, see Chih-yu Shih, *China's Just World* (Boulder: Lynne Rienner, 1993).

58. See Kenneth Lieberthal, "The Background in Chinese Politics," in H. J. Ellison (ed.), *The Sino-Soviet Conflict* (Seattle: University of Washington Press, 1982), pp. 3–28.

59. One expression of this anxiety is to ask, "why do teachers always beat us students?" To answer the question, Zi Zhongyun, a leading expert on

international politics in China, believes that one must first deny the validity of the question. Anti-imperialist sentiment only serves imperialism. The real enemy accordingly is in China, namely, corruption and nationalist pretension. See Zi Zhongyun, "How Should Chinese View International Situations and Pose Themselves?" (*Zhongguoren yinggai ruhe kandai guoji xingshi yu ruhe zichu*), *China Review* (*Zhongguo pinglun*) 24 (December 1999): 20–25.

60. Zi calls this "abnormal enclosure," ibid., p. 21.

61. There are numerous statements on this point. See, e.g., Li Peng, "Report on Work of Government" (March 20, 1992).

62. This tendency is manifested in, e.g., Ann Kent, *Between Freedom and Subsistence* (Hong Kong: Cambridge University Press, 1993).

63. See Information Office of the State Council, *Human Rights in China* (*Zhongguo de renquan zhuangkuang*) (Beijing: Central Literature Press, 1992).

64. For a more recent rebuttal that is universal in logic, see Information Office of the State Council, *Human Rights Record of the United States in 1999* (*Yijiujiujiu meiguo de ren quan jilu*), New China New Agency script (February 27, 2000); or Zhou Wei, "The Anatomy of the View that Human Rights Prevail over Sovereignty" (*Renquan gaoyu zhuquan ren toushi*), *Renmin Ribao* (March 28, 2000): 6.

65. In the beginning of the twenty-first century, this means economic globalization, maintenance of international political economic order, stable economic growth, and equal trade relationships with the rest of the world. See the section on international situations and diplomatic work in "Political Resolution of the Ninth National Commission of Political Consultative Conference" (March 11, 1999), http: www.mac.gov.tw/ rpir/project/990311.htm as of March 24, 2000.

3 The Nationalist Clue: Defending People's Heart

1. For example, Kuo-hsing Chen, "Caution Conflict Called upon the Pass of China's National Defense Act" (*Dui zhongguo zhiding guofang fa ying you de jingti*), *Taiwan Times* (March 10, 1997): 4.

2. For different perspectives on the exercises, see Forum, *China Journal* (July 1997): 87–134.

3. For further information, see Chinese Communist Party Center Literature Commission (ed.), *Selected Work of Deng Xiaoping, III* (*Deng xiaoping wen xuan*) (Beijing: People's Press, 1994), pp. 72–76.

4. For legal provisions concerning the domestic use of the National Defense Force, see *China Times* (March 4, 1997): 9.

5. See, e.g., Philip Snow, *The Star Raft: China's Encounter with Africa* (New York: Weidenfeld & Nicolson, 1988), pp. 69–104.

6. Jonathan Adelman and Chih-yu Shih, *Symbolic War: The Chinese Use of Force, 1840–1980* (Taipei: Institute of International Relations, 1993).

7. James Der Derian and Michael Shapiro, *International/Intertextual Relations* (Lexington: Lexington Books, 198); Jim George, *Discourses of Global Politics* (Boulder: Lynne Rienner, 1994); Jens Bartelson, *A Genealogy of Sovereignty* (Cambridge: Cambridge University Press, 1995).

8. V. Spike Peterson, *Feminist (Re)Visions of International Relations Theory* (Boulder: Lynne Rienner, 1992); Ann Tickner, *Gender in International Politics* (New York: Columbia University Press ,1992); Cynthia Enloe, *Bananas, Beaches and Bases* (Berkeley: University of California Press, 1990).

9. Lily Ling, "Democratization under Internationalization," *Democratization* 3, 2 (1996); Chih-yu Shih, A Postcolonial Reading of Cross-Strait Relations, *The Journal of Contemporary China* 17 (January 1998); Sankaran Krishna, "The Improvement of Being Ironic," *Alternatives* 18 (1993): 385–417; David Blaney and Naeem Inayatullah, "Knowing Encounters," in Yosef Lapid and Friedrich Kratochwil (eds.), *The Return of Culture and Identity in IR Theory* (Boulder: Lynne Rienner, 1996).

10. Michael J. Shapiro and Hayward R. Alker (eds.), *Challenge Boundaries* (Minneapolis: University of Minnesota Press, 1995); Keith Krause, and Michael C. Williams (eds.), *Critical Security Studies* (Minneapolis: University of Minnesota Press,1997).

11. R. B. J. Walker, *Inside/Outside: International Relations as Political Theory* (Cambridge: Cambridge University Press, 1993)

12. David Campbell, *Writing Security* (Minneapolis: University of Minnesota Press, 1992)

13. James Der Derian, *On Diplomacy* (Cambridge: Blackwell, 1987); *Anti-Diplomacy* (Cambridge: Blackwell, 1992).

14. Lewis F. Richardson, *Armaments and Security* (Pittsburgh: The Boxwood Press, 1960).

15. David S. Landes, "Some Thoughts on the Natures of Economic Imperialism," *Journal of Economic History* 21 (1961): 496–512.

16. David Campbell, *Writing Security* (Minneapolis: University of Minnesota Press, 1992).

17. R. B. J. Walker, *Inside/Outside: International Relations as Political Theory* (Cambridge: Cambridge University Press, 1993).

18. Cynthia Weber, *Simulating Sovereignty: Intervention, the State and Symbolic Intervention* (Cambridge: Cambridge University Press, 1995), ch. 1.

19. Stanley Hoffmann, *Duties Beyond Borders* (Syracuse: Syracuse University Press, 1981).

20. E. H. Carr, *Nationalism and After* (New York: Macmillan, 1945).

21. D. A. Bell, D. Brown, K. Jayasuriya, and D. M. Jones (eds.), *Towards Illiberal Democracy in Pacific Asia* (New York: St. Martin's Press, 1995).

22. See, e.g., Samuel Huntington, *Political Order in Changing Societies* (New Haven: Yale University Press, 1968).

23. Editors, *Selected Historical Documents on Yellow Peril* (Huanghuo lun lishi ziliao xuan ji) (Beijing: Chinese Social Science Press, 1979).

24. Bigo Didder, "Security, Borders and the State," in A. Sweedler and J. Scott (eds.), *Border Regions in Functional Transition* (Berlin: Institute of Regional Development, IRS, 1996)

25. Ole Barru Bizab Waever, Morton Kelstrup, and Pieere Lematire, *Identity, Migration and the New Security Agenda in Europe* (New York: St. Martin's Press, 1993).

26. Stelin Siglev, *The Empire of the Dragon* (*Long de diguo*) (Taipei: Think Tank, 1996).

27. Michael H. Hunt, "Chinese National Identity and the Strong State: The Late-Qing-Republican Crisis," in L. Dittmer and S. Kim (eds.), *China's Quest for National Identity* (Ithaca: Cornell University Press, 1993), pp. 62–79.

28. See the discussion in Michael Hunt, *The Genesis of Chinese Communist Foreign Policy* (New York: Columbia University Press, 1996) and Shih, "A Postcolonial Reading".

29. Wang Hui, "The Fate of `Mr. Science' in China: The Concept of Science and Its Application in Modern Chinese Thought," in Tani Barlow (ed.), *Formations of Colonial Modernity in East Asia* (Durham: Duke University Press, 1997), p. 56.

30. Ibid., p. 52

31. Zhuang Hanlong and Yang Ming, *Historical Discourse on the Strategy of Peaceful Evolution in the West* (*Xifang heping yanbian zhanlyue shi hua*) (Beijing: Long March Publisher, 1991), pp. 119–120.

32. Tani Barlow, "Introduction," in T. Barlow (ed.), *Formations of Colonial Modernity in East Asia* (Durham: Duke University Press, 1997), p. 8.

33. For a related theme of Awaking Lion, see Jianfei Qin, *The World Views China* (*Shijie de zhongguo guan*) (Shanghai: Xuelin, 1992).

34. Kuan-sheng Liao, *Anti-Foreignism and Modernization in China, 1860–1980* (New York: St. Martin's Press, 1984).

35. Qian Qichen, "Seriously Studying Zhou Enlai's Diplomatic Thoughts and Practices," in Pei Jianzhang (ed.), *Studying Zhou Enlai: Diplomatic Thoughts and Practices* (*Yanjiu zhou enlai—waijiao sixiang yu shijian*) (Beijing: World Knowledge, 1989), p. 1.

36. These documents and responses to them are collected in Liuzi Shih (ed.), *The Ten-Thousand-Word and Other Underground Writings in Beijing* (*Beijing dixia wan yan shu*) (Hong Kong: Mirror Books, 1997).

37. See the discussion by Ta-ning Hsie, "The Origin and the Contents of the Great Unity Conception" (*Da yitong guannian de laiyuan ji qi neirong*), presented at the Conference on Prospects and Retrospect, annual meeting of the Association for Unity and Self-strengthening (Taipei), January 4, 1998.

38. Ah Ying, "On the National Crisis of the Year of Geng Zi" (*Geng zi guo bian ji*), in *Literature on the Incident of the Year of Gengzi* (*Gengzi shijian wenxian ji*) (Beijing: Chinese Bookstore, 1959), pp. 947–951.

39. Wu Hsiang-hsiang, *The History of the Second Sino-Japanese War* (*Di erci zhong ri zhangzheng shi*) (Taipei: Scooper Press, 1973), p. 402.
40. Lowell Dittmer and Samuel Kim (eds.), *China Quest for National Identity* (Ithaca: Cornell University Press, 1993).
41. The Headquarter of the Chinese People Opposing America, Assisting Korea Movement (ed.), *The Great Opposing American, Assisting Korea Movement* (*Weida de kang mei yuan chao yundong*) (Beijing: New China Bookstore, 1954), pp. 36–37.
42. Melvin Gurtov and Byng-Moo Hwang, *China under Treat* (Baltimore: The Johns Hopkins University Press, 1980).
43. Ibid., pp. 142, 156.
44. Reihuan Li (1992), quoted in the *United Daily* (October 30) (Taipei).
45. See Dru Gladney, "Ethnic Identity in China," in William Joseph (ed.), *China Briefing, 1994* (Boulder: Westview, 1995), pp. 171–192.
46. For example, see Gerald Segal, *Defending China* (Oxford: Oxford University Press, 1985).
47. See Alastair Ian Johnston, *Cultural Realism: Strategic Culture and Great Strategy in Ming China* (Princeton: Princeton University Press, 1995) and his critics in *Journal of Asian Studies* 56, 3 (August 1997): 769–773.
48. *Records of Barbarian Affairs* (*Duban yiwu shimo*), Daoguang years, 54: 1.
49. Luo Chuanli, "The Origin and Development of Sino-French Warfare," in Chinese History Association (eds.), *The Sino-French War* (*Zhong fa zhangzheng*) (Shanghai: New Knowledge Publication, 1955).
50. "Archive of Telegram in the Guanxu Period," in C. L. Yang (ed.), *Collected Literature on the Sino-Japanese War* (*Zhong ri zhangzheng wenxian hui bian*) (Taipei: Tingwen Bookstore, 1973), July 17, 20 (*Guangxu* years).
51. Ibid., December 10, 20 (*Guangxu* years).
52. Chuanli Luo, " On the National Crisis in the Year of Gengzi" (*Gengzi guo bian ji*), in Ah, Y. (ed.), *Collected Literature on the Events in the Year of Gengzi* (*Gengzi shibian wenxue ji*) (Beijing: Chinese Bookstore, 1959) pp. 945–958.
53. Lancelot Giles, *The Siege of the Peking Legations: A Diary* (Nedlands: University of West Australian Press, 1970), p. 88.
54. Hua Yuan, *Crystal Lesson from Bitter History* (*Tong shi ming jian*) (Beijing: Beijing Press, 1991), p. 139.
55. See Wei-kuo Chiang, *The History of National Revolution* (*Guomin geming shi*) (Taipei: Liming, 1979), pp. 7–8.
56. Wu, op. cit., pp. 796, 798.
57. Steve Chan, "Chinese Conflict Calculus and Behavior," *World Politics* 30 (April 1978): 391–410.
58. Zhou Enlai, "A Report to the Chinese People's Political Consultative Conference," in *The Great Opposing America, Assisting Korea Movement*, op. cit., pp. 25, 27.

59. Allen Whiting, *China Crosses the Yalu* (New York: Macmillan, 1960), p. 84.

60. Thomas Stolper, *China, Taiwan, and the offshore Island* (New York: M. E. Sharpe, 1985).

61. Spokesman of the Foreign Ministry, "A Declaration Concerning the Stopping of Shelling of Quemoy," *The People's Republic of China Foreign Relations Documents 1958 (Zhonghua renmin gongheguo duiwai guanxi wenjianji)* (Beijing: World Knowledge, 1959), p. 178.

62. Peng Dehuai, "A Letter to the Taiwanese," October 25, 1958; ibid., p. 182.

63. *Collection of Original Materials Concerning the Disputes Between Bandits and Russia (Fei e douzheng yuanshi ziliao huibian)*, Vol. 14 (Taipei: Institute of International Relations, 1971), pp. 27–28.

64. See Gong Huiping, "The Airport Meeting of Zhou Enlai and Kosygin and Its Lessons," in Pei (ed.), op. cit., pp. 170–178.

65. Xie Yixian, *Diplomatic Wisdom and Stratagem: The Theory and Principles of New Chinese Diplomacy (Waijiao zhihui yu moulyue: xin zhongguo waijiao lilun yu yuanze)* (Zhengzhou: Henan People's Press, 1993), pp. 262–263.

66. Chih-yu Shih, *China's Just World: The Morality of Chinese Foreign Policy* (Boulder: Lynne Rienner, 1993).

67. En-han Li, *Revolutionary Diplomacy Before and After the North Expedition, 1925–1931 (Beifa qian hou de geming waijiao, 1925–1931)* (Taipei: The Institute of Modern History, Academic Sinica, 1993).

68. In almost every armed conflict, the PLA claimed defense. For one typical example, see *Collected Literature on the PRC Foreign Relations (Zhonghua renmin gongheguo duiwai guanxi wenjian ji)*, 1962 (Beijing: World Knowledge, 1964), p. 114.

69. Editors (ed.), *The Military Work of Contemporary Chinese Military (Dangdai zhongguo jundui de junshi gongzuo)* (Beijing: Chinese Social Science Press, 1989), p. 460.

70. Liu Zhongxin, *The Business of Blood and Fire (Xie yu huo de shiye), Modern National Defense Series (Xiandai guofang congshu)* (Chengdu: Sichuan Education Press, 1991), pp. 173–174.

71. G. C. Spivak, "Can the Subaltern Speak?" in C. Nelson and L. Grossberg (eds.), *Marxism and Interpretation of Culture* (Chicago: University of Illinois Press, 1988).

72. Lee Teng-hui's inauguration speech in *China Times* (May 20, 1996): 2.

73. See the *Symposium of the Conference on China Policy (Min jin dang zhongguo zhengce yantaohui)* (Taipei: Democratic Progressive Party, February 13–15, 1998).

74. Editorial of *PLA Daily*, reprinted in *People's Daily (Renmin Ribao)* (January 31, 1996).

75. Shih-min Chen, *The Origin and the Evolution of China's Nuclear Strategy (Zhonggong hewu zhanlyue de xingcheng yu zhuanbian)*, Masters

Thesis (Graduate Institute of Politic Science, National Taiwan University, 1992) (Taipei).

76. Stuart Harris, "The PRC's Quest for Great Power Status," presented at An International Conference on the PRC After the Fifteenth Party Congress, Taipei (February 20, 1998).

77. Jorn Brommelhorster and John Frankenstein, *Mix Motives, Uncertain Outcomes: Defense Conversion in China* (Boulder: Lynne Rienner, 1997).

78. Cui Yuchen, *The Nascent Contention in Fighting for the Soft Border Lines* (*Zheng duo ran bian jiang de xin jiaozhu*), *Mondern National Defense Series* (Chengdu: Sichuan Education Press), p. 196.

79. Ibid., pp. 206–207

80. See Li Jiaquan, "On the Root and Its Outlet of Lee Tenghui's Sense of Pity" (*li denghui beiai de genyou ji qi chulu*), *Straits Review (Haixia pinglun)* 47 (November 1994).

81. Chi Haotian, Vice Chairman of Central Military Commission, quoted in *Renmin Ribao* (oversees edition) (June 11, 1996).

82. Chi Haotian quoted in *Renmin Ribao* (December 12, 1996).

83. Joseph B. Underhill-Cady, *Doing Battle with Death*, Ph.D. dissertation University of Michigan (Ann Arbor, 1995).

84. According to Ellis Joffe, the Chinese military's self-image "is inseparable from the pride and patriotism," and "until Jiang Zemin demonstrate that he is a worthy standard bearer of Chinese nationalist aspirations...the military will tend to view him with some suspicion and presumably consider it necessary to keep a close watch..." in his "The PLA and Politics," presented at An International Conference on the PRC After the Fifteenth Party Congress, Taipei (February 19, 1998).

85. Li Peng quoted in *Renmin Ribao* (January 31, 1996).

86. Liu Huaqing, Central Military Commission, quoted by *Renmin Ribao* (August 31, 1995).

87. Huang Jiashu, *Can Taiwan Become Independent?* (*Taiwan neng duli ma?*), *Strategic Studies Series of International Strategic Research Foundation* (Haikou: South Sea Press, 1994), p. 278.

88. Richard Bernstein and Ross H. Munro, *The Coming Conflict with China* (New York: Alfred A. Knopf, 1997); Samuel Huntington, *The Clash of Civilizations and the Making of World Order* (New York: Simon & Schurster, 1996); for a related discussion see Andrew Nathan and Robert Ross, *The Great Wall and the Empty Fortress* (New York: W. W. Norton, 1997).

4 THE RATIONAL CHOICE CLUE: CURING EPISTEMOLOGICAL AMNESIA

1. For exceptions, see Quincy Wright, *The Study of War* II (Chicago: Chicago University Press, 1942); Anthony Smith, "Nationalism and the Historians," *International Journal of Comparative Sociology* 33, 1–2

(1992): 55–80; Anthony Smith, *The Ethnic Revival in the Modern World* (Cambridge: Cambridge University Press, 1981).

2. Kenneth Waltz, *Theory of International Politics* (Reading, MA: Addison-Wesley, 1979).

3. Robert Keohane and Joseph Nye, *Power and Interdependence* (Boston: Little, Brown & Company, 1978).

4. Karl Marx and Friedrich Engels, *Basic Writings on Politics and Philosophy*, L. S. Feuer (ed.) (Glasgow: The Fontana Library, 1959); Frank H. Simond and Brooks Emeny, *The Great Powers in World Politics: International Relations and Economic Nationalism* (New York: American Book Company, 1939).

5. Herbert Kelman, "Patterns of Personal Involvement in the National System: A Social-Psychological Analysis of Political Legitimacy," in James Rosenau (ed.), *International Politics and Foreign Policy* (New York: Free Press, 1969), p. 277; Cynthia H. Enloe, "Ethnicity, the State, and the New International Order," in J. F. Stack, Jr. (ed.), *The Primordial Challenge: Ethnicity in the Contemporary World* (New York: Greenwood, 1986), pp. 25–42; William Bloom, *Personal Identity, National Identity and International Relations* (Cambridge: Cambridge University Press, 1990); Wendell Bell, "New States in the Caribbean: A General Theoretical Account," in S. N. Eisenstadt and S. Rokkan (eds.), *Building States and Nations* II (London: Sage, 1974), pp. 177–209.

6. Francis Fukuyama, *The End of History and the Last Man* (New York: Aron, 1992); Kwame Anthony Appiah, *In My Father's House: Africa in the Philosophy of Culture* (Oxford: Oxford University Press, 1992).

7. Barry Posen, "The Security Dilemma and Ethnic Conflict," *Survival* 35 1 (1993): 27–47; John Mearsheimer, "Back to the Future: Instability in Europe After the Cold War," *International Security* 15 (1990): 5–56; Steven Krasner, "State Power and the Structure of International Trade," *World Politics* 28 (1976): 317–347; Robert Gilpin, *The Political Economy of International Relations* (Princeton: Princeton University Press, 1987); Anthony H. Birch, *Nationalism & National Integration* (London: Unwin Hyman, 1989); Steven Krasner, *Defining the National Interest* (Stanford: Stanford University Press, 1978).

8. James Mayall, *Nationalism and International Society* (Cambridge: Cambridge University Press, 1990); Barry Buzan, "From International System to International Society: Structural Realism and Regime Theory Meet the English School," *International Organization* 47 (1993): 327–352.

9. David Campbell, "Political Prosaics, Transversal Politics, and the Anarchical World," in M. J. Shapiro and H. R. Alker (eds.), *Challenging Boundaries* (Minneapolis: University of Minnesota Press, 1996), pp. 7–31; Richard Ashley, "Untying the Sovereign State: A Double Reading of the Anarchy Problematique," *Millennium* 17 (1988): 227–263.

10. Walker, *Inside/Outside: International Relations as Political Theory* (Cambridge: R. B. J. Cambridge University Press, 1993); Jens Bartelson, *A Genealogy of Sovereignty* (Cambridge: Cambridge University Press, 1995).

11. Yaccov Y. I. Vertzberger, *The World in Their Minds: Information Processing, Cognition, and Perception in Foreign Policy Decisionmaking* (Stanford: Stanford University Press, 1990); Martha Cottam and Chih-yu Shih, *Contending Dramas: A Cognitive Approach to International Organizations* (New York: Praeger, 1992).

12. Arthur Schlesinger, *The Disuniting of America: Reflections on a Multicultural Society* (New York: Norton, 1992); Stuart Hall, "The Local and the Global: Globalization and Ethnicity," in A. McClintock, A. Mufti, and E. Shohat (eds.), *Dangerous Liaisons: Gender, Nation, & Postcolonial Perspectives* (Minneapolis: University of Minnesota Press, 1997), pp. 173–187.

13. Benedict Anderson, *Imagined Communities* (London: Verso, 1983).

14. Friedrich Kratochwil, "Citizenship: On the Border of Order," in Y. Lapid and F. Kratochwil (eds.), *The Return of Culture and Identity in IR Theory* (Boulder: Lynne Rienner, 1997), pp. 181–197.

15. Hans Kohn, *The Idea of Nationalism* (New York: Collier-Macmillan, 1967); Eric Hobsbawn, *Nations and Nationalism Since 1780* (Cambridge: Cambridge University Press, 1990).

16. Eric Hobsbawn and Terence Ranger (eds.), *The Invention of Tradition* (Cambridge: Cambridge University Press, 1983).

17. Joseph M. Grieco, "Understanding the Problem of International Cooperation: The Limits of Neoliberal Institutionalism and the Future of Realist Theory," in D. A. Baldwin, *Neorealism and Neoliberalism: The Contemporary Debate* (New York: Columbia University Press, 1993).

18. Unlike the case $\delta = 0$, where people forgive the past completely and render grievances meaningless, here people suffer from grievances but do not act upon past grievances while computing only to manage future grievances.

19. Ernest Gellner, *Nations and Nationalism* (Oxford: Basil Blackwell, 1983).

20. Edward Said, *Culture and Imperialism* (New York: Vintage Books, 1991).

21. Stephen D. Krasner, "State Power and the Structure of International Trade," *World Politics* 28 (1976).

22. Montserrat Guibernau, *Nationalisms: The Nation-State and Nationalism in the Twentieth Century* (Cambridge: Polity Press, 1996), pp. 143–150; Jehua Reinharz and George L. Mosse (eds.), *The Impact of Western Nationalisms* (New Delhi: Sage, 1992).

23. Yael Tamir, *Liberal Nationalism* (Princeton: Princeton University Press, 1993); Liah Greenfeld, *Nationalism: Five Roads to Modernity* (Cambridge: Harvard University Press, 1992), pp. 25–87.

24. Franz Fanon, "On National Culture," in F. Fanon, *The Wretched of the Earth* (New York: Grove, 1964).

25. Ann Cvetkovich and Douglas Kellner (eds.), *Articulating the Global and the Local: Globalization and Cultural Studies* (Boulder: Westview, 1997).

26. Lily Ling, "Democratization under Internationalization: Media Reconstructions of Gender Identity in Shanghai," *Democratization* 3, 2 (1996): 140–157; Naeem Inayatullah and David L. Blaney, "Knowing Encounters: Beyond Parochialism in International Relations Theory," in Y. Lapid and F. Kratochwil (eds.), *The Return of Culture and Identity in IR Theory* (Boulder: Lynne Rienner, 1996), pp. 65–84.

27. Ashis Nandy, *The Intimate Enemy: Loss and Recovery of Self Under Colonialism* (Oxford: Oxford University Press, 1983).

28. I owe my conceptualization of civilizer state to Peter Van Ness, who in an unpublished manuscripts details the characteristics of civilizer states and identifies the United States and China to be two of the foremost examples.

29. Young-tsu Wong, *Search for Modern Nationalism: Zhang Binglin and Revolutionary China, 1869–1936* (Hong Kong: Oxford University Press, 1983); James Townsend, "Chinese Nationalism," *The Australian Journal of Chinese Affairs* 27 (1992); Kauko Laitinen, *Chinese Nationalism in the Late Qing Dynasty* (London: Curzon Press, 1990); Edward Friedman, *New National Identities in Post-Leninist Transformations: The Implications for China* (Hong Kong: Chinese University of Hong Kong Press, 1992).

30. Chih-yu Shih, "A Postcolonial Reading of Cross-Taiwan Straits Relations," *The Journal of Contemporary China* 7, 17 (Winter 1998).

31. Kuan-sheng Liao, *Anti-Foreignism and Modernization in China, 1860–1980* (New York: St. Martin's Press, 1984).

32. Lucian Pye, "How China's Nationalism Was Shanghaied," *The Australian Journal of Chinese Affairs* 29 (1993).

33. Greenfeld, *Five Roads to Modernity*, pp. 397–484.

34. Rein Müllerson, *Human Rights Diplomacy* (New York: Routledge, 1997).

35. Samuel Berger, "Building a New Consensus on China," delivered at the Council on Foreign Relations, New York on June 6, 1997, at the web site, www.ait.gov.tw.

36. Arthur Schlesinger, *The Cycles of American History* (Boston: Houghton Mifflin, 1986); Chih-yu Shih, *The Spirit of Chinese Foreign Policy: A Psychocultural View* (London: Macmillan, 1990); Jack Holm, *Mood/Interest theory of American Foreign Policy* (Lexington: University of Kentucky Press, 1985); Lowell Dittmer and Samuel Kim, *China's Quest of National Identity* (Ithaca: Cornell University Press, 1993).

37. State Council of the People's Republic of China, *Human Rights in China* (Beijing: Information Office of the State Council, 1991).

38. Licheng Ma and Zhijun Ling, *Battling: The Records of Three Thought Liberation Campaigns in Contemporary China* (*Jiaofeng: dangdai*

zhongguo san ci sixiang jiefang shilu) (Beijing: Today's China Press, 1998).

39. Ann Kent, *Between Freedom and Subsistence: China and Human Rights* (Hong Kong: Cambridge University Press, 1993).
40. Bill Clinton, "China and the National Interest," speech delivered on October 24, 1997, Washington D. C., at the web site, www.ait.gov.tw.
41. Richard Madsen, *China and the American Dream* (Berkeley: University of California Press, 1995).
42. Neil J. Smelser, "The Rational and the Ambivalent in the Social Sciences," *American Sociological Review* 63 (1998): 1–16.
43. Yosef Lapid and Friedrich Kratochwil, "Revisiting the "National": Toward an Identity Agenda in Neorealism?" in Y. Lapid and F. Kratochwil (eds.), *The Return of Culture and Identity in IR Theory* (Boulder: Lynne Rienner, 1996).
44. Alexander Wendt, "Collective Identity Formation and the International State," *American Political Science Review* 88 (1994): 384–396.
45. David Campbell, *Writing Security: United States Foreign Policy and the Politics of Identity* (Minneapolis: Minnesota University Press, 1992); Johann P. Arnason, "Nationalism, Globalization and Modernity," in M. Featherstone (ed.), *Global Culture: Nationalism, Globalization and Modernity* (London: Sage, 1990), pp. 207–236; Yosef Lapid and Friedrich Kratochwil, "Theorizing the 'National' in International Relations Theory," in F. Kratochwil and R. Mansfield (eds.), *International Organizations* (New York: Harper Collins, 1994).
46. Scott Burchill and Andrew Linklater (eds.), *Theories of International Relations* (New York: St. Martin's, 1996), pp. 188–193; Jaques Derrida, *Positions* (Chicago: University of Chicago Press, 1981).

5   THE POSTCOLONIAL CLUE: BRINGING JAPAN BACK IN

1. For a useful discussion, see Lowell Dittmer and Samuel Kim (eds.), *China's Quest for National Identity* (Ithaca: Cornell University Press, 1993).
2. I have discussed this in *China's Just World: The Morality of Chinese Foreign Policy* (Boulder: Lynne Rienner, 1993), pp. 133–166.
3. See Kenneth B. Pyle, *The New Generation in Meiji Japan: Problems of Cultural Identity, 1885–1895* (Stanford: Stanford University Press, 1969).
4. See the analysis of Mark Mancall, *China at Center: 300 Years of Foreign Policy* (New York: Free Press, 1984).
5. For reference see Lyon Sharman, *Sun Yat-sen: His Life and Its Meaning* (Stanford: Stanford University Press, 1968).
6. Michael Hunt, "Chinese National Identity and the Strong State: The Late Qing-Republic Crisis," in L. Dittmer and S. Kim (eds.), *China's Quest for National Identity* (Ithaca: Cornell University Press, 1993).

7. See Kenneth B. Pyle, "In Pursuit of a Grand Design: Nakasone Betwix the Past and the Future," *Journal of Japanese Studies* 13, 2 (1987).

8. The Chinese version of the article appeared in *Independence Evening* (*Zili wanbao*) (April 30–May 2, 1994): 2.

9. Here, Shiba refers to Chiang Kai-shek and his successor and son Chiang Ching-kuo.

10. Li Jaiquan, "How Much Intimacy Toward the Chinese is there Left?" (*Haiyou duoshao zhongguoren de ganqing*), *Wenhui Bao* (June 10, 1994).

11. Telegram of New China News Agency of June 13, 1994, quoted in *Wenhui Bao* (June 14, 1994).

12. Zhu Chengxiu, "How Far will Lee Teng-hui Go?" (*Li denghui haiyao zou duo yuan*), *Dagong Bao* (June 19, 1994).

13. Ibid.

14. See *Straits Review* (*Haixia pinglun*) 47 (November 1994): 21.

15. Cui Zhiqin, "The Dangerous Tendency in the Lee Teng-hui Group's Mainland China Policy" (*Li denghui jituan dalu zhengce de weixian dongxiang*), presented at the 4th Annual Meeting of the Scholarly Exchange Between the Two Sides of the Taiwan Straits, Beijing, August 1–6, 1994.

16. Liu Hong, "A Brief Note on Lee Teng-hui's Theory of 'People's Sovereignty'" (*Jian ping li denghui de zhuquan zaimin lun*), presented at the 4th Annual Meeting of the Scholarly Exchange between the Two Sides of the Taiwan Straits, Beijing, August 1–6, 1994.

17. Li Jiaquan, "The Root and Its Outlet of Lee Teng-hui's Sense of Pity" (*Li denghui beiai de genyou ji qi chulu*), *Straits Review* 47 (November 1994): 44.

18. *China Times Evening* (*Zhong Shi Wanbao*) (September 9, 1994): 2.

19. *United Evening (Lianhe Wanbao)* (August 18, 1994): 1

20. *United Daily (Lianhe Bao)* (August 20, 1994): 2.

21. *United Daily* (August 24, 1994): 4

22. *United Daily* (August 24, 1994): 4.

23. *China Times (Zhongguo Shibao)* (August 27, 1994): 4.

24. *The Masses Daily (Minzhong Ribao)* (October 4, 1994): 2.

25. *The Masses Daily* (September 8, 1994): 3.

26. *United Daily* (September 10, 1994): 3.

27. *China Times* (September 17, 1994): 3.

28. *China Times* (September 18, 1994): 4.

30. *China Times* (September 17, 1994): 3.

31. *United Daily* (September 18, 1994): 4.

32. *China Times* (September 23, 1994): 2.

33. *China Times* (September 24, 1994): 2.

34. *China Times* (September 27, 1994): 1.

35. *United Evening* (September 30, 1994): 1.

36. Anthony Kuhn, "Ping-Pong Politics," *Far Eastern Economic Review* (December 8, 1994): 44–45.

37. Ibid.

38. For a theoretical discussion of this perspective, see David Campbell, *Writing Security* (Minneapolis: University of Minnesota Press, 1992).

39. See *Central Daily (Zhongyang Ribao)* (December 26, 1994): 7.

6 THE GLOBALIZATION CLUE: ESTRANGING THE PARTTIME SELF

1. For detailed discussion and a case study, see David Campbell, *Writing Security* (Minneapolis: University of Minnesota Press, 1992).

2. James Der Derian, *On Diplomacy* (Oxford: Blackwell, 1987), ch. 2.

3. Rob B. J. Walker, *"International Relations" as Political Theory* (Cambridge: Cambridge University Press, 1993), ch. 1.

4. Alexander Wendt, *Social Theory of International Politics* (Cambridge: Cambridge University Press, 1999).

5. He means the mediation of the estrangement of man from a universal utopia. *On Diplomacy.*

6. For more discussion, see David S. G. Goodman and Gerald Segal (eds.), *China Rising: Nationalism and Interdependence* (London: Routledge, 1997).

7. Ippei Yamazawa and Ken-Ichi Imai (eds.), *China Enters WTO: Pursuing Symbiosis with the Global Economy* (Tokyo: Institute of Developing Economies, Japan External Trade Organization, 2001).

8. See Chih-yu Shih, *The Spirit of Chinese Foreign Policy* (London: Macmillan, 1990).

9. See, e.g., Yuan Weishi, "The Two Great Chronic Diseases that Block China from Achieving Modernization and Integrating with the World" (*Fangai zhongguo rongru shijie shixian xiandaihua de liang da wan zheng*), *Nanfang Zhoumo* (Southern Weekly) (November 27, 2001); or Zhu Xueqin, "From Macartney's Trip to China to China's entry into the WTO" (*Cong magaerni fang hua dao zhongguo jiaru wto*), *Nanfang Zhoumo* (Southern Weekly) (November 29, 2001).

10. An article critical of the Party's and Jiang Zemin's reconceptualization of socialism for the purpose of incorporating private entrepreneurs into the Party, dated July 15, 2001, was widely circulated on the Internet. This article was written in the name of Hu Angang, an outstanding policy analyst known for his concern about the state's financial capacity. Hu denied the authorship later on. The article incurred widespread discussion nonetheless.

11. They include Han Deqiang, Zuo Dapei, Wang Shaoguang, Lu Dequan, Yang Fang, and Shao Lixin.

12. The literature generally shares the concern about the ethnic moving in, see Stephen Castles and Alastair Davidson, *Citizenship and Migration: Globalization and the Politics of Belonging* (London: Routledge, 2000); Alan Wolfe, "The Return of the Melting Pot," *The New Republic* 31 (December 1990); Nevzat Soguk, *States and Strangers: Refugees and Displacements of Statecraft* (Minneapolis: University of Minnesota Press,

1999); Bonnie Honig, *Democracy and the Foreigner* (Princeton: Princeton University Press, 2001).

13. See the discussion by Bonnie Honig in "Ruth, the Model Emigré: Mourning and the Symbolic Politics of Immigration," in D. Campbell and M. J. Shapiro (eds.), *Moral Spaces: Rethinking Ethics and World Politics* (Minneapolis: University of Minnesota Press, 1999), pp. 184–210.

14. Australia, New Zealand, and Israel.

15. For the experiences of expatriates, see Jan Selmer, *General Adjustment, Interaction Adjustment, Work Adjustment, and Subjective Well-being of Western Expatriate Managers in China* (Hong Kong: Business Research Center, School of Business, Hong Kong Baptist University, 1996).

16. A point also raised by Honig, see Donald Winnicott, "Transitional Objects and Transitional Phenomenon," in R. Minsky (ed.), *Psychoanalysis and Gender* (London: Routledge, 1996).

17. James Der Derian, *Anti-Diplomacy: Spies, Speed, Terror and War* (Oxford: Blackwell, 1992).

18. See Samuel Kim, *China, the United Nations and World Order* (Princeton: Princeton University Press, 1979).

19. For a detailed account of the thought fluctuation, see Ma Licheng and Ling Zhijun, *Crossfire: Accounts of Thought Liberation in Contemporary China (Jiaofeng: dangdai zhongguo sixiang jiefang shilu)* (Beijing: Jinri Zhongguo, 1998)

20. For one example, Chinese Social Science Academy (ed.), *The Call of Chinese Humanistic Spirit (Zhonghua renwen jinshen de huhuan)* (Beijing: Jiouzhou, 1998); for another, see Yan Jin et al. (eds.), *Chinese and Western Economic Conceptions and Modernization (Zhong xi fang jingji guan yu xiandaihua)* (Shanghai: Shanghai Social Science Academy, 1999); for a third, see Chinese Social Science Academy (ed.), *The Call of Chinese National Cultural Spirit (Zhonghua minzu wenhua jinshen de huhuan)* (Beijing: Jingji Guanli Press, 2000).

21. Li Shitao (ed.), *The Positions of Intellectuals (Zhishifenzi lichang)* (Changchuen: Times Art, 2000).

22. A cartoon on the first page of *Washington Post* on July 1, 1997, shows that the Chinese are adopting Boxer Mike Tyson's way in treating the British. This was right after Tyson bite his opponent's ear. In the drawing, the Chinese had a whole mouth of Tyson's teeth while the British have an injured ear.

23. No English newspapers I read (over 20) failed to discuss the implications of Chinese troops entering Hong Kong.

24. "Hong Kong—'Safeguard': Chinese Promise Early Elections," *The Times* (June 30, 1997): 1.

25. For example, see Jonathan Unger (ed.), *Chinese Nationalism* (Armonk, NY: M. E. Sharpe, 1996); Zheng Yongnian, *Discovering Chinese Nationalism in China: Modernization, Identity and International Relations* (Cambridge: Cambridge University Press, 1999).

26. James Sasser interviewed in "Rocks, Paint and MREs: Under Siege The U.S. ambassador's firsthand account of the attack on the Beijing embassy," *Newsweek* (May 24, 1999).

27. I discuss reflexive Orientalism in *Negotiating Ethnicity in China* (London: Routledge, 2002), ch. 4.

28. Chih-yu Shih, "How Ethnic is Ethnic Education: The Issue of School Enrollment in Meigu's Yi Community," *Prospect Quarterly* 2, 3 (July 2001).

29. Chih-yu Shih, "Between the Mosque and the State," *Religion, State and Society* 28, 2 (June 2000).

30. Song Qiang, Zhang Zangzang, and Qiao Bian, *China Can Say No* (*Zhongguo keyi shuo bu*) (Beijing: Zhonghua Gong Shang Lianhe Press, 1996); they published *China Still Can Say No* two years later; also see Shen Jiru, *China Is Not Mr. No* (*Zhongguo budang bu xiansheng*) (Beijing: Jinri Zhongguo Press, 1998).

31. Richard Maxwell, "Technologies of National Desire," in M. Shapiro and H. R. Alker (eds.), *Challenging Boundaries* (Minneapolis: University of Minnesota Press, 1996), pp. 327–351.

32. It is implied in the choice of people regarding the price they are willing to pay for nationalism or the choice of the government regarding the cost it is willing to bear to mobilize nationalism.

33. Translated from French by Aaron Asher (New York: Harper Perennial, 1996).

34. For the emergence of postmodern identity under a similar circumstance, see David Michael Green, "The End of Identity? The Implications of Postmodernity for Political Identification," *Nationalism & Ethnic Politics* 6, 3 (Autumn 2000): 68–90.

35. This is an argument symbolized by the bestseller in political science, Francis Fukuyama, *The End of History and the Last Man* (New York: Aron, 1992); also see Alan Charles Kros, "The West at the Dawn of the 21 Century: Triumph without Self-belief," *Watch on the West* 2, 1 (February 2001); for criticism, see David Campbell, *National Deconstruction: Violence, Identity and Justice in Bosnia* (Minneapolis: University of Minnesota Press, 1998); or Yosef Lapid and Friedrich Kratochwil, "Revisiting the 'National': Toward an Identity Agenda in Neorealism?" in Y. Lapid and F. Kratochwil (eds.), *The Return of Culture and Identity in IR Theory* (Boulder: Lynne Rienner, 1996), pp. 105–126.

36. For example, see Deng Zhenglai, *Research and Reflections* (*Yanjiu yu fansi*) (Shengyang: Liaoning University Press, 1998), especially chs. 2–3; see also Brantly Womack, "Transfigured Community: New-Traditionalism and Work Unit Socialism in China," *China Quarterly* 126 (June 1991).

7 The Confucian Clue: Practicing Anti-Negotiation Toward Taiwan

1. See, e.g., Martha Cottam, *Images and Intervention* (Pittsburgh: University of Pittsburgh Press, 1994); Yaacov Vertzberger, *The World in Their Minds* (Stanford: Stanford University Press, 1990); Bruce Mazlish, *The Revolutionary Ascetic* (New York: Basic Books, 1976).

2. See, e.g., Kenneth Waltz, *Theory of International Politics* (Menlo Park, A: Addison-Wesley, 1979); Immanuel Wallerstein, *The Capitalist World Economy* (Cambridge: Cambridge University Press, 1979).

3. See Theda Skocpol, *States and Social Revolutions* (Cambridge: Cambridge University Press, 1979), ch. 1.

4. For further discussion, see Samuel Kim, "New Directions and Old Puzzles in Chinese Foreign Policy," in S. Kim (ed.), *China and the World* (Boulder: Westview, 1994), pp. 16–20; Michael Ng-Quinn, "Effects of Bipolarity in Chinese Foreign Policy," *Survey* 26, 2 (1982): 102–130; Richard Wich, *Sino-Soviet Crisis Politics* (Cambridge: Harvard University Press, 1980).

5. See the discussion in Quansheng Zhao, *Interpreting Chinese Foreign Policy* (Oxford: Oxford University Press, 1996); Chih-yu Shih, *The Spirit of Chinese Foreign Policy* (London: Macmillan, 1990).

6. For nontraditional writers in this regard, see Alexander Wendt, "Collective Identity Formation and the International State," *American Political Science Review* 88, 2 (1994): 84–96; Ira J. Cohen, *Structuration Theory* (New York: St. Martin, 1989); Anthony Giddens, *The Constitution of Society* (Berkeley: University of California Press, 1986).

7. See John Ruggie, *Winning the Peace* (New York: Columbia University Press, 1998); and his "Continuity and Transformation in the World Polity," *World Politics* 35, 2 (1983): 261–285.

8. See various chapters in Yosef Lapid and Friedrich Kratochwil (eds.), *The Return of Culture and Identity in IR Theory* (Boulder: Lynne Rienner, 1996).

9. For an effective critique, see Carol Gilligan, *Mapping the Moral Domain* (Cambridge: Harvard University Press, 1988).

10. For further analysis from this perspective, see James Der Derian and Michael Shapiro (eds.), *International/Intertexual Relations* (Lexington: Lexington Books, 1989); Jean Bethke Elshtain, *Women and War* (New York: Basic Books, 1987).

11. See his "On Zhou Enlai" (*Lun zhou enlai*), *Bandit Information Monthly* (*Fei qing yuebao*) 15, 5 (July 1983); *Collected Work on the Problems of Communist China* (*Zhonggong wenti lunji*) (Taipei: Institute of International Relations, 1976).

12. This is what is called "the discursive overkill of the social and the political as volunteered by social scientists." For a critical review of the work of Chinese political scientists from the postcolonial perspectives, see Fred Y. L. Chiu, "Politics and the Body Social in Colonial Hong Kong," in

T. Barlow (ed.), *Formations of Colonial Modernity in East Asia* (Durham: Duke University Press, 1997), especially pp. 302–309.

13. See the articles collected in Tun-jen Cheng, Chi Hwang, and Samuel Wu (eds.), *The Inherited Rivalry* (Boulder: Lynne Rienner, 1994); Forum: The Taiwan Crisis, *The China Journal* 36 (July 1997): 87–134.

14. Robert Lifton, *Revolutionary Immortality* (New York: Random House, 1969); Lucian Pye, *The Spirit of Chinese Politics* (Cambridge: MIT Press, 1968); Richard Solomon, *Mao's Revolution and the Chinese Political Culture* (Berkeley: University of California Press, 1968)

15. See his enlightening piece, "China: Erratic State, Frustrated Society," *Foreign Affairs* 69, 4 (1990).

16. The poverty of language of a similar sort is common in all postcolonial areas, see Gayatri Chakravorty Spivak, "Can the Subaltern Speak?" in P. Williams and L. Chrisman (eds.), *Colonial Discourse and Post-Colonial Theory* (New York: Columbia University Press, 1994).

17. *Issues & Studies* contains most articles in this regard, see, e.g., Ming Xia, "U.S.-PRC Trade-Related Negotiations," *Issues & Studies* 32, 4 (April 1996): 61–88; Milton Yeh and Liang Yu-ying, "Beijing's Negotiation Habits as Seen from the Talks over Hong Kong's New Airport Project," *Issues & Studies* 31, 5 (May 1995); Sheng Lijun, "Peking-Washington Bargaining, 1981–84," *Issues & Studies* 30, 6 (June 1994).

18. For a social scientific discussion of how human relations constrain Chinese social behavior, see Kwang-kuo Hwang, "Face and Favor," *American Journal of Sociology* 92, 4 (1987).

19. This is thoroughly analyzed in Lucian Pye, *The Dynamics of Chinese Politics* (Cambridge: Oelgeschlage, Gunn & Hain, 1981).

20. *Heqin* was popular between the Chinese court and its neighboring nations throughout history; *dianzhi* prevailed during the Spring–Autumn Period and the Warring Period; and the Communist Party in China during the 1950s and the 1960s most frequently practiced *jiaoxin*.

21. This helps explain why Chinese People's Congresses at all levels are always docile during sessions, see Kevin O'Brien, *Reform without Liberalization* (Cambridge: Cambridge University Press, 1990).

22. This is politics of performing (*biaoxian*). For more discussion, see Andrew Walder, *Communist Neo-traditionalism* (Berkeley: University of California Press, 1986).

23. For further analysis, see Richard Solomon, *Chinese Political Negotiating Behavior, 1967–1984* (Santa Monica: Rand, 1995). Solomon notes, "the Chinese instinctively seek to enmesh the foreign negotiator in the same web of attractions and pressure that operate in their own society and political system," p. 9.

24. See Martha Cottam, "Image Change and Problem Presentation after the Cold War," presented at the International Studies Association Annual Meeting, Washington D.C. (March 29–April 1, 1994).

25. See James Der Derian, *Antidiplomacy* (Cambridge: Blackwell, 1992); and also his *On Diplomacy* (Oxford: Blackwell, 1987).

26. See Chih-yu Shih, "Democratic Personality," presented at International Congress of Applied Psychology annual Meeting, San Francisco (August 9–14, 1998).

27. A similar psychology is found in the Chinese gift-giving behavior, see Mayfair Yang, *Gifts, Favors and Banquets* (Ithaca: Cornell University Press, 1994).

28. One observer calls the Chinese selfless drama a show of flexible rigidity, see Zhao Quansheng, "Achieving Maximum Advantage," presented at the American Political Science Association Annual Meeting, San Francisco (September 1, 1990).

29. For further discussion of Chinese moral politics, see Chih-yu Shih, "The Decline of China's Moral Regime," *Comparative Political Studies* 27, 2 (July 1994).

30. The Institute of Diplomacy in Beijing has all these principles written down in an unpublished textbook, which was later printed for the public in 1993, see Xie Yixian, *Diplomatic Wisdom and Stratagem* (*Waijiao zhihui yu moulyue*) (Zhengzhou: Henan People's Press, 1993).

31. Although clothed with an entirely different interpretation, this style of unilateral withdrawal is noted in Steve Chan, "Chinese Conflict Calculus and Behavior," *World Politics* 30 (April 1978): 391–410.

32. For a classic analysis, see Franz Schurmann, *Ideology and Organization in Communist China* (Berkeley: University of California, 1968).

33. This is also a noteworthy style in Beijing's Taiwan policy, see Yun-han Chu, "Making Sense of Beijing's Policy Toward Taiwan," presented at An International Conference on the PRC After the Fifteenth Party Congress, Taipei (February 20, 1998).

34. Lin Biao was condemned specifically for mistaking an adventurist policy for a revolutionary position, see Xie, op. cit., pp. 65–67.

35. Ibid., pp. 265–266.

36. For a rundown of these labels, refer to *Collection of Original Materials Concerning the Dispute between China and Russia, 1966–1969*, all volumes (*Fei e douzheng yuanshi ziliao huibian*) (Taipei: Institute of International Relations, 1967–1971).

37. See ibid., for all those synonymous names.

38. Thus on human rights issues, China is self-portrayed as a victim of imperialism, see State Council, *The Human Rights Situation in China* (*Zhongguo de renquan zhuangkuang*) (Beijing: Central Literature Press, 1991). For a further analysis, see Ann Kent, *Between Freedom and Subsistence* (Oxford: Oxford University Press, 1993).

39. See Jonathan Adelman and Chih-yu Shih, *Symbolic War* (Taipei: Institute of International Relations, 1992)

40. Ibid., pp. 210–216.

41. Ibid., pp. 201–206.

42. See various perspectives on this issue in Peter Nan Ness (ed.), *Debating Human Rights* (New York: Routledge, 1998).

43. Chen yi, a veteran Chinese diplomat who died 20 years ago is praised today precisely because of his fearless performance in front of imperialism, see Wang Jingke, *The Diplomatic Art of Chen Yi (Chen yi de waijiao yishu)* (Jinan: Shandong University Press, 1994).

44. For more details, see Xie Yixian, *Engagement and Coexistence (Zhechong yu gongchu)* (Zhengzhou: Henan People's Press, 1990).

45. These talks are recorded in *New China Monthly* (April 1979) and subsequent issues.

46. Longsheng Gu, Introduction to *Mao Zedong's Economic Thought (Mao zedong jingji sixiang yinlun)* (Taiyuan: Shanxi Economic Press, 1992), p. 173.

47. Ibid., pp. 173–176.

48. Ibid., p. 281.

49. Ibid., p. 261.

50. For more details, see Qizhi Lai, *All Aspects of Chris Patten's Political Reform Programs (Peng dingkang zhenggai fangan mianmian guan)* (Hong Kong: Guangyu Press, 1993).

51. The one China principle is noted in both *Shanghai Communiqué* and *Normalization Communiqué* between Beijing and Washington.

52. *The National Unification Guidelines* calls Beijing to recognize Taipei as an equal entity with international legal status.

53. The National Unification Commission in 1992 passed the clarification.

54. A peace approach first appeared in 1954, but only after 1979 Sino-U.S. rapprochement did Beijing seriously promote a peaceful solution to ending China's Civil War. Chairman of People's Congress Ye Jianying announced a nine-point conciliatory statement on January 1, 1979 to call for the reunification of China, followed by Deng Xiaoping's six-point statement in 1983 to a similar effect.

55. This loyalty performance parallels what Tani Barlow calls colonial modernity, see her edited volume, *Formations of Colonial Modernity in East Asia* (Durham: Duke University Press, 1997), Introduction.

56. All this targeted President Lee Teng-hui personally, see Jiang Dianming (ed.), *Taiwan 1995* (Beijing: Jiouzhou Books, 1996), pp. 482–505.

57. See Keith Richburg, "Lee Stands Firm on 'Independent' Taiwan," *The Washington Post* (November 8, 1997): A1.

58. Noted by Wang Daohan, a senior statesman then heading the board of directors of the Association for Cross-Taiwan Strait Exchanges, see *China Times* (November 17, 1997): 1.

59. Lee Teng-hui made this remark on December 20, 1997. See *China Times* (December 21, 1997): 1, 3; or *United Daily* (December 21, 1997): 1, 3.

60. The opposition as well as the ruling party seems to share this problematic, for more information on the opposition's China policy, see *Symposium of Democratic Progressive Party Conference on China Policy*

(*Minzhu jinbu dang zhongguo zhengce yantaohui yuhuidaibiao shumian yijian huibian*) (Taipei: Party Center, Democratic Progressive Party, February 13–15, 1998).

61. For a summary of Taipei's China policy, see King-yu Chang, *Cross-Strait Relations* (Taipei: Mainland Affairs Council, 1997).

62. *Symposium*, op. cit., pp. 148–150.

63. For more information, see the joint press statement by President Clinton and President Jiang Zemin.

REFERENCES

Adelman, Jonathan and Chih-yu Shih (1993), *Symbolic War: The Chinese Use of Force, 1840–1980* (Taipei: Institute of International Relations).

Adsen, Richard (1995), *China and the American Dream* (Berkeley: University of California Press).

Ah, Ying (1959), "On the National Crisis of the Year of Geng Zi" (*Geng zi guo bian ji*) in editors n.a., *Literature on the Incident of the Year of Gengzi* (*Gengzi shijian wenxian ji*) (Beijing: Chinese Bookstore), pp. 947–951.

Anderson, Benedic (1983), *Imagined Communities* (London: Verso).

Anderson, James H. (1999), "Tensions Across the Strait," *The Heritage Foundation Backgrounder* 1328 (September 28).

Appiah, Kwame Anthony (1992), *In My Father's House: Africa in the Philosophy of Culture* (Oxford: Oxford University Press).

Arnason, Johann P. (1990), "Nationalism, Globalization and Modernity," in M. Featherstone (ed.), *Global Culture: Nationalism, Globalization and Modernity* (London: Sage), pp. 207–236.

Ashley, Richard (1988) "Untying the Sovereign State: A Double Reading of the Anarchy Problematique," *Millennium* 17: 227–263.

Barlow, Tani (1997), "Introduction," in T. Barlow (ed.), *Formations of Colonial Modernity in East Asia* (Durham: Duke University Press).

Bartelson, Jens (1995), *A Genealogy of Sovereignty* (Cambridge: Cambridge University Press).

Bell, D. A., D. Brown, K. Jayasuriya and D. M. Jones (eds.) (1995), *Towards Illiberal Democracy in Pacific Asia* (New York: St. Martin's Press).

Bell, Wendell (1974), "New States in the Caribbean: A General Theoretical Account," in S. N. Eisenstadt and S. Rokkan (eds.), *Building States and Nations* II (London: Sage, 1973), pp. 177–209.

Bennett, Gordon (1979), "Traditional, Modern and Revolutionary Values on New Social Groups in China," in Richard Wilson et al. (eds.), *Value Change in Chinese Society* (New York: Routledge).

Berger, Samuel (1997), "Building a New Consensus on China," delivered at the Council on Foreign Relations (New York: June 6) at the website, www.ait.gov.tw.

Bernstein, Richard and Ross H. Munro (1997), *The Coming Conflict with China* (New York: Alfred A. Knopf).

Bhabha, Homi K. (Summer 1993), "The World and the Home," *Social Text* 31–32: 141–153.

Birch, Anthony H. (1989), *Nationalism & National Integration* (London: Unwin Hyman).

Blaney, David and Naeem Inayatullah (1996), "Knowing Ecounters," in Yosef Lapid and Friedrich Kratochwil (eds.), *The Return of Culture and Identity in IR Theory* (Boulder: Lynne Rienner).

Bloom, William (1990), *Personal Identity, National Identity and International Relations* (Cambridge: Cambridge University Press).

Brommelhorster, Jorn and John Frankenstein (1997), *Mix Motives, Uncertain Outcomes: Defense Conversion in China* (Boulder: Lynne Rienner).

Burchill, Scott and Andrew Linklater (eds.) (1996), *Theories of International Relations* (New York: St. Martin's Press), pp. 188–193.

Buzan, Barry (1993), "From International System to International Society: Structural Realism and Regime Theory Meet the English School," *International Organization* 47: 327–352.

Campbell, David (1992), *Writing Security: United States Foreign Policy and the Politics of Identity* (Minneapolis: Minnesota University Press).

Campbell, David (1996), "Political Prosaics, Transversal Politics, and the Anarchical World," in M. J. Shapiro and H. R. Alker (eds.), *Challenging Boundaries* (Minneapolis: University of Minnesota Press), pp. 7–31.

Campbell, David (1998), *National Deconstruction: Violence, Identity and Justice in Bosnia* (Minneapolis: University of Minneapolis Press).

Carr E. H. (1945), *Nationalism and After* (New York: Macmillan).

Castles, Stephen and Alastair Davidson (2000), *Citizenship and Migration: Globalization and the Politics of Belonging* (London: Routledge).

Chan, Steve (1978), "Chinese Conflict Calculus and Behavior," *World Politics* 30 (April): 391–410.

Chang, King-yu (1997), *Cross-Strait Relations* (Taipei: Mainland Affairs Council).

Chang, Parris and Martin Lasater (eds.) (1993), *If China Crosses the Taiwan Strait* (Lanham, MD: University Press of America).

Chao, Linda and Ramon Myers (1997), *The First Chinese Democracy* (Baltimore: The Johns Hopkins University Press).

Chen, Chih-chi (1993), *Chinese Diplomatic History* (*Zhongguo waijiao shi*) (Taipei: Nantian).

Chen, Kuo-hsing (1997), "Caution Conflict Called upon the Pass of China's National Defense Act" (*Dui zhongguo zhiding guofang fa ying you de jingti*), *Taiwan Times* (March 10): 4.

Chen, Shih-min (1992), *The Origin and the Evolution of China's Nuclear Strategy* (*Zhonggong hewu zhanlyue de xingcheng yu zhuanbian*), Masters Thesis (Graduate Institute of Political Science, National Taiwan University, Taipei).

Chen, Xiao-mei (1995), *Occidentalism* (Oxford: Oxford University Press).

Cheng, Tun-jen, Hwang Chi and Wu Samuel (eds.) (1994), *The Inherited Rivalry* (Boulder: Lynne Rienner).

Chiang, Wei-kuo (1979), *The History of National Revolution* (*Guomin geming shi*) (Taipei: Liming).

Chinese Communist Party Center Literature Commission (ed.) (1994), *Selected Work of Deng, Xiaoping, III* (*Deng xiaoping wen xuan*) (Beijing: People's Press).

Chinese Social Science Academy (ed.) (1998), *The Call of Chinese Humanistic Spirit* (*Zhonghua renwen jinshen de huhuan*) (Beijing: Jiouzhou).

Chinese Social Science Academy (ed.) (2000), *The Call of Chinese National Cultural Spirit* (*Zhonghua minzu wenhua jinshen de huhuan*) (Beijing: Jingji Guanli Press).

Chiu, Fred Y. L. (1997), "Politics and the Body Social in Colonial Hong Kong," in T. Barlow (ed.), *Formations of Colonial Modernity in East Asia* (Durham: Duke University Press).

Chu, Yun-han (1998), "Making Sense of Beijing's Policy Toward Taiwan," presented at An International Conference on the PRC After the Fifteenth Party Congress, Taipei (February 20).

Cui, Zhiqin (1994), "The Dangerous Tendency in the Lee Teng-hui Group's Mainland China Policy" (*Li denghui jituan dalu zhengce de weixian dongxiang*), presented at the 4th Annual Meeting of the Scholarly Exchange Between the Two Sides of the Taiwan Straits (Beijing: August 1–6).

Cohen, Ira J. (1989), *Structuration Theory* (New York: St. Martin's Press).

Cottam, Martha and Chih-yu Shih (1992), *Contending Dramas: A Cognitive Approach to International Organizations* (New York: Praeger).

Cottam, Martha (1994), "Image Change and Problem Presentation after the Cold War," presented at the International Studies Association Annual Meeting, Washington D.C. (March 29–April 1, 1994).

Cottam, Martha (1994), *Images and Intervention* (Pittsburgh: University of Pittsburgh Press).

Cui, Yuchen (1996), *The Nascent Contention in Fighting for the Soft Border Lines* (*Zheng duo ran bian jiang de xin jiaozhu*), *Modern National Defense Series* (Chengdu: Sichuan Education Press).

Cvetkovich, Ann and Douglas Kellner (eds.) (1997), *Articulating the Global and the Local: Globalization and Cultural Studies* (Boulder: Westview).

Deng, Zhenglai (1998), *Rationality and Reflections* (*Lixing yu fansi*) (Shenyang: Shenyang People's Press).

Deng, Zhenglai (1998), *Research and Reflections* (*Yanjiu yu fansi*) (Shenyang: Liaoning University Press).

Der Derian, James (1987), *On Diplomacy* (Oxford: Blackwell).

Der Derian, James (1992), *Antidiplomacy: Spies, Speed, Terror and War* (Cambridge: Blackwell).

Der Derian, James and Michael Shapiro (eds.) (1989), *International/ Intertexual Relations* (Lexington: Lexington Books).

Derrida, Jaques (1981), *Positions* (Chicago: University of Chicago Press).

Diamond, Larry (2000), "Forward," in L. Diamond (ed.), *China and Democracy: The Prospect for a Democratic China* (New York: Routledge).

Didder, Bigo (1996), "Security, Borders and the State," in A. Sweedler and J. Scott (eds.), *Border Regions in Functional Transition* (Berlin: Institute of Regional Development, IRS).

Dittmer, Lowell and Samuel Kim (eds.) (1993), *China's Quest for National Identity* (Ithaca: Cornell University Press).

Editors n.a. (1964), *Collected Literature on the PRC Foreign Relations (Zhonghua renmin gongheguo duiwai guanxi wenjian ji)*, 1962 (Beijing: World Knowledge).

Editors n.a. (1971), *Collection of Original Materials Concerning the Disputes Between Bandits and Russia (Fei e douzheng yuanshi ziliao huibian)*, Vol. 14 (Taipei: Institute of International Relations).

Editors n.a. (1979), *Selected Historical Documents on Yellow Peril (Huanghuo lun lishi ziliao xuan ji)* (Beijing: Chinese Social Science Press).

Editors n.a. (1989), *The Military Work of Contemporary Chinese Military (Dangdai zhongguo jundui de junshi gongzuo)* (Beijing: Chinese Social Science Press).

Editors n.a. (1998), *Symposium of Democratic Progressive Party Conference on China Policy (Minzhu jinbu dang zhongguo zhengce yantaohui yuhuidaibiao shumian yijian huibian)* (Taipei: Party Center, Democratic Progressive Party, February 13–15), mimeo.

Editors n.a. (1998), *Symposium of the Conference on China Policy (Min jin dang zhongguo zhengce yantaohui)* (Taipei: Democratic Progressive Party, February 13–15).

Editors n.a. (1989), *Contemporary Neo-Confucianists (Dangdai xin lujia)* (Shanghai: Sanlian).

Elshtain, Jean Bethke (1987), *Women and War* (New York: Basic Books).

Enloe, Cynthia (1990), *Bananas, Beaches and Bases* (Berkeley: University of California Press).

Enloe, Cynthia H. (1986), "Ethnicity, the State, and the New International Order," in J. F. Stack, Jr. (ed.), *The Primordial Challenge: Ethnicity in the Contemporary World* (New York: Greenwood), pp. 25–42.

Fan, Qinlin (2000), "Caveats of National Dignity and the Choice of Modern Culture" *(Minzu zizun de wuqu yu xiandai wenhua de xuanze)* in Shitao Li (ed.), *Positions of Intellectuals: Turbulence between Radicalism and Conservatism (Jijin yu baoshou zhijian de dongdang)* (Changchuen: Times Art), pp. 336–342.

Fanon, Franz (1964), "On National Culture," in F. Fanon (ed.), *The Wretched of the Earth* (New York: Grove).

Friedman, Edward (1992), *New National Identities in Post-Leninist Transformations: The Implications for China* (Hong Kong: Chinese University of Hong Kong Press).

Friedman, Edward (1995), *National Identity and the Democratic Prospects for Socialist China* (Armonk: M. E. Sharpe).

Fukuyama, Francis (1992), *The End of History and the Last Man* (New York: Aron).

Gellner, Ernest (1983), *Nations and Nationalism* (Oxford: Basil Blackwell).

George, Jim (1994), *Discourses of Global Politics* (Boulder: Lynne Rienner).

Giddens, Anthony (1986), *The Constitution of Society* (Berkeley: University of California Press).

Giles, Lancelot (1970), *The Siege of the Peking Legations: A Diary* (Nedlands: University of West Australian Press), p. 88.

Gilligan, Carol (1988), *Mapping the Moral Domain* (Cambridge: Harvard University Press).

Gilpin, Robert (1987), *The Political Economy of International Relations* (Princeton: Princeton University Press).

Gladney, Dru (1995), "Ethnic Identity in China," in W. Joseph (ed.), *China Briefing, 1994* (Boulder: Westview), pp. 171–192.

Gold, Thomas B. (1998), "Taiwan Society at *Fin de Siécle*," in D. Shambaugh (ed.), *Contemporary Taiwan* (Oxford: Oxford University Press), pp. 47–70.

Goldman, Merle (1994), *Sowing the Seeds of Democracy in China* (Cambridge: Harvard University Press).

Gong, Huiping (1989), "The Airport Meeting of Zhou Enlai and Kosygin and Its Lessons," in Pei Jianzhang (ed.), *Studying Zhou Enlai: Diplomatic Thoughts and Practices (Yanjiu zhou enlai—waijiao sixiang yu shijian)* (Beijing: World Knowledge), pp. 170–178.

Goodman, David S. G. and Gerald Segal (1997) (eds.), *China Rising: Nationalism and Interdependence* (London: Routledge).

Green, David Michael (2000), "The End of Identity? The Implications of Postmodernity for Political Identification," *Nationalism & Ethnic Politics* 6, 3 (Autumn 2000): 68–90.

Greenfeld, Liah (1992), *Nationalism: Five Roads to Modernity* (Cambridge: Harvard University Press).

Gregor, James A. and Maria Hsia Chang (1984), *The Iron Triangle* (Stanford: Hoover Institution Press).

Grieco, Joseph M. (1993), "Understanding the Problem of International Cooperation: The Limits of Neoliberal Institutionalism and the Future of Realist Theory," in D. A. Baldwin (ed.), *Neorealism and Neoliberalism: The Contemporary Debate* (New York: Columbia University Press).

Gu, Changsheng (1991), *Missionary and Modern China (Chuanjiaoshi yu jindai zhongguo)* (Shanghai: Shanghai People's Press).

Gu, Longsheng (1992), *Introduction to Mao, Zedong's Economic Thought (Mao zedong jingji sixiang yinlun)* (Taiyuan: Shanxi Economic Press).

Guibernau, Montserrat (1996), *Nationalisms: The Nation-State and Nationalism in the Twentieth Century* (Cambridge: Polity Press), pp. 143–150.

Gurtov, Melvin and Byng-Moo Hwang (1980), *China under Treat* (Baltimore: The Johns Hopkins University Press).

Hall, Stuart (1997), "The Local and the Global: Globalization and Ethnicity," in A. McClintock, A. Mufti and E. Shohat (eds.), *Dangerous Liaisons: Gender, Nation, & Postcolonial Perspectives* (Minneapolis: University of Minnesota Press), pp. 173–187.

Harris, Stuart (1998), "The PRC's Quest for Great Power Status," presented at An International Conference on the PRC After the Fifteenth Party Congress (Taipei: February 20).

Hickey, Dennis Van Vranken (1997), *Taiwan's Security in the Changing International System* (Boulder: Lynne Rienner).

Hobsbawn, Eric (1990), *Nations and Nationalism Since 1780* (Cambridge: Cambridge University Press).

Hobsbawn, Eric and Terence Ranger (eds.) (1983), *The Invention of Tradition* (Cambridge: Cambridge University Press).

Hoffmann, Stanley (1981), *Duties beyond Borders* (Syracuse: Syracuse University Press).

Holm, Jack (1985), *Mood/Interest theory of American Foreign Policy* (Lexington: University of Kentucky Press).

Honig, Bonnie (1999), "Ruth, the Model Emigré: Mourning and the Symbolic Politics of Immigration," in D. Campbell and M. J. Shapiro (eds.), *Moral Spaces: Rethinking Ethics and World Politics* (Minneapolis: University of Minnesota Press), pp. 184–210.

Honig, Bonnie (2001), *Democracy and the Foreigner* (Princeton: Princeton University Press).

Hsi, Hsian-te (1991), *The Image of the United States Presented in the Chinese Journals During the Late Qing Period (Qing mo zhongwen baokan chengxian de mei guo xing xiang)* (Taipei: Wenzhang Press).

Hsie, Ta-ning (1998), "The Origin and the Contents of the Great Unity Conception" (*Da yitong guannian de laiyuan ji qi neirong*), presented at the Conference on Prospects and Retrospect, annual meeting of the Association for Unity and Self-strengthening (Taipei: January 4).

Hu, Xiwei (1996), "Rationality and Utopia" (*Lixing yu wutuobang*) in Ruiquan Gao (ed.), *Currents of Social Thoughts in Modern China (Zhongguo jindai shehui sichao)* (Shanghai: Eastern China Normal University Press), pp. 224–250.

Hua, Yuan (1991), *Crystal Lesson from Bitter History (Tong shi ming jian)* (Beijing: Beijing Press).

Huang, Jiashu (1994), *Can Taiwan Become Independent? (Taiwan neng duli ma?), Strategic Studies Series of International Strategic Research Foundation* (Haikou: South Sea Press).

Hunt, Michael (1996), *The Genesis of Chinese Communist Foreign Policy* (New York: Columbia University Press).

Hunt, Michael H. (1993), "Chinese National Identity and the Strong State: The Late-Qing-Republican Crisis," in L. Dittmer and S. Kim (eds.), *China's Quest for National Identity* (Ithaca: Cornell University Press), pp. 62–79.

Huntington, Samuel (1968), *Political Order in Changing Societies* (New Haven: Yale University Press).

Huntington, Samuel (1996), *Clash of Civilization and the Remaking of World Order* (New York: Simon & Schuster).

Hwang Kwang-kuo (1987), "Face and Favor," *American Journal of Sociology* 92: 4.

Inayatullah, Naeem and David L. Blaney (1996), "Knowing Encounters: Beyond Parochialism in International Relations Theory," in Y. Lapid and F. Kratochwil (eds.), *The Return of Culture and Identity in IR Theory* (Boulder: Lynne Rienner), pp. 65–84.

Information Office of the State Council (2000), *Human Rights Record of the United States in 1999* (*Yijiujiujiu meiguo de ren quan jilu*), New China New Agency script (2.27).

Jiang Dianming (ed.) (1996), *Taiwan 1995* (*Taiwan 1995*) (Beijing: Jiouzhou Books).

Jin, Yuelin (1934), *The Outlet for Chinese Culture* (*Zhongguo wenhua de chulu*) (Shanghai: The Commerce Press).

Joffe, Ellis (1998), "The PLA and politics," presented at An International Conference on the PRC After the Fifteenth Party Congress (Taipei: February 19).

Johnston, Alastair Ian (1995), *Cultural Realism: Strategic Culture and Great Strategy in Ming China* (Princeton: Princeton University Press).

Kelman, Herbert (1969), "Patterns of Personal Involvement in the National System: A Social-Psychological Analysis of Political Legitimacy," in James Rosenau (ed.), *International Politics and Foreign Policy* (New York: Free Press).

Kent, Ann (1993), *Between Freedom and Subsistence: China and Human Rights* (Hong Kong: Cambridge University Press).

Keohane, Robert and Joseph Nye (1978), *Power and Interdependence* (Boston: Little, Brown & Company).

Kim, Samuel (1979), *China, the United Nations and World Order* (Princeton: Princeton University Press).

Kim, Samuel (1994), "New Directions and Old Puzzles in Chinese Foreign Policy," in S. Kim (ed.), *China and the World* (Boulder: Westview).

Kohn, Hans (1967), *The Idea of Nationalism* (New York: Collier-Macmillan).

Koichi, Nomura (1999), *The China Knowledge in Modern Japan* (*Jindai riben de zhongguo renshi*) Xuefeng Zhang (trans.) (Beijing: Central Translation and Editorial Press).

Krasner, Steven (1976), "State Power and the Structure of international Trade," *World Politics* 28: 317–347.

Krasner, Steven (1978), *Defining the National Interest* (Stanford: Stanford University Press).

Kratochwil, Friedrich (1997), "Citizenship: On the Border of Order," in Y. Lapid and F. Kratochwil (eds.), *The Return of Culture and Identity in IR Theory* (Boulder: Lynne Rienner), pp. 181–197.

Krause, Keith and Williams, Michael C. (eds.) (1997), *Critical Security Studies* (Minneapolis: University of Minnesota Press).

Krishna, Sankaran (1993), "The Improvement of Being Ironic," *Alternatives* 18: 385–417.

Kros, Alan Charles (2001), "The West at the Dawn of the 21 Century: Triumph without Self-belief," *Watch on the West* 2, 1 (February).

Kuhn, Anthony (1994), "Ping-Pong Politics," *Far Eastern Economic Review* (December 8): 44–45.

Kundera, Milan (1996), *The Book of Laughter and Forgetting*, Aaron Asher (trans.) (New York: Harper Perennial).

Kuo, Hua-lun (1976), *Collected Work on the Problems of Communist China* (*Zhonggong wenti lunji*) (Taipei: Institute of International Relations).

Kuo, Hua-lun (1983), "On Zhou Enlai" (*Lun zhou enlai*), *Bandit Information Monthly* (*Fei qing yuebao*) 15, 5 (July).

Lai, Qizhi (1993), *All Aspects of Chris Patten's Political Reform Programs* (*Peng dingkang zhenggai fangan mianmian guan*) (Hong Kong: Guangyu Press).

Laitinen, Kauko (1990), *Chinese Nationalism in the Late Qing Dynasty* (London: Curzon Press).

Landes, David S. (1961), "Some Thoughts on the Natures of Economic Imperialism," *Journal of Economic History* 21: 496–512.

Lapid, Yosef and Friedrich Kratochwil (1996), "Revisiting the 'National': Toward an Identity Agenda in Neorealism?" in Y. Lapid and F. Kratochwil (eds.), *The Return of Culture and Identity in IR Theory* (Boulder: Lynne Rienner), pp. 105–126.

Lapid, Yosef and Friedrich Kratochwil (1994), "Theorizing the 'National' in International Relations Theory," in F. Kratochwil and R. Mansfield (eds.), *International Organizations* (New York: Harper Collins).

Lapid, Yosef and Friedrich Kratochwil (1996) (eds.), *The Return of Culture and Identity in IR Theory* (Boulder: Lynne Rienner).

Li, En-han (1993), *Revolutionary Diplomacy Before and After the North Expedition, 1925–1931* (*Beifa qian hou de geming waijiao, 1925–1931*) (Taipei: The Institute of Modern History, Academic Sinica).

Li, Jaiquan (1994), "How Much Intimacy Toward the Chinese is There Left?" (*Haiyou duoshao zhongguoren de ganqing*), *Wenhui Bao* (June 10).

Li, Jiaquan (1994), "On the Root and Its Outlet of Li, Tenghui's Sense of Pity" (*Li denghui beiai de genyou ji qi chulu*), *Straits Review* (*Haixia pinglun*) 47 (November).

Li, Peng (March 20, 1992), "Report on Work of Government," mimeo.

Li, Shitao (ed.) (2000), *Positions of Intellectuals: Debates on Liberalism and the Division of Chinese Intellectual Circles* (*Zhishifenzi lichang: ziyouzhuyi zhi zheng yu zhongguo sixiang jie de fenhua*) (Changchuen: Times Art).

Li, Ting-yi (1978), *Early Sino-American Diplomatic History* (*Zhong mei zaoqi waijiao shi*) (Taipei: Chuan-chi Literature).

Li, Xiguang and Liu Kang (1996), *Behind Demonization of China* (*Yaomohua zhongguo de beihou*) (Beijing: Chinese Social Science Press).

Liang, Qichao (1984), *Selected Writings of Liang, Qichao* (*Liang qichao xuan ji*) (Shanghai: Shanghai People's Press).

Liao, Kuan-sheng (1984), *Anti-Foreignism and Modernization in China, 1860–1980* (New York: St. Martin's Press).

Lieberthal, Kenneth (1982), "The Background in Chinese Politics," in H. J. Ellison (ed.), *The Sino-Soviet Conflict* (Seattle: University of Washington Press), pp. 3–28.

Lifton, Robert (1969), *Revolutionary Immortality* (New York: Random House).

Lilley, James and David Shambaugh (1999), *China's Military Faces the Future* (Armonk: M. E. Sharpe).

Ling, Lily L. H. M. (1996), "Democratization under Internationalization: Media Reconstructions of Gender Identity in Shanghai," *Democratization* 3, 2: 140–157.

Ling, Lily L. H. M. and Chih-yu Shih (1998), "Confucianism with a Liberal Face," *Review of Politics* 60, 1: 55–82.

Liu, Hong (1994), "A Brief Note on Lee Teng-hui's Theory of 'People's Sovereignty'" (*Jian ping li denghui de zhuquan zaimin lun*), presented at the 4th Annual Meeting of the Scholarly Exchange between the Two Sides of the Taiwan Straits (Beijing: August 1–6).

Liu, Zhongxin (1991), *The Business of Blood and Fire* (*Xie yu huo de shiye*), *Modern National Defense Series* (*Xiandai guofang congshu*) (Chengdu: Sichuan Education Press).

Luo, Chuanli (1995), "The Origin and Development of Sino-French Warfare," in Chinese History Association Editors (eds.), *The Sino-French War* (*Zhong fa zhangzheng*) (Shanghai: New Knowledge Publication).

Luo, Chuanli (1959), "On the National Crisis in the Year of Gengzi" (*Gengzi guo bian ji*), in Ah Ying (ed.), *Collected Literature on the Events in the Year of Gengzi* (*Gengzi shibian wenxue ji*) (Beijing: Chinese Bookstore), pp. 945–958.

Müllerson, Rein (1997), *Human Rights Diplomacy* (New York: Routledge).

Ma, Licheng and Zhijun Ling (1998), *Battling: The Records of Three Thought Liberation Campaigns in Contemporary China* (*Jiaofeng: dangdai zhongguo san ci sixiang jiefang shilu*) (Beijing: Today's China Press).

Mancall, Mark (1984), *China at Center: 300 Years of Foreign Policy* (New York: Free Press).

Marx, Karl and Friedrich Engels (1959), *Basic Writings on Politics and Philosophy*, (ed.), L. S. Feuer (Glasgow: The Fontana Library).

Maxwell, Richard (1996), "Technologies of National Desire," in M. Shapiro and H. R. Alker (eds.), *Challenging Boundaries* (Minneapolis: University of Minnesota Press), pp. 327–351.

Mayall, James (1990), *Nationalism and International Society* (Cambridge: Cambridge University Press).

Mazlish, Bruce (1976), *The Revolutionary Ascetic* (New York: Basic Books).

Mearsheimer, John (1990), "Back to the Future: Instability in Europe After the Cold War," *International Security* 15: 5–56.

Ming, Xia (1996), "U.S.–PRC Trade-Related Negotiations," *Issues & Studies* 32, 4 (April): 61–88.

Mizoguchi, Mineo (1996), *Sinology in the Japanese Perspectives* (*Riben shiye zhong de zhongguoxue*), Li Suping, Gong Ying, Xue Tao (trans.) (Chinese People's University Press).

Nandy, Ashis (1983), *The Intimate Enemy: Loss and Recovery of Self Under Colonialism* (Oxford: Oxford University Press).

Nathan, Andrew (1990), *China's Crisis: Dilemmas of Reform and Prospect for Democracy* (New York: Columbia University Press).

Nathan, Andrew (1996), "China's Goals in the Taiwan Strait," *The China Journal* 36 (July): 87–93.

Nathan, Andrew (2000), "Chinese Democracy: The Lessons of Failure," in L. Diamond (ed.), *China and Democracy: The Prospect for a Democratic China* (New York: Routledge).

Nathan, Andrew and Robert Ross (1997), *The Great Wall and Empty Fortress* (New York: W. W. Norton).

Naughton, Barry (1994), "The Foreign Policy Implications of China's Economic Development Strategy," in T. Robinson and D. Shambaugh (eds.), *Chinese Foreign Policy* (Oxford: Oxford University).

Ng-Quinn, Michael (1982), "Effects of Bipolarity in Chinese Foreign Policy," *Survey* 26, 2: 102–130.

O'Brien, Kevin (1990), *Reform without Liberalization* (Cambridge: Cambridge University Press).

Pei, Minxin (1994), *From Reform to Revolution* (Cambridge: Harvard University Press).

Peng, Dehuai (1959), "A Letter to the Taiwanese," October 25, 1958, *The People's Republic of China Foreign Relations Documents 1958* (*Zhonghua renmin gongheguo duiwai guanxi wenjianji*) (Beijing: World Konwledge), p. 182.

Peterson, Spike V. (1992), *Feminist (Re)Visions of International Relations Theory* (Boulder: Lynne Rienner).

Posen, Barry (1993), "The Security Dilemma and Ethnic Conflict," *Survival* 35, 1: 27–47.

Pye, Lucian (1968), *The Spirit of Chinese Politics* (Cambridge: MIT Press).

Pye, Lucian (1981), *The Dynamics of Chinese Politics* (Cambridge: Oelgeschlage, Gunn & Hain).

Pye, Lucian (1990), "China: Erratic State, Frustrated Society," *Foreign Affairs* 69, 4: 56–74.

Pye, Lucian (1991), "The State and the Individual," *China Quarterly* 127: 443–466.

Pye, Lucian (1993), "How China's Nationalism Was Shanghaied," *The Australian Journal of Chinese Affairs* 29.

Pyle, Kenneth B. (1969), *The New Generation in Meiji Japan: Problems of Cultural Identity, 1885–1895* (Stanford: Stanford University Press).

Pyle, Kenneth B. (1987), "In Pursuit of a Grand Design: Nakasone Betwix the Past and the Future," *Journal of Japanese Studies* 13, 2.

Qian, Qichen (1989), "Seriously Studying Zhou Enlai's Diplomatic Thoughts and Practices," in Jianzhang Pei (ed.), *Studying Zhou Enlai: Diplomatic Thoughts and Practices* (*Yanjiu zhou enlai—waijiao sixiang yu shijian*) (Beijing: World Knowledge).

Records of Barbarian Affairs (*Duban yiwu shimo*), Daoguang years.

Reinharz, Jehua and George L. Mosse (eds.) (1992), *The Impact of Western Nationalisms* (New Delhi: Sage).

Richardson, Lewis F. (1960), *Armaments and Security* (Pittsburgh: The Boxwood Press).

Richburg, Keith (1997), "Lee Stands Firm on 'Independent' Taiwan," *The Washington Post* (November 8): A1.

Ross, Robert (1991), "China Learns to Compromise," *The China Quarterly* 128: 742–773.

Ross, Robert (1995), *Negotiating Cooperation* (Stanford: Stanford University Press).

Ruggie, John (1983), "Continuity and Transformation in the World Polity," *World Politics* 35, 2: 261–185.

Ruggie, John (1998), *Winning the Peace* (New York: Columbia University Press).

Said, Edward (1978), *Orientalism* (New York: Random House).

Said, Edward (1991), *Culture and Imperialism* (New York: Vintage Books).

Schlesinger, Arthur (1986), *The Cycles of American History* (Boston: Houghton Mifflin).

Schlesinger, Arthur (1992), *The Disuniting of America: Reflections on a Multicultural Society* (New York: Norton).

Schurmann, Franz (1968), *Ideology and Organization in Communist China* (Berkeley: University of California).

Segal, Gerald (1985), *Defending China* (Oxford: Oxford University Press).

Segal, Gerald (ed.) (1982), *The China Factor* (London: Croom Helm).

Segal, Gerald and David Goodman (1994), *China Deconstructs* (New York: Routledge).

Selmer, Jan (1996), *General Adjustment, Interaction Adjustment, Work Adjustment, and Subjective Well-being of Western Expatriate Managers in China* (Hong Kong: Business Research Center, School of Business, Hong Kong Baptist University).

Shapiro, Michael J. (1999), "The Ethics of Encounter: Unreading, Unmapping the Imperium," in D. Campbell and M. J. Shapiro (eds.), *Moral Spaces: Rethinking Ethics and World Politics* (Minneapolis: University of Minnesota Press).

Shapiro, Michael J. and Hayward R. Alker (eds.) (1995), *Challenge Boundaries* (Minneapolis: University of Minnesota Press).

Sharman, Lyon (1968), *Sun Yat-sen: His Life and Its Meaning* (Stanford: Stanford University Press).

Shen, Jiru (1998), *China Is Not Mr. No* (*Zhongguo budang bu xiansheng*) (Beijing: Jinri Zhongguo Press).

Sheng, Lijun (1994), "Peking-Washington Bargaining, 1981–84," *Issues & Studies* 30, 6 (June).

Shih, Chih-yu (1990), *The Spirit of Chinese Foreign Policy: A Psychocultural View* (London: Macmillan).

Shih, Chih-yu (1993), *China's Just World: The Morality of Chinese Foreign Policy* (Boulder: Lynne Rienner).

Shih, Chih-yu (1994), "The Decline of China's Moral Regime," *Comparative Political Studies* 27, 2 (July).

Shih, Chih-yu (1996), "How Flexible is Peking's Foreign Policy?" in B. Lin and J. Myers (eds.), *Contemporary China in the Post-Cold War Era* (University of South Carolina Press), pp. 306–327.

Shih, Chih-yu (1998), "Democratic Personality," presented at International Congress of Applied Psychology Annual Meeting, San Francisco (August 9–14, 1998).

Shih, Chih-yu (1998), "A Postcolonial Reading of Cross-Strait Relations," *The Journal of Contemporary China* 17, 7 (January): 125–139.

Shih, Chih-yu (1999), *Collective Democracy* (Hong Kong: The Chinese University Press).

Shih, Chih-yu (2000), "Between the Mosque and the State," *Religion, State and Society* 28, 2 (June 2000).

Shih, Chih-yu (2000), *Reform, Identity and Chinese Foreign Policy* (Taipei: Vanguard Institute for Policy Studies).

Shih, Chih-yu (2001), "How Ethnic is Ethnic Education: The Issue of School Enrollment in Meigu's Yi Community," *Prospect Quarterly* 2, 3 (July).

Shih, Chih-yu (2002), *Negotiating Ethnicity in China* (London: Routledge).

Shih, Chih-yu (2002), "The Eros of International Politics: Madame Chiang Kaishek and the State Question in China," *Comparative Civilizations Review* 46 (Spring): 91–119.

Shih, Liuzi (ed.) (1997), *The Ten-thousand-Word and Other Underground Writings in Beijing (Beijing dixia wan yan shu)* (Hong Kong: Mirror Books).

Siglev, Stelin (1996), *The Empire of the Dragon (Long de diguo)* (Taipei: Think Tank).

Simond, Frank H. and Brooks Emeny (1939), *The Great Powers in World Politics: International Relations and Economic Nationalism* (New York: American Book Company).

Skocpol, Theda (1979), *States and Social Revolutions* (Cambridge: Cambridge University Press).

Smelser, Neil J. (1998), "The Rational and the Ambivalent in the Social Sciences," *American Sociological Review* 63: 1–16.

Smith, Anthony (1981), *The Ethnic Revival in the Modern World* (Cambridge: Cambridge University Press).

Smith, Anthony (1992), "Nationalism and the Historians," *International Journal of Comparative Sociology* 33, 1–2: 55–80.

Snow, Philip (1988), *The Star Raft: China's Encounter with Africa* (New York: Weidenfeld & Nicolson).

Soguk, Nevzat (1999), *States and Strangers: Refugees and Displacements of Statecraft* (Minneapolis: University of Minnesota Press).

Solinger, Dorothy J. (ed.) (1983), *Three Visions of Chinese Socialism* (Boulder: Westview).

Solinger, Dorothy (1984), *China's Business under Socialism* (Berkeley: University of California).

Solomon, Richard (1968), *Mao's Revolution and the Chinese Political Culture* (Berkeley: University of California Press).

Solomon, Richard (1995), *Chinese Political Negotiating Behavior, 1967–1984* (Santa Monica: Rand).

Song, Qiang, Zhang Zangzang and Bian Qiao (1995), *China Can Say No (Zhongguo keyi shuo bu)* (Beijing: Zhonghua Gong Shang Lianhe Press).

Spivak, Gayatri Chakravorty (1994), "Can the Subaltern Speak?" in P. Williams and L. Chrisman (eds.), *Colonial Discourse and Post-Colonial Theory* (New York: Columbia University Press). Also in C. Nelson and L. Grossberg (eds.) (1998), *Marxism and Interpretation of Culture* (Chicago: University of Illinois Press).

Spokesman of the Foreign Ministry (1959), "A Declaration Concerning the Stopping of Shelling of Quemoy," *The People's Republic of China Foreign Relations Documents 1958 (Zhonghua renmin gongheguo duiwai guanxi wenjianji)* (Beijing: World Knowledge), p. 178.

State Council of the People's Republic of China (1991), *Human Rights in China* (Beijing: Information Office of the State Council).

State Council of the People's Republic of China (1991), *The Human Rights Situation in China (Zhongguo de renquan zhuangkuang)* (Beijing: Central Literature Press).

Stolper, Thomas (1985), *China, Taiwan, and the Offshore Island* (New York: M. E. Sharpe).

Tamir, Yael (1993), *Liberal Nationalism* (Princeton: Princeton University Press).

The Headquarter of the Chinese People Opposing America, Assisting Korea Movement (ed.) (1954), *The Great Opposing American, Assisting Korea Movement (Weida de kang mei yuan chao yundong)* (Beijing: New China Bookstore).

Tickner, Ann (1992), *Gender in International Politics* (New York: Columbia University Press).

Townsend, James (1992), "Chinese Nationalism," *The Australian Journal of Chinese Affairs* 27.

Underhill-Cady, Joseph B. (1995), *Doing Battle with Death*, Ph.D. dissertation (University of Michigan, (Ann Arbor)).

Unger, Jonathan (ed.) (1996), *Chinese Nationalism* (Armonk, NY: M. E. Sharpe).

Van Ness, Peter (ed.) (1999), *Debating Human Rights* (New York: Routledge).

Van Ness, Peter and Satish Raichur (1981), "Dilemmas of Socialist Development," *Bulletin of Concerned Asian Scholars* 15, 1.

Vertzberger, Yaacov (1990), *The World in Their Minds: Information Processing, Cognition, and Perception in Foreign Policy Decisionmaking* (Stanford: Stanford University Press).

Waever, Ole Barru Bizab, Morton Kelstrup and Pieere Lematire (1993), *Identity, Migration and the New Security Agenda in Europe* (New York: St. Martin's Press).

Walder Andrew (1986), *Communist Neo-Traditionalism* (Berkeley: University of California Press).

Walker R. B. J. (1993), *Inside/Outside: International Relations as Political Theory* (Cambridge: Cambridge University Press).

Wallerstein, Immanuel (1979), *The Capitalist World Economy* (Cambridge: Cambridge University Press).

Waltz, Kenneth (1979), *Theory of International Politics* (Menlo Park, CA: Addison-Wesley).

Wang, Daohan (1997) (a senior statesman then heading the board of directors of the Association for Cross-Taiwan Strait Exchanges), *China Times* (November 17): 1.

Wang, Gongwu (1996), *The Revival of Chinese Nationalism* (Leiden: Leiden University).

Wang, Hui (1997), "The Fate of 'Mr. Science' in China: The Concept of Science and Its Application in Modern Chinese Thought," in T. Barlow (ed.), *Formations of Colonial Modernity in East Asia* (Durham: Duke University Press).

Wang, Hui (2000), "The Situation of Contemporary Chinese Thoughts and the Issue of Modernity" (*Dangdai zhongguo de sixiang zhuangkuang yu xiandaixing wenti*), in Li Shitao (ed.), *Debates on Liberalism*, (Changchuen: Times Art), pp. 83–123.

Wang, Jingke (1994), *The Diplomatic Art of Chen Yi (Chen yi de waijiao yishu)* (Jinan: Shandong University Press).

Weber, Cynthia (1995), *Simulating Sovereignty: Intervention, the State and Symbolic Intervention* (Cambridge: Cambridge University Press).

Wendt, Alexander (1992), "Anarchy is What States Make of it: The Social Construction of Power Politics," *International Organization* 46: 391–392, 397, 402, 424–426.

Wendt, Alexander (1994), "Collective Identity Formation and the International State," *American Political Science Review* 88: 384–396.

Wendt, Alexander (1999), *Social Theory of International Politics* (Cambridge: Cambridge University Press).

White, Gordon (1993), *Riding the Tiger* (Stanford: Stanford University Press).

Whiting, Allen (1960), *China Crosses the Yalu* (New York: Macmillan).

Whiting, Allen (1974), *The Chinese Calculus of Deterrence* (Ann Arbor: University of Michigan Press).

Wich, Richard (1980), *Sino-Soviet Crisis Politics* (Cambridge: Harvard University Press).

Winnicott, Donald (1996), "Transitional Objects and Transitional Phenomenon," in R. Minsky (ed.), *Psychoanalysis and Gender* (London: Routledge).

Wolfe, Alan (1990), "The Return of the Melting Pot," *The New Republic* 31 (December).

Womack, Brantly (1991), "Transfigured Community: New-Traditionalism and Work Unit Socialism in China," *China Quarterly* 126 (June).

Wong, Young-tsu (1983), *Search for Modern Nationalism: Zhang, Binglin and Revolutionary China, 1869–1936* (Hong Kong: Oxford University Press).

Wright, Quincy (1942), *The Study of War II* (Chicago: Chicago University Press).

Wu, Hsiang-hsiang (1973), *The History of the Second Sino-Japanese War* (*Di erci zhong ri zhangzheng shi*) (Taipei: Scooper Press).

Xiao, Gongqin (1998), *History has Refused Romanticism* (*Lishi jujue langman*) (Taipei: Zhiliang).

Xie, Xialing (1989), "Reinterpreting May Fourth Spirit, Absorbing Confucian Thoughts" (*Chongshi wu si jingshen, xishou luxue sixiang*), *Fudan Xuebao* 3.

Xie, Yixian (1990), *Engagement and Coexistence* (*Zhechong yu gongchu*) (Zhengzhou: Henan People's Press).

Xie, Yixian (1993), *Diplomatic Wisdom and Stratagem: The Theory and Principles of New Chinese Diplomacy* (*Waijiao zhihui yu moulyue: xin zhongguo waijiao lilun yu yuanze*) (Zhengzhou: Henan People's Press).

Xin, Jianfei (1992), *The World Views China* (*Shijie de zhongguo guan*) (Shanghai: Xuelin).

Yamazawa, Ippei and Ken-Ichi Imai (eds.) (2001), *China Enters WTO: Pursuing Symbiosis with the Global Economy* (Tokyo: Institute of Developing Economies, Japan External Trade Organization).

Yan, Jin et al. (eds.) (1999), *Chinese and Western Economic Conceptions and Modernization* (*Zhong xi fang jingji guan yu xiandaihua*) (Shanghai: Shanghai Social Science Academy).

Yang C. L. (ed.) (1973), *Collected Literature on the Sino-Japanese War* (*Zhong ri zhangzheng wenxian hui bian*) (Taipei: Tingwen Bookstore).

Yang, Mayfair (1994), *Gifts, Favors and Banquets* (Ithaca: Cornell University Press).

Yeh, Milton and Liang Yu-ying (1995), "Beijing's Negotiation Habits as Seen from the Talks over Hong Kong's New Airport Project," *Issues & Studies* 31, 5 (May).

Yuan, Weishi (2001), "The Two Great Chronic Diseases That Block China from Achieving Modernization and Integrating with the World" (*Fangai zhongguo rongru shijie shixian xiandaihua de liang da wan zheng*), *Nanfang Zhoumo* (Southern Weekly) (November 27).

Zhang, Zuo (1993), *Chinese Civilization and Lu, Xun's Critique* (*Zhongguo wenming yu lu xun de piping*) (Taipei: Guiguan).

Zhao, Quansheng (1990), "Achieving Maximum Advantage," presented at the American Political Science Association Annual Meeting, San Francisco (September 1, 1990).

Zhao, Quansheng (1996), *Interpreting Chinese Foreign Policy* (Oxford: Oxford University Press).

Zheng, Yongnian (1999), *Discovering Chinese Nationalism in China: Modernization, Identity and International Relations* (Cambridge: Cambridge University Press).

Zhou, Enlai (October 1, 1950), "Struggling for the Sake of Consolidating and Developing People's Victory" (*Wei gonggu he fazhan renmin de shengli er fendou*), a lecture given to All-nation Commission, National

Political Consultative Conference, in editors n.a., *Selected Work by Zhou Enlai (Zhou enlai xuan ji)* (1984) (Beijing: People's Press), p. 43.

Zhou Enlai, "On Current Financial Situations and the Few Relationships in New China's Economy" (*Dangqian caijing xingshi he xin zhongguo jinji de jizhong guanxi*), in editors n.a., *Selected Work by Zhou Enlai (Zhou enlai xuan ji)* (1984) (Beijing: People's Press), pp. 10–11.

Zhou, Pei Jianzhang (ed.) (1989), *Studying Zhou Enlai (Yanjiu zhou enlai)* (Beijing: World Knowledge Press).

Zhou, Wei (2000), "The Anatomy of the View that Human Rights Prevail over Sovereingty" (*renquan gaoyu zhuquan ren toushi*), *Renmin Ribao* (3.28): 6.

Zhu, Chengxiu (1994), "How Far will Lee Teng-hui Go?" (*Li denghui haiyao zou duo yuan*), *Dagong Bao* (June 19).

Zhu, Xueqin (2001), "From Macartney's Trip to China to China's entry into the WTO" (*Cong magaerni fang hua dao zhongguo jiaru wto*), *Nanfang Zhoumo* (Southern Weekly) (November 29).

Zhu, Zhixin (1979), *Collection of Zhu, Zhixin's Writing (Zhu zhixin ji)* (Shanghai: Chinese Bookstore).

Zhuang, Hanlong and Yang Ming (1991), *Historical Discourse on the Strategy of Peaceful Evolution in the West (Xifang heping yanbian zhanlyue shi hua)* (Beijing: Long March Publisher).

Zi, Zhongyun (1999), "How Should Chinese View International Situations and Pose Themselves? (*Zhongguoren yinggai ruhe kandai guoji xingshi yu ruhe zichu*), *China Review (Zhongguo pinglun)* 24 (December): 20–25.

INDEX